WOMEN & MEN
IN MANAGEMENT 4

EDITION

To Laura Graves for her love and support
and
to the memory of my grandmother
Edna Powell
for all the quarters and much more

WOMEN & MEN
IN MANAGEMENT 4
EDITION

GARY N. POWELL
University of Connecticut

Los Angeles | London | New Delhi
Singapore | Washington DC

For information:

SAGE Publications, Inc.
2455 Teller Road
Thousand Oaks,
    California 91320
E-mail: order@sagepub.com

SAGE Publications India Pvt. Ltd.
B 1/I 1 Mohan Cooperative
    Industrial Area
Mathura Road, New Delhi 110 044
India

SAGE Publications Ltd.
1 Oliver's Yard
55 City Road
London EC1Y 1SP
United Kingdom

SAGE Publications Asia-Pacific Pte. Ltd.
33 Pekin Street #02-01
Far East Square
Singapore 048763

Printed in the United States of America

Library of Congress Cataloging-in-Publication Data

Powell, Gary N.
Women and men in management/Gary N. Powell. — 4th ed.
    p. cm.
Includes bibliographical references and index.
ISBN 978-1-4129-7284-0 (pbk. : acid-free paper)
    1. Women executives. 2. Executives. 3. Sex role in the work environment. I. Title.

HD6054.3.P69 2011
658.4'095—dc22   2010009451

This book is printed on acid-free paper.

10   11   12   13   14   10   9   8   7   6   5   4   3   2   1

Acquisitions Editor:	Lisa Cuevas Shaw
Editorial Assistant:	MaryAnn Vail
Production Editor:	Libby Larson
Typesetter:	C&M Digitals (P) Ltd.
Proofreader:	Wendy Jo Dymond
Indexer:	Terri Corry
Cover Designer:	Candice Harman
Marketing Manager:	Helen Salmon

Contents

Foreword

Belle Rose Ragins[1]

"We ask justice, we ask equality, we ask that all the civil and political rights that belong to citizens of the United States, be guaranteed to us and our daughters forever."

—Susan B. Anthony (1820–1906)

"Our struggle today is not to have a female Einstein get appointed as an assistant professor. It is for a woman schlemiel to get as quickly promoted as a male schlemiel."

—Bella Abzug (1920–1998)

"The truth will set you free. But first, it will piss you off."

—Gloria Steinem (1934–)

When the first edition of *Women & Men in Management* was published in 1988, the field was just emerging as an established area of scientific inquiry. Groundswells of new studies were being published, and excitement was in the air. We felt like we were discovering vast new frontiers of knowledge—the Wild West of Research. But our excitement was quickly tempered when we looked at the data. The picture was bleak: gender discrimination was rampant, the glass ceiling was glacier-thick, and women earned 70% of the pay of their male counterparts.[2] But we were optimistic. Surely things would change once the inequities were uncovered? We remained confident that gender equity was just around the corner and that by the turn of the century women would receive equal status in the workplace.

Time passed, and over 20 years later, we have made precious little progress toward that goal. In the United States, women are more likely than men to pursue undergraduate and most graduate degrees, but earn only 80% of the pay of their male counterparts.[3] It appears that the glass ceiling is made of kryptonite; only 13.5% of women have made it to the *Fortune* 500 executive suite, and women are actually losing ground in some states.[4] Even as women are poised to become the majority of the workforce, they increasingly encounter workplaces replete with harassment and discrimination, experiences that are amplified for women who face a double or triple "whammy" based on their race, ethnicity, disability, weight, religion, socioeconomic class, or sexual orientation.[5]

But the critical challenge before us is not our lack of progress, it is *the myth of equity*: the unfounded belief that stereotyping and discrimination are things of the past. Whether it is based on wishful thinking, myopia, or just plain propaganda, the myth of equity is perhaps most damaging when held by the younger generation of women. These young women can be seen thanking the early "trailblazers" for forging the path to workplace equity, as if somehow the trailblazers banished sexism with a swift wave of their laser sword or magic wand. The trailblazers shake their heads; they recognize that gender equity remains more of a wish than a reality, that misogyny is alive and well within and outside the workplace, and that the bright young women marching into the workforce will be greeted with virulent new strains of modern sexism that are more pernicious and damaging than ever. These resistant new strains are entrenched deep in our psyche and, like the strains of old, distort our perceptions and frame our expectations. The classic 1950s film clip of the female secretary being chased around the desk by her lecherous male boss has been replaced with a new DVD featuring either Sigourney Weaver perched on her throne of a desk, ready to be toppled, or Sandra Bullock, realizing—thank God not too late—that work can never take the place of a real man. These young women are now told that they can have it all—and they believe it. And if they don't get it all—well, they have only themselves to blame. We rarely witness their male counterparts grappling with these issues. The myth of equity persists and permeates our expectations of ourselves and of others.

So it is now, more than ever before, that we need this new edition of *Women and Men in Management*. This gem of a book shines the brightest in these dark times. Gary Powell has once again produced a volume that documents the current state of research on gender in the workplace.

The author does a spectacular job of synthesizing an array of over 700 studies and articles that document not only the current state of gender in the workforce, but also the full range of developmental, social, and societal variables that have led to this current state of affairs. This book not only challenges the myth of equity—it roundly refutes it—and not a moment too soon.

We are grateful for such a fine volume. Now, if only it came out in DVD.

Notes

1. Belle Rose Ragins is Professor of Human Resource Management at the University of Wisconsin-Milwaukee.

2. Powell, G. (1988). *Women and men in management.* Newbury Park, CA: Sage; U.S. Department of Labor, Bureau of Labor Statistics. (1987). *Employment and Earnings 34* (6), computed from p. 46, table A-22.

3. U.S. Census Bureau. (2006). *Majority of undergrads and grad students are women, Census Bureau reports.* Retrieved January 5, 2010, from http://www.census .gov/Press-Release/www/releases/archives/education/007909.html; Marklein, M. (October, 19, 2005). College gender gap widens: 57% are women. *USA Today.* Retrieved January 5, 2010, from http://www.usatoday.com/news/education/ 2005-10-19-male-college-cover_x.htm; U.S. Census Bureau. (2009). *Census Bureau releases data showing relationship between education and earnings.* Retrieved January 5, 2010, from http://www.census.gov/Press-Release/www/releases/archives/education/ 013618.html; U.S. Department of Labor. (2008). *Quick stats on women workers, 2008.* Retrieved January 5, 2010, from http://www.dol.gov/wb/stats/main.htm; Institute for Women's Policy Research (2009). *The gender wage gap: 2008.* Retrieved January 5, 2010 from http://www.iwpr.org/pdf/C350.pdf.

4. Catalyst. (2009). *2009 Catalyst Census of the* Fortune *500 reveals women missing from critical business leadership.* Retrieved December 28, 2009, from http://www.catalyst.org/press-release/161/2009-catalyst-census-of-the-fortune- 500-reveals-women-missing-from-critical-business-leadership; Milwaukee Women Inc. (2007). *Missed opportunities in corporate leadership: 2007 Executive summary report.* Retrieved July 10, 2009, from http://www.milwaukeewomeninc.org/ research.php.

5. Rampell, C. (February 5, 2009). As layoffs surge, women may pass men in job force. *New York Times.* Retrieved January 5, 2010, from http://www.nytimes.com/ 2009/02/06/business/06women.html; Ragins, B. R., Cornwell, J. M., & Miller, J. S. (2003). Heterosexism in the workplace: Do race and gender matter? *Group and Organization Management, 28,* 1, 45–74; Dipboye, R. L., & Colella, A. (Eds.) (2005). *Discrimination at work: The psychological and organizational bases.* Mahwah, NJ: Erlbaum.

Acknowledgments

M any people contributed to the preparation of this fourth edition of *Women and Men in Management*. I wish to express my deepest gratitude to:

1. Laura Graves for being a terrific collaborator on Chapters 4 and 5 of this edition as well as coauthor of the previous edition.

2. Tony Butterfield for being my great mentor, collaborator, colleague, and friend.

3. The School of Business of the University of Connecticut, for giving me the opportunity to teach the course on Women and Men in Management that won the American Assembly of Collegiate Schools of Business (AACSB) Committee on Equal Opportunity for Women Innovation Award and inspired the writing of this book.

4. My colleagues in the Gender and Diversity in Organizations Division (formerly Women in Management Division) of the Academy of Management, for providing both a forum for the sharing of research findings and a stimulus for creative thinking on this topic.

5. My parents, Norm and Zina Powell, for being as encouraging and supportive as parents could ever be.

6. Tiger the Cat for unlimited love, affection, and play.

7. Again, and most of all, Laura Graves, my wife and favorite colleague, for standing by me all the way.

CHAPTER 1

Sex, Gender, and Work

On the Psychology of Sex

There is perhaps no field aspiring to be scientific where flagrant personal bias, logic martyred in the cause of supporting a prejudice, unfounded assertions, and even sentimental rot and drivel, have run riot to such an extent as here.[1]

Psychologists love dichotomies. There are always two kinds of people.[2]

Our story begins from a pithy word from the first psychologist to undertake an extensive and systematic examination of the psychological characteristics of the sexes.[3] In 1910, Helen Thompson Woolley issued a stinging indictment of research about the topic of sex differences that is quoted at the beginning of this chapter. Since then, thousands of studies on the topic of have been published by scholars around the world. Has anything changed?

One century later, Susan Fiske, a prominent modern-day psychologist, offered the humorous take on psychologists who conduct research about sex differences that appears in the second quote above. When psychologists consider the characteristics of two groups such as men and women, they tend to view members of the two groups as opposite in traits. This tendency in turn influences the psychologists' research, including the topics studied, the labels assigned to traits, and the interpretation of results and conclusions reached. It is also exhibited in popular conceptions of how the sexes differ. For example, John Gray's best-selling book, *Men Are from Mars, Women Are from Venus,* asserted that women and men are so different in personal traits that they might as well be from different planets. Not all people agree; on a Web site titled *The Rebuttal from Uranus,* Susan Hamson slammed Gray's book as "a sexist, patronizing, male-centered invective which does little more than perpetuate long-held negative gender stereotypes." However, even if psychologists and other observers are predisposed to believe that sex differences in personal traits are prevalent, this does not necessarily mean that sex differences are absent. Moreover, even if sex differences in personal traits that men and women bring to the workplace are minimal, their experiences in the workplace may differ dramatically.[4]

Women and Men in Management, Fourth Edition, examines the evolving roles and experiences of women and men in the global workplace. Significant changes have occurred over the last half-century in the status of women and men and in their interactions at work. However, sharply different views have been offered about the implications of these changes for the workplace of the future. Some believe that all of the needed changes have taken place and remaining sex-based inequalities in the workplace will continue to erode. According to an **optimistic view** of trends toward gender equality, the inevitable consequence of egalitarian values among parents to provide their daughters and sons with similar opportunities, among citizens to support legal interventions such as antidiscrimination laws and requirements for family leaves, and among organizations to offer women-friendly programs such as on-site child care will be equal opportunities and pay for women and men. In short, the day will come when a person's sex no longer matters at work.[5]

However, others believe that needed changes have stalled and remaining sex-based inequalities are now entrenched. According to a **pessimistic view,** although men are doing more housework, they are not exactly embracing the opportunity to take on equal responsibility with their female partners for child care and other household demands. Also, although women have sought access to male-intensive occupations (those in which two thirds or more of the workforce is male) in greater numbers, fewer men have sought access to female-intensive occupations (those in which two thirds or more of the workforce is female). Further, the legal requirement of equal opportunities for women and men in the workplace is not equivalent to a societal commitment to ensure that they will be similarly oriented to take advantage of such opportunities. Although we do not know whether the future will offer greater support for the optimistic or pessimistic view, the evidence about the present state of affairs in the workplace offers a more mixed picture.

The role of women in the workplace has been expanding steadily world-wide. In the United States, the proportion of women in the labor force (i.e., the proportion of all adults employed or seeking employment who are women), which was 42% in 1980, has risen to 47%. This proportion varies widely across countries, for example, 14% in Saudi Arabia, 27% in Morocco, 37% in Chile, and 48% in Finland. However, the trend in almost all countries has been in the same direction, toward the increased employment of women. Similarly, although the proportion of women in management in different countries varies widely due to differences in national culture and definitions of the term *manager,* the trend in almost all countries has been toward the increased representation of women in the managerial ranks.[6]

Despite these trends, female managers are concentrated in the lower management levels and hold positions with less authority than men. The higher the level of the organization, the fewer women are found. Although definitions of what constitutes "top management" vary among companies, the proportion of female executive officers, typically considered as top management, is only 14% in *Fortune* 500 corporations and less than 5% in many nations. Women are also underrepresented in corporate boards, consisting of 15% of board directors in *Fortune* 500 corporations (the 500 highest-grossing closely held and public U.S. corporations), 12% of board directors in FTSE 100 companies (the 100 most highly capitalized United Kingdom companies listed on the London Stock Exchange), and about 10% of board directors in the largest companies listed on the national stock exchange of European Union member states. Around the world, a **glass ceiling** appears to restrict women's access to top management positions solely because they are women. Women are not allowed to advance in managerial hierarchies as far as men with equivalent credentials.[7]

The economic status of women in the workplace remains lower than that of men. The average female full-time worker continues to be paid less than the average male full-time worker. This gap is partly due to the lower average wages of workers in female-intensive occupations than that of workers in male-intensive occupations. Also, women are paid less than men in the same occupation and often in the same job. The ratio of female-to-male wages for similar work is below 100% in all nations for which the World Economic Forum reports data, with the highest value for Uzbekistan (83%) and the lowest value for Bolivia (45%); the ratio for the United States is 67%, ranking 64th out of 125 nations.[8]

The global labor force also remains sharply segregated on the basis of sex. In recent years, women have shown more interest in entering male-intensive occupations than men have shown in entering female-intensive occupations, which is not surprising because workers in male-intensive occupations are the higher paid. However, women continue to be crowded into a lower-paying set of occupations than are men.[9]

Thus, differences in workplace status according to biological sex remain strong, even though there have been considerable changes. Is it only a matter of time until the proportions of women and men in all managerial levels and all occupations become essentially equal, until women and men are paid equal wages for equal work, and until individuals' work experiences are unaffected by their biological sex? As we shall see, it will depend on actions that organizations and individuals take.

Sex Versus Gender

In this book, we make a distinction between two frequently used terms: *sex* and *gender*. The term *sex* (or biological sex) refers to the binary categories of male and female, which are determined by biological characteristics of individuals such as their physiological properties and reproductive apparatus. The term *gender* refers to the psychosocial implications of being male or female, such as beliefs and expectations about what kinds of attitudes, behaviors, skills, values and interests are more appropriate for or typical of one sex than the other. Thus, gender is a term used in a social context to refer to the role associated with being male or female.[10]

The study of **sex differences** examines how males and females actually differ. In contrast, the study of **gender differences** focuses on how people believe that males and females differ. For example, a sex difference in leadership style would exist if female leaders were more considerate of their subordinates than were male leaders. There would be a gender difference in leadership style if people believed that female leaders were more considerate of their subordinates than were male leaders. However, there could be a gender difference in leadership style without a corresponding sex difference, and vice versa. Furthermore, gender differences can *cause* sex differences. For example, if parents believe that the developmental needs of their sons differ from those of their daughters, they may raise their children in ways that reinforce that belief. In the same vein, if supervisors believe that the skills and interests of their female and male subordinates differ, they may assign tasks to their subordinates in ways that reinforce that belief. In each case, the result is a **self-fulfilling prophecy**—when expectations cause behavior that makes the expectations come true. We identify many workplace situations in which self-fulfilling prophecies are likely to occur.[11]

As we consider the effects of sex differences on work-related behavior, we also need to consider the effects of gender differences. Sex differences influence how people are disposed to behave in work settings. Gender differences influence how people react to others' behavior in such settings. Gender differences are manifested in stereotypes, prejudice, and discrimination. A **stereotype** is a set of beliefs about the personal attributes of a group of people. Stereotyping is a cognitive activity, related to thinking, learning, and remembering distinctions between various groups of people. In contrast, people who display **prejudice,** or a negative attitude toward members of other groups, are engaging in an emotional activity. Finally, **discrimination,** a behavioral activity, is exhibited in how people treat members of other groups and in the decisions they make about others. We have reason to be concerned about all three of these phenomena. All of us may be targets of stereotyping, prejudice, and discrimination. In addition, we may engage in stereotyping, prejudice, and discrimination.[12]

Dimensions of Diversity

Sex represents only one of many personal characteristics that may influence individuals' experiences in the workplace. People differ in many ways, some of which are changeable, others less amenable to change. **Primary dimensions of diversity** are essentially unchangeable personal characteristics that exert significant lifelong impacts. Sex is a primary dimension of diversity, along with race, ethnicity, age, sexual orientation, and physical abilities/disabilities. Together, primary dimensions of diversity shape our basic self-image and sense of identity. They affect our early learning experiences, and there is typically no escaping their impact throughout the course of our lives.[13]

Secondary dimensions of diversity, on the other hand, are changeable personal characteristics. These characteristics are acquired and may be modified or abandoned throughout life. Education, income, marital and parental status, religion, political affiliation, and work experience are some secondary dimensions of diversity of importance to many people. People also distinguish themselves in many other ways, such as in their choices of collegiate fraternities or sororities, hobbies, activities, voluntary associations, clothing and grooming style, and music preferences. Of course, a person does not completely determine his or her secondary characteristics. For instance, educational background, work experience, income, or marital status will be affected by other people's decisions. However, people generally have more control over the secondary dimensions of diversity in their lives than over the primary dimensions of diversity.

The primary dimensions of diversity may fall into different categories, including whether group membership is visible and whether it is regarded as changeable. For example, sexual orientation is not necessarily observable and opinions differ as to whether it is changeable. As a result, gays and lesbians face decisions about "coming out." They may decide to disclose their sexual orientation to family members and friends on a person-to-person basis based on the level of trust in the relationship and the anticipated reaction to the disclosure. However, they are unlikely to disclose their sexual orientation to coworkers if they perceive or fear workplace discrimination on the basis of sexual orientation.[14]

In contrast, sex is highly visible and not easily changed. People have little choice about "coming out" as female or male. The psychologist Sandra Bem once asked audience members if they had ever known anyone personally without noticing that person's sex. Few could answer yes. Sex is an important characteristic to most people when forming their impression of someone. Even if sex is not important to a particular person's own sense of identity, other people may be influenced by their beliefs and expectations associated with that person's sex.

Thus, people categorize themselves and may be categorized by others along many different dimensions of diversity, both primary and secondary. The focus of this book is the influence of categorizations of people according to sex on what transpires in the workplace. However, sex is not isolated from other dimensions of diversity. The effect of sex on how people develop their senses of identity and on how they are treated in the workplace cannot be separated from the effects of race, ethnicity, age, sexual orientation, physical abilities/disabilities, and various secondary dimensions of diversity.

Researchers often ignore the interdependence of sex and other dimensions of diversity. For example, many studies of sex or gender differences have not reported the racial or ethnic group of the individuals who were the focus of the study. By ignoring issues of race and ethnicity, such studies reflect an underlying assumption that sex and gender differences are similar across all racial and ethnic groups. That is, White women, Black women, Hispanic women, Asian women, and women of other racial and ethnic groups are assumed to have similar personal characteristics and experiences, as are White men, Black men, Hispanic men, Asian men, and so on. We need to guard against making such assumptions ourselves.[15]

In addition, people often compare the effects of stereotyping, prejudice, and discrimination on the basis of different dimensions of diversity and offer conclusions about which "ism" (e.g., sexism, racism, ageism, heterosexism) has worse consequences. For example, Hillary Clinton, a White woman, and Barack Obama, a man often characterized as Black although he is of mixed race, were leading contenders for the nomination of the Democratic Party for the U.S. presidency in the 2008 election; Obama won the nomination and subsequent election. During the campaign, considerable debate took place in the media over which candidate was subject to greater discrimination, Clinton on the basis of sex or Obama on the basis of race. Clinton was the target of sexism in comments about her display of emotions, whereas Obama was the target of racism in comments about his Muslim-sounding middle name, Hussein. Gloria Steinem, a prominent feminist, argued that sexism trumped racism in the campaign to the disadvantage of Clinton, asserting that "gender is probably the most restricting force in American life, whether the question is who must be in the kitchen or who could be in the White House." However, Obama faced a challenge in handling issues of both gender and race; a political observer noted, "As a Black man, he must be careful not to appear too hostile toward a White woman."[16]

Although the comparison of sexism and racism in media accounts of the Clinton–Obama contest may have educated some people about the kinds of stereotyping, prejudice, and discrimination that may occur, it oversimplified the complex issues involved. It seems more reasonable to acknowledge that sex, race, and a host of other dimensions of diversity may be used as the basis for stereotyping, prejudice, and discrimination. We need to guard against all "isms" in the workplace and not be distracted by comparisons of their strength.

Watching Out for Biases

People have strong beliefs about whether there are fundamental differences between the capabilities of females and males. In fact, speculation about such differences is a universal phenomenon. People seldom wonder whether children who differ in eye color or height also differ in personality, behavioral tendencies, or intellectual abilities. However, they do care if there are such differences between girls and boys.[17]

Researchers may bring either of two types of bias to the study of sex differences, alpha bias and beta bias. **Alpha bias** consists of the tendency to exaggerate sex differences. **Beta bias** consists of the tendency to minimize or ignore sex differences. Either type of bias can lead to a distortion of how the researcher sees reality.[18]

Such biases may be the result of the personal prejudices of researchers. If the researcher's goal is to prove that traditional stereotypes of the sexes are inaccurate and that females and males are essentially equivalent in their personalities, behavioral tendencies, and intellectual abilities, he or she is likely to demonstrate beta bias by concluding that any sex differences that are found are trivial. On the other hand, if the researcher's goal is to prove that one sex is superior to the other in some way or to justify a status quo in which women and men are seen as naturally suited to different roles and thereby deserving of different treatment, he or she is likely to demonstrate alpha bias by concluding that sex differences in personal characteristics are large and fundamental to human functioning.[19]

Also, as Susan Fiske suggested in the opening quote, the mere presence of a two-category system leads psychologists as well as other people to view the two categories as opposites. For example, parents with two children tend to describe each in contrast to the other (e.g., "Tom is more of a leader and Joe is more of a follower"). However, parents with three or more children tend to focus on the unique aspects of each child (e.g., "Kristin enjoys rooting for her favorite baseball team, Melissa likes to produce school plays, Rob likes camping, Will enjoys music and photography, and Nate likes to bang the drums"). Similarly, anthropologists who have done fieldwork in only two cultures tend to emphasize the differences between these cultures, whereas anthropologists with wider field experience are more aware of the diversity of human experience. The same phenomenon may occur for sex. Because there are only two categories, no one has the opportunity to gain "wider field experience" with a third or fourth sex. As a result, people tend to focus on the differences between males and females, thereby reinforcing alpha bias. Also, every researcher of sex differences belongs to one of the two groups being examined. Researchers may be more likely to report sex differences that reflect favorably on members of their own sex. Moreover, the popular media exhibit alpha bias in their choice of which research results to publicize. Findings of sex differences are glamorized and magnified, whereas findings of sex similarities receive much less media attention.[20]

Overall, it seems realistic to expect that some sex differences will be small to nonexistent, others will be moderate, and still others will be large. However, we need to be aware of the possibility of biases, both in researchers and in media accounts of research on sex differences, that affect what research findings are reported and how they are interpreted. We also need to guard against two dangerous assumptions that may be made about the results of research. First, if a sex difference is found in some aspect of human behavior, this does not mean that all males do something and all females do something quite different. Second, sex differences that are found are not necessarily biologically based and therefore automatically present and not subject to change. Indeed, the behavior of the sexes is highly subject to social influences, as we shall see throughout the book.[21]

Organization of the Book

The book begins its analysis of the transition in female/male work relationships by looking back in time. Chapter 2 considers the evolution of women's and men's work roles during the 20th century. It examines the effects of historical influences such as the occurrence of two major world wars, the passage of equal employment opportunity laws, and the development of a women's liberation movement. The current status of women and men in today's workforce is described in terms of sex differences in labor force participation, occupation, and pay.

Chapter 3 examines sex and gender differences that affect the behavior of women and men in the workplace. This chapter reviews some of the major findings of psychological research on sex differences. Key concepts such as gender stereotypes, gender roles, sexism, and gender identity that are critical to understanding male/female interactions are introduced. The ways in which parents, schools, and the mass media convey gender role expectations to children, as well as the limitations of strict adherence to gender roles in adults, are explored.

Chapter 4, coauthored with Laura Graves, considers how individuals and organizations make decisions about establishing employment relationships. For individuals, these decisions entail choosing which job opportunities to pursue and which job offers to accept; for organizations, they entail choosing which applicants to hire. The chapter describes how differences in men's and women's job search strategies and reactions to specific jobs and organizations lead them to seek and obtain very different employment opportunities. It also examines sex discrimination in organizations' hiring decisions, including how and when sex discrimination occurs and who discriminates against whom. Recommendations are offered for reducing sex and gender effects on the employment decisions of individuals and organizations.

Chapter 5, also coauthored with Laura Graves, considers the effects of sex and gender on behavior in diverse teams. The chapter analyzes differences in how men and women behave and are evaluated in mixed-sex teams. It also examines how the sex composition of the team influences the experiences of male and female team members and the team's effectiveness. It suggests that mixed-sex teams are susceptible to a host of problems, the severity of which depends on a number of situational factors. The chapter concludes with recommendations for actions that team members and leaders may take to facilitate the functioning of mixed-sex teams.

Chapter 6 examines the effects of leader preferences, leader and gender stereotypes, and attitudes toward female leaders on how leadership is exhibited in organizations. Despite the increased proportion of women in management, people who express a choice still prefer to have a male boss, and stereotypes continue to reflect the beliefs of "think manager—think male" and "think manager—think masculine." Sex differences in actual leader behavior and effectiveness are examined to determine whether there is any basis to these stereotypes. The chapter concludes that, contrary to leader stereotypes, women may actually be better prepared to handle managerial roles in today's work environment. Organizations are urged to take actions to ensure that capable leaders of both sexes have equal chances to succeed.

Chapter 7 explores issues pertaining to the expression of sexuality in the workplace, which includes sexual harassment (unwelcome sexual attention directed toward others) and workplace romances (mutually desired relationships between two people at work). It examines the causes and consequences of both types of sexually oriented behavior. Actions are recommended for both organizations and individuals to deal with sexual harassment and to minimize the disruption caused by workplace romances.

Chapter 8 considers what it takes for individuals to achieve a sense of work–family balance, whatever their family structure may be; even single employees are likely to have a family life that is important to them. It examines the increasing diversity of family structures. It describes how individuals' experiences of the work–family interface may be both positive and negative at different times and in different ways, depending on the extent to which they segment or integrate these two roles. It examines sex differences in how people define and measure "success," including the paradox that women and men are similarly satisfied with their careers despite the fact that men's careers appear to be the more successful in objective terms. It reviews sex differences in how family factors influence important work decisions. The chapter concludes with actions that organizations may take to enhance employees' work–family balance as well as actions that individuals may take on their own behalf.

Chapters 1 through 8 identify numerous issues related to sex and gender that arise in today's workplace. Chapter 9 offers solutions to these problems. It details the relevant laws and regulations with which organizations must comply to avoid discrimination. The chapter presents the business case for going beyond legal compliance to promote diversity (i.e., representation of members of different groups in all jobs and levels) and inclusion (i.e., acceptance of members of all groups in the organizational culture). Actions are outlined for organizations to achieve nondiscriminatory, diverse, and inclusive cultures.

In summary, *Women and Men in Management, Fourth Edition,* covers a wide range of topics. It describes female and male work roles in the past and the present. The effects of sex and gender on childhood development and adult behavior are considered. It examines how sex and gender influence individuals' experiences as job candidates, team members, and managers. Issues associated with the expression of sexuality in the workplace are explored. Finally, this book offers concrete recommendations for individuals and organizations to ensure that all people feel successful according to their own definition of success, regardless of their biological sex.

Notes

1. Woolley, H. T. (1910). A review of the recent literature on the psychology of sex. *Psychological Bulletin, 7,* 335.

2. Fiske, S. T. (2007). *Venus and Mars, or down to earth: Stereotypes and realities of gender differences.* Presented in M. Gernsbacher (Chair), Presidential symposium, Meeting of the Association for Psychological Science, Washington, DC.

3. Milar, K. S. (2000). The first generation of women psychologists and the psychology of women. *American Psychologist, 55,* 616–619.

4. Gray, J. (1992). *Men are from mars, women are from Venus: A practical guide for improving communication and getting what you want in your relationships.* New York: HarperCollins; Hamson, S. (2003). *The rebuttal from Uranus.* Retrieved May 19, 2009, from http://ourworld.compuserve.com/homepages/women_rebuttal_from_uranus/.

5. Blau, F. D., Brinton, M. C., & Grusky, D. B. (Eds.) (2006). *The declining significance of gender?* (pp. 3–34). New York: Russell Sage Foundation.

6. U.S. Department of Labor, Bureau of Labor Statistics. (2009). *Labor force statistics from the Current Population Survey,* table A-19. Retrieved December 22, 2009, from http://www.bls.gov/cps; International Labour Office. (2009). *LABORSTA-Internet: Statistics by country,* table 2A. Retrieved December 22, 2009, from http://laborsta.ilo.org; International Labour Office. (1993). Unequal race to the top. *World of Work: The Magazine of the International Labour Office* (U.S. ed.), no. 2, 6–7.

7. Catalyst. (2009). *2009 Catalyst census:* Fortune *500 women executive officers and top earners.* New York: Author. Retrieved January 18, 2010, from http://www.catalyst.org; Catalyst. (2009). *2009 Catalyst census:* Fortune *500 women board directors.* New York: Author. Retrieved January 18, 2010, from http://www.catalyst.org; Sealy, R., Vinnecombe, S., & Singh, V. (2008). *The Female FTSE Report 2008: A decade of delay.* Cranfield, UK: Cranfield University School of Management. Retrieved May 29, 2009, from http://www.som .cranfield.ac.uk; European Commission. (2007). *Women and men in decision-making 2007: Analysis of the situation and trends.* Luxembourg, Belgium: Office for Official Publications of the European Communities. Retrieved May 20, 2009, from http://ec.europa.eu/employment_social; Powell, G. N. (1999). Reflections on the glass ceiling: Recent trends and future prospects. In G. N. Powell (Ed.), *Handbook of gender and work* (pp. 325–345). Thousand Oaks, CA: Sage.

8. Hausmann, R., Tyson, L. D., & Zahidi, S. (2009). *The global gender gap report 2009.* Geneva, Switzerland: World Economic Forum. Retrieved October 27, 2009, from http://www.weforum.org; Roos, P. A., & Gatta, M. L. (1999). The gender gap in earnings: Trends, explanations, and prospects. In G. N. Powell (Ed.), *Handbook of gender and work* (pp. 95–123). Thousand Oaks, CA: Sage.

9. England, P. (2006). Toward gender equality: Progress and bottlenecks. In F. D. Blau, M. C. Brinton, & D. B. Grusky (Eds.), *The declining significance of gender?* (pp. 245–264). New York: Russell Sage Foundation; Jacobs, J. A. (1999). The sex segregation of occupations: Prospects for the 21st century. In G. N. Powell (Ed.), *Handbook of gender and work* (pp. 125–141). Thousand Oaks, CA: Sage.

10. Archer, J., & Lloyd, B. (2002). *Sex and gender* (2nd ed.). Cambridge, UK: Cambridge University Press; Korabik, K. (1999). Sex and gender in the new millennium. In G. N. Powell (Ed.), *Handbook of gender and work* (pp. 3–16). Thousand Oaks, CA: Sage.

11. Eden, D. (2003). Self-fulfilling prophecies in organizations. In J. Greenberg (Ed.), *Organizational behavior: The state of the science* (2nd ed., pp. 91–122). Mahwah, NJ: Erlbaum; Geis, F. L. (1993). Self-fulfilling prophecies: A social psychological view of gender. In A. E. Beall & R. J. Sternberg (Eds.), *The psychology of gender* (pp. 9–54). New York: Guilford.

12. Fiske, S. T. (1998). Stereotyping, prejudice, and discrimination. In D. T. Gilbert, S. T. Fiske, & G. Lindzey (Eds.), *The handbook of social psychology*

(4th ed., Vol. 2, pp. 357–411). Boston: McGraw-Hill; Hunter, T. D. (Ed.). (2009). *Handbook of prejudice, stereotyping, and discrimination.* New York: Psychology Press.

13. Loden, M., & Rosener, J. B. (1991). *Workforce America: Managing employee diversity as a vital resource.* Homewood, IL: Business One Irwin.

14. Ragins, B. R. (2004). Sexual orientation in the workplace: The unique work and career experiences of gay, lesbian and bisexual workers. In J. J. Martocchio (Ed.), *Research in personnel and human resources management* (Vol. 23, pp. 35–120). Amsterdam: Elsevier; Ragins, B. R., Singh, R., & Cornwell, J. M. (2007). Making the invisible visible: Fear and disclosure of sexual orientation at work. *Journal of Applied Psychology, 92,* 1103–1118; Griffith, K. H., & Hebl, M. R. (2002). The disclosure dilemma for gay men and lesbians: "Coming out" at work. *Journal of Applied Psychology, 87,* 1191–1199; Ragins, B. R., & Cornwell, J. M. (2001). Pink triangles: Antecedents and consequences of perceived workplace discrimination against gay and lesbian employees. *Journal of Applied Psychology, 86,* 1244–1261.

15. Ferdman, B. M. (1999). The color and culture of gender in organizations: Attending to race and ethnicity. In G. N. Powell (Ed.), *Handbook of gender and work* (pp. 17–34). Thousand Oaks, CA: Sage; Reid, P. T. (1988). Racism and sexism: Comparisons and conflicts. In P. A. Katz & D. A. Taylor (Eds.), *Eliminating racism: Profiles in controversy* (pp. 203–221). New York: Plenum.

16. Steinem, G. (2008, January 8). Women are never front-runners. *New York Times.* Retrieved January 8, 2008, from http://www.nytimes.com; Crary, D. (2008, January 14). Presidential campaign fuels debate over sexism, racism: Is one more taboo than the other? *Associated Press.* Retrieved January 14, 2008, from http://www.ap.org.

17. Jacklin, C. N. (1989). Female and male: Issues of gender. *American Psychologist, 44,* 127–133.

18. Hare-Mustin, R. T., & Maracek, J. (1988). The meaning of difference: Gender theory, postmodernism, and psychology. *American Psychologist, 43,* 455–464; Hyde, J. S., & Mezulis, A. H. (2001). Gender difference research: Issues and critique. In J. Worell (Ed.), *Encyclopedia of women and gender* (Vol. 1, pp. 551–559). San Diego: Academic Press.

19. Eagly, A. H. (1995). The science and politics of comparing women and men. *American Psychologist, 50,* 145–158; Hyde, J. S. (2005). The gender similarities hypothesis. *American Psychologist, 60,* 581–592.

20. Fiske (2007); Belle, D. (1985). Ironies in the contemporary study of gender. *Journal of Personality, 53,* 400–405.

21. Lippa, R. A. (2006). The gender reality hypothesis. *American Psychologist, 61,* 639–640; Lippa, R. A. (2005). *Gender, nature, and nurture* (2nd ed). Mahwah, NJ: Erlbaum; Caplan, P. J., & Caplan, J. B. (2009). *Thinking critically about research on sex and gender* (3rd ed.). Boston: Pearson Allyn & Bacon.

CHAPTER 2

Yesterday and Today

Girl Power at School, but Not at the Office

I was born in 1982—about 20 years after the women's rights movement began. . . . "Girl power" was celebrated, and I felt that all doors were open to me. . . . Then I left the egalitarianism of the classroom for the cubicle, and everything changed. The realization that the knowledge and skills acquired at school don't always translate at the office is something that all college graduates, men and women, must face. But for women, I have found, the adjustment tends to be much harder.[1]

Women and men are entering a very different work world, with new expectations of what they will encounter as well as new expectations of others that they will have to meet. But how different are the current roles that women and men play in the workplace compared with those of the past? If traditional gender roles have been tossed aside, what has replaced them?

Traditional gender roles emphasize the differences rather than the similarities between women and men. They suggest that women should behave in a "feminine" manner, consistent with presumed feminine attributes, and that men should behave in a "masculine" manner, consistent with presumed masculine attributes. Traditionally, to deviate from these roles is to engage in abnormal behavior. Gender roles have had a profound impact on relations between women and men in all spheres of our society—the family, the educational system, the legal system, and the workplace.

In this chapter, we first consider the evolution of the work roles of women and men over the twentieth century. We trace the impact of diverse historical events, such as the advent of industrialization, two world wars, and the development of the women's liberation movement. Second, we look at the roles of men and women in the workforce today, considering differences between sexes and among various racial and ethnic groups. Finally, we consider the impact of the changes in traditional workplace gender roles on current economic realities and on the work relationships between men and women.

The 20th Century: A Century of Change

The First Half

As the 20th century began, men were firmly established as the dominant sex in the workplace, both in numbers and in positions of authority. The stay-at-home wife who devoted herself exclusively to household and family responsibilities was a status symbol in U.S. society. This practice was the product of the existing patriarchal social system and the Industrial Revolution of the late 18th and early 19th centuries, which removed paid employment from the home. Although the role of stay-at-home wife was largely based on the experiences of White middle-class families that could afford to forgo the wife's wages, society embraced the notion that a woman's proper place was in the home.[2]

Thus, the U.S. labor force was clearly differentiated by sex at the beginning of the 20th century. Census statistics regarding **labor force participation rates** showed that 19% of women and 80% of men were in the labor force (Table 2.1). In other words, four of every five women *were not* engaged in paid employment, whereas four out of every five men *were*.

In the decades between 1900 and 1940, labor force participation rates for men and women remained essentially unchanged, despite the occurrence of several major events. World War I (1914 to 1918) created new jobs for women at higher wages than previous levels as large numbers of men went off to war. However, no sustained change in the employment of women resulted. In fact, the labor force participation rate of women in 1920 (21%) was slightly lower than it had been in 1910 (23%). Labor unions, government, and society in general were not ready for more than a temporary change in the economic role of women. Men received first

Table 2.1 Labor Force Participation Rates

	Percentage in the U.S. Labor Force	
Year	Women	Men
1900	19	80
1910	23	81
1920	21	78
1930	22	76
1940	25	79
1950	31	80
1960	35	79
1970	43	80
1980	51	77
1990	58	76
2000	60	75
2009	59	72

SOURCES: **1900–1960**: U.S. Department of Commerce, Bureau of the Census. (1975). *Historical statistics of the United States: Colonial times to 1970* (pp. 127–128, series D11-25). Washington, DC: Government Printing Office; **1970–2000**: U.S. Department of Labor, Bureau of Labor Statistics. (2002). *Labor force statistics from the Current Population Survey,* table 2. Retrieved April 22, 2002, from http://www.bls.gov/cps; **2009**: U.S. Department of Labor, Bureau of Labor Statistics (2009). *Labor force statistics from the Current Population Survey*, table A-3. Retrieved December 23, 2009, from http://www.bls.gov/cps.

NOTE: **1900–1930**: data for persons 10 years old and over; **1940–1960**: data for persons 14 years old and over; **1970–2009**: data for persons 16 years old and over.

priority in hiring when they returned from the war, and many women were driven from the labor force.

The passage of the Nineteenth Amendment to the U.S. Constitution in 1920, which gave women the right to vote, failed to influence economic roles. Backers of the amendment had hoped that ending sex discrimination in the right to vote would lead to the dismantling of sex discrimination in other areas and usher in a new era of equality between the sexes. However, women's suffrage brought about little change in women's economic status.[3]

The Great Depression, extending from the U.S. stock market crash in 1929 to the Japanese bombing of Pearl Harbor in 1941, threw millions of Americans out of work. The unemployment rate rose considerably, peaking at 25% during 1933. These conditions contributed to an identity crisis for unemployed men of all races. In the book *Puzzled America*, published in 1935, Sherwood Anderson concluded, "The breaking down of the moral fiber of the American man through being out of a job, losing that sense of being some part of the moving world of activity, so essential to an American man's sense of his manhood—the loss of this essential something in the jobless can never be measured in dollars."[4] The Depression caused great strains in family relations, as unemployed men suffered loss of status in their families. Those who relied upon holding an authoritative role in the family and society felt humbled and disgraced. In addition, the Depression triggered resentment toward working women, especially working wives. The attention being expended on the problems of men intensified the attitude that working women were depriving male breadwinners of employment. However, these dynamics were not reflected in the labor force participation rates of women and men shown in Table 2.1 because unemployed workers were still counted in the labor force.[5]

World War II, which closely followed the Depression, marked a turning point in the distribution of economic roles between women and men, although it did not necessarily cause the massive changes that were to follow. Similar to World War I, World War II created what was expected to be a temporary high demand for female labor. Women were attracted to war-related industries by an advertising campaign appealing to their patriotism, and they were given access to the more skilled, higher-paying jobs usually held by men. However, after the war was won in 1945, the labor force did not quickly "return to normal" as it did after World War I. Instead, a new sense of what was normal emerged.

The Second Half

Changes in the economic roles played by the sexes in the second half of the 20th century took several forms. The labor force participation rate of women rose steadily from 31% in 1950 to 60% by 2000, with the largest increase in labor force participation seen among non-Hispanic White women. In contrast, the labor force participation rate of men declined from 80% in 1950 to 75% in 2000. Although the gap between men and women remained at 15% in 2000, it had narrowed considerably over the 20th century.

This was the result of significant change in the composition of the female labor force. In 1900, 6% of married women and 44% of single (never married) women worked. In 1950, 24% of married women and 51% of single women worked. However, in 2000, 62% of married women and 65% of single women worked. Thus, the gap between the labor force participation rates of married and single women virtually disappeared over the century. In 2000, 53% of the female labor force was married, close to the 59% of male labor force that was married.[6]

Postwar changes in the female labor force demonstrated increasing disregard for the idea that the woman's proper place was in the home. In 1900, the women most accepted into the workplace were single, making up two thirds of the female labor force. Employment of single women required the least adjustment to public opinion; the notion that the *mother's* proper place was in the home could still be held as a standard when single women worked. The next group to enter the labor force in large numbers was older married women. Between 1940 and 1960, the proportion of 45- to 64-year-old women who worked went from 20% to 42%. These women were past their peak child-raising years. Their increasing presence in the workplace could be accepted begrudgingly by defenders of the status quo as long as *young* mothers stayed at home. The final group of women to increase its labor force participation consisted of younger married women with preschool or school-age children. By 2000, 81% of mothers with children between 14 and 17 years old, 78% of those with children between 6 and 13 years old, 74% of those with children between 3 and 5 years old, and 63% of those with children 2 years old or under were in the labor force. The increased employment of mothers of young children ended adherence to the belief that women belong at home.[7]

The **educational attainment** of women also changed considerably in the postwar years. In the United States, the proportion of college degrees earned by women increased between 1950 and 2000 from 24% to 57% at the bachelor's level and from 29% to 58% at the master's level. As Table 2.2 indicates, these increases were exhibited among members of the major racial and ethnic groups. Moreover, the proportion of college degrees in business earned by women increased between 1960 and 2000 from only 7% to 50% at the bachelor's level, and from only 4% to 40% at the master's level. These trends reflect a major societal shift toward the enhancement of women's academic credentials as well as an increased commitment of women to managerial and professional careers.

These changes may in part be attributed to the power of "the pill," female oral contraceptives, regarded by *The Economist* as the most

Table 2.2   College Degrees Earned in the United States

	Percentage of Degrees Earned by Women						
	1950	1960	1970	1980	1990	2000	2007
Bachelor's Level:							
Total, all disciplines:	24	35	43	50	53	57	57
White	–	–	–	50	53	57	56
Black	–	–	–	60	62	66	66
Hispanic		–	–	50	55	60	61
Asian	–	–	–	46	50	54	55
Total, business	–	7	9	34	47	50	49
Master's Level:							
Total, all disciplines:	29	32	40	50	53	58	61
White	–	–	–	52	55	60	62
Black	–	–	–	64	64	69	71
Hispanic		–	–	52	55	60	64
Asian	–	–	–	40	43	53	54
Total, business	–	4	4	22	34	40	44

SOURCES: **1950–2000**: U.S. Department of Education, National Center for Education Statistics (2002). *Digest of education statistics 2001* (computed from tables 247, 268, 271, and 284). Retrieved April 23, 2002, from http://nces.ed.gov; **2007**: U.S. Department of Education, National Center for Education Statistics (2009). *Digest of education statistics 2008* (computed from tables 268, 284, 287, and 300). Retrieved May 28, 2009, from http://nces.ed.gov.

NOTE: – indicates data not available.

important advance in science and technology in the 20th century. The pill was approved for use by U.S. women in 1960 and was dispensed rapidly first to married women and, after several federal and state court actions, to single women. The pill greatly increased the reliability of contraception and reduced uncertainty about the consequences of sexual activity. Women could invest in a lengthy education without fearing that it would be interrupted by an unplanned pregnancy. Because the pill led to the postponing of marriage by most young women regardless of their educational aspirations, career women could delay marriage until completing their initial career preparation without being forced to choose from a reduced pool of eligible bachelors. Thus, the pill facilitated women's preparation for managerial and professional careers.[8]

The increased employment and educational attainment of women coincided with a rise in the proportion of **white-collar jobs** in the economy. "White-collar" jobs are those that do not require manual labor, including managerial jobs, professional jobs (e.g., engineers, teachers, lawyers, computer scientists, health care practitioners), sales jobs (e.g., sales representatives and proprietors), and administrative support jobs (e.g., administrative assistants and clerical workers). In 1950, 36% of all jobs were white-collar, and women held 40% of these jobs. By 2000, over half of all jobs were white-collar, and women held over half of these jobs.[9]

The women who entered the U.S. labor force after World War II came increasingly from the non-Hispanic White middle class. The growth in white-collar occupations created jobs that were compatible with middle-class status. Aspirations for a higher standard of living, consumerism, the desire to send children to college, and inflation made it necessary for some middle-class women to work to maintain a middle-class standard of living.

However, traditional attitudes concerning women's proper place in society persisted. During the 1950s, the mass media promoted an image of family togetherness that defined the mother's role as central to all domestic activity. According to Betty Friedan's *The Feminine Mystique*, women supposedly found true fulfillment as follows:

> Their only dream was to be perfect wives and mothers; their highest ambition to have five children and a beautiful house, their only fight to get and keep their husbands. They had no thought for the unfeminine problems of the world outside the home; they wanted the men to make the major decisions. They gloried in their role as women, and wrote proudly on the census blank: "Occupation: housewife."[10]

Women were supposed to revel in this role and happily surrender control of and participation in economic and public life to men. According to opinion polls, both women and men accepted such gender roles. Yet the statistics that have been presented show that something else was actually happening in the workplace. As one observer put it, "A visitor from another planet who read the magazines and newspapers of the 1950s would never have guessed that the women portrayed as being engaged exclusively in homemaking activities were also joining the job market in unprecedented numbers."[11]

During this period, women workers were not perceived as crusading to achieve economic equality with men. Instead, their increased economic activity could be interpreted as consistent with their primary role as helpmates to their spouses. Most women who worked were citing economic need as the reason for their employment, even when the family income was solidly in the middle-class range. If women had not been portrayed, or portrayed themselves, as working temporarily to help meet immediate needs, male resistance to their entry into the labor force might have been greater.

Nonetheless, the contradiction between traditional attitudes and actual behavior could not last, especially when that contradiction became greater each year. What eventually changed was the public perception of traditional gender roles. In the late 1960s and early 1970s, a **women's liberation movement** emerged that had a major impact on the attitudes of women and, indirectly, men about their roles. This change was spurred both by the experiences of women in the civil rights movement of the 1960s and by the increasing resentment of middle-class business and professional women toward the barriers that held back their progress. This discontent found an early voice in Friedan's *The Feminine Mystique,* but mere recognition of the limits on women's achievements placed by society's attitudes was not enough. A full-fledged push for legislative and economic action ensued that would bring closer the goal of equality, or at least of equal opportunity, for men and women.[12]

The National Organization of Women (NOW), the first avowedly feminist organization since women gained the right to vote, held its inaugural meeting in 1966 with Betty Friedan the chief organizer. Its statement of purpose expressed concerns about discrimination in employment, education, and the legal system. It also called for a true partnership between the sexes to be brought about by equitable sharing of the responsibilities of home and children and their economic support. Women's groups such as NOW were successful in promoting change in many areas. Through lawsuits or the threat of legal action, large corporations were pressured into initiating "affirmative action" programs to increase their hiring and promotion of women. The federal government was pressured into investigating sex discrimination in federally funded contracts and federally sponsored programs and then devising programs to end it. Women's studies courses were added to the curriculum at many colleges and universities. Pressure from the women's liberation movement reduced the emphasis on gender stereotypes in children's books, stimulated the opening of day care centers, and contributed to the elimination of sexist language in professional journals and of separate advertising for "women's jobs" and "men's jobs" in the classified sections of newspapers. The women's movement had impact in many ways, large and small, and a whole generation of women became aware of the possibilities that could be open to them if they did not follow traditional norms.[13]

Starting in the 1960s, **equal employment opportunity (EEO) laws** were passed in many countries to restrict sex discrimination, as well as other types of discrimination. In the United States, Title VII of the Civil Rights Act of 1964 prohibited discrimination on the basis of sex, race, color, religion, or national origin in any employment condition, including hiring, firing, promotion, transfer, compensation, and access to training programs. Title VII was later extended to ban discrimination on the basis of pregnancy or childbirth and to ban sexual harassment. The Equal Pay Act of 1963 made it illegal to pay members of one sex less than the other if they are in equivalent jobs. All organizations with 50 or more employees and federal contracts exceeding $50,000 per year were required to file affirmative action programs with the federal government detailing the steps they were taking to eliminate discrimination. In addition, Title IX of the Education Amendments of 1972 banned sex discrimination in educational institutions receiving federal funds. Among other benefits, Title IX led to an enormous increase in opportunities for women to participate in college athletics.[14]

Ironically, the Title VII ban on sex discrimination in the United States was proposed as a last-minute amendment by a civil rights opponent as a strategy to prevent passage of the bill. Opponents felt the male-dominated Congress would be more reluctant to pass the legislation if sex was included. Indeed, one representative justified his opposition with the phrase, "Vive la difference!" However, women's rights advocates joined civil rights opponents to pass the amendment, and then joined civil rights advocates to pass the entire bill, amendment and all. Thus, Title VII opened the door for significant gains for women in the workplace despite the intent of the representative who offered the amendment.[15]

The women's movement and EEO laws elicited mixed reactions from men. The men most threatened by these social and legal developments were those most committed to traditional roles in the family, the workplace, and public affairs. They were alarmed because their power in a patriarchal social system was being challenged. Other men were concerned about the impact on their job security and future advancement as more women entered the workplace. These men were inclined to dismiss newly mandated affirmative action programs as promoting "reverse discrimination." Most men, however, viewed the women's movement and EEO laws with ambivalence and anxiety. They took these developments seriously, but they did not know what to make of them or how to respond to them.[16]

Many women, on the other hand, complained of a backlash against the women's liberation movement and were frustrated at the incomplete achievement of its goals. One woman characterized feminism as the Great Experiment That Failed, with its perpetuators as the casualties. Younger women, however, tended to see such complaints as tales from "the old days when, once upon a time, women had trouble getting into the schools or jobs they now hold."[17]

In the last decade of the 20th century, tensions between women and men over public issues and events repeatedly emerged. **Sexual harassment,** or the directing of unwelcome sexual attention by one workforce member toward another, became a matter of considerable public discussion due to several highly publicized incidents. For example, the National Football League fined players on the New England Patriots professional football team for locker-room sexual harassment of a female journalist, Lisa Olson. The response of the team's owner, Victor Kiam, to the charge of harassment was to call Olson a "classic bitch." Hounded by fans of the team when she returned to the Patriots' stadium to cover later games, Olson eventually left the country to pursue her profession in Australia. This was one of many incidents in which female sportswriters experienced intimidation and blatant sexism as they entered terrain where previously there had been no female presence.[18]

The U.S. Secretary of the Navy resigned and other naval officers were disciplined or dismissed after rampant sexual harassment and assault at the annual convention of the Tailhook Association, a group of retired and active naval aviators, came to public light. Female naval aviators were sexually assaulted by reportedly several hundred men as they were forced to walk a gauntlet of drunken officers lining the corridor outside hospitality suites at the convention hotel. The navy helicopter pilot who was the first to complain to navy officials about her treatment, Lt. Paula Coughlin, subsequently was the subject of a smear campaign by some of her fellow officers.[19]

In a "she said, he said" incident that raised issues of sexism and racism, Clarence Thomas, a Black nominee for the U.S. Supreme Court who was eventually confirmed as a Justice, was accused by Anita Hill, a Black law professor and former subordinate of Thomas, of sexual harassment. In televised hearings, Hill's graphic charges were dramatically aired and vehemently denied by Thomas, who claimed he was a victim of racism. Battle lines were drawn over the merits of Hill's charges; polls suggested that White women, who were less sensitive to Thomas's charge of racism, were most favorable to Hill, whereas Black women, who were more sensitive to racism, were most favorable to Thomas. Publicity from the Thomas–Hill hearings increased public sensitivity to the issue of sexual harassment. In the first half of the next year, sexual harassment charges filed with the U.S. Equal Employment Opportunity Commission were up by more than 50% over the same period the year before.[20]

Workplace romance, or the sharing of welcome sexual attention by two workforce members, became a hotly contested public issue after it became known that U.S. President Bill Clinton had engaged in sexual activity with a White House intern, Monica Lewinsky. Clinton was impeached by the U.S. House of Representatives but was not convicted of the impeachment charges by the U.S. Senate, which would have forced him to leave office. Clinton claimed that the investigation of the affair infringed on his private life. However, the fact that the incidents occurred on White House premises and placed a burden on his office staff made it a very public affair.[21]

Although of less consequence than sexual activity in the workplace involving a president and intern, the merits of flirting by professional women were hotly debated. After the *Wall Street Journal* reported that younger women were more inclined to "let their femininity show" and use it to get ahead professionally than their mothers had been, readers took sides. A female reader complained that giving the impression that young women were using their sexual appeal to compete in the workplace perpetuated the stereotype of women as sex objects and harmed women perceived as less attractive who were working hard to get ahead based on merit. A male reader complained that if he risked a sexual harassment complaint by flaunting his sexuality in the office, professional women should not be allowed to flaunt their feminine lures either. The only people who seemed to be happy about the situation were the women who enjoyed and benefited from flirting and the men who welcomed their attention.[22]

A Snapshot of the Present

Let us now consider the current status of men and women in the workplace. Review of key events and trends in the 20th century suggests that the economic roles played by the sexes became more similar over time.

Sex differences in U.S. labor force participation, educational attainment, and employment in white-collar occupations and the marital status of labor force participants decreased dramatically over the course of the century.

In the early years of the 21st century, as Table 2.1 suggests, the proportion of men in the labor force decreased slightly (from 75% in 2000 to 72%); however, the proportion of women in the labor force, 59%, remained essentially the same as it had been in 1990 (58%) and 2000 (60%). As Table 2.2 indicates, the proportion of master's degrees earned by women continued to rise, both overall (from 58% to 61%) and in business (from 40% to 44%); however, the proportion of women earning undergraduate degrees held steady at 57%. Also, the proportion of women in the labor force held steady since 2000 at 47%.[23] Overall, the rate of change in the economic roles played by women and men and their educational attainment in preparation for these roles appears to have slowed considerably in the 21st century.

These changes, or lack of changes, have left significant differences in the employment status and workplace experiences of men and women firmly in place. In the opening passage of this chapter, Hannah Seligson, a journalist, describes her dismay upon personally discovering these differences. She expected to find that the workplace is a meritocracy in which distinctions based on seemingly irrelevant factors such as an individual's sex are minimal or nonexistent. Instead, she found something quite different. In a sense, the rest of this book documents what Hannah found.[24]

Moreover, the employment status and workplace experiences differ for men and women of various racial and ethnic groups. First, a note on the terminology used to represent race and ethnicity in this book: The terms "White," "Black," and "Asian" are used to designate racial groups and "Hispanic" to designate an ethnic group because these are the terms most frequently used in U.S. government reports and employment statistics. However, the terms "Caucasian," "African American," "Pacific Islander," and "Latino/Latina" or "Chicano/Chicana" may just as well be used. Further, each of these groups may be divided into multiple subgroups. Employment statistics about other racial and ethnic groups are often incomplete if compiled at all and are not reported in this chapter. Also, employment statistics do not recognize the fact that many members of the labor force are multiracial and multiethnic; this is a limitation in the way in which the statistics are compiled. For example, if the U.S president had been included in employment statistics compiled after the winner of the 2008 presidential election began his term, the president (Barack Obama) could have been classified as either Black or White.

The three largest racial groups in the U.S. labor force according to government data are Whites (81%), Blacks (11%), and Asians (5%); other racial groups (e.g., Native Americans) represent a combined total of about 3% of the labor force. Hispanics represent the largest ethnic group in the labor force tracked in government data (14%). Hispanics as an ethnic group may be classified according to race; about 95% of Hispanics in the labor force are classified as White and the remaining 5% are scattered across other racial groups. For purposes of comparison, we will examine the employment status of White, Black, Asian, and Hispanic men and women.[25]

Table 2.3 reports the percentage of women and men in the labor force for each of the four racial and ethnic groups examined. The sex difference in labor force participation rates varies across racial and ethnic groups, ranging from 6% for Blacks to 24% for Hispanics. As we shall see, there are other significant differences in the employment status of members of different racial and ethnic groups.

Table 2.3 Labor Force Participation Rates by Racial/Ethnic Group

	Percentage in the U.S. Labor Force		
Racial/Ethnic Group	**Women**	**Men**	**Difference**
White	59	74	15
Black	61	67	6
Asian	59	75	16
Hispanic	56	80	24
ALL RACES AND ETHNIC GROUPS	60	73	13

SOURCES: U.S. Department of Labor, Bureau of Labor Statistics (2009). *Labor force statistics from the Current Population Survey*, tables 3 and 4. Retrieved December 23, 2009, from http://www.bls.gov/cps.

The Sex Segregation of Occupations

If the workplace were completely integrated with regard to sex, the percentages of the male and female labor force in each occupation would be equal. For example, if 5% of all males were engineers, 5% of all females would be engineers, and the same would hold true for all occupations. As one sex increased in proportion in the labor force relative to the other, the percentages of members of that sex in different occupations would remain equal to the equivalent percentages for the other sex.

Occupations may be characterized as segregated with regard to sex when females and males are *not* similarly distributed across occupations. The level of **sex segregation of occupations** has dropped in most countries since the 1970s, primarily due to the increased employment of women in male-dominated occupations. However, the level of sex segregation remains very high. About half of the female or male labor force in the United States, and over half of the female or male labor force in many other countries, would have to change occupations for sex segregation to be eliminated completely. Although there have been increases in the labor force participation of women worldwide, the sex segregation of occupations is one of the most enduring features of the global economy.[26]

The nature of sex segregation in the U.S. workplace may be understood best by examining the employment of women and men in specific occupational categories. As Table 2.4 indicates, women hold 46.7% of all jobs in the labor force. Occupations are classified as male-intensive, female-intensive, or sex-neutral based on the proportion of women in the occupation. **Male-intensive occupations** are defined as those in which one third (33.3%) or less of the work force is female. **Female-intensive occupations** are defined as those in which two thirds (66.7%) or more of the work force is female. **Sex-neutral occupations** consist of occupations in which women hold more than one third and less than two thirds of the jobs (33.4% to 66.6%).

Taking into account the size of the labor force in various occupations, only 9.6% of women work in male-intensive occupations, and only 13.5% of men work in female-intensive occupations. In contrast, 46.0% of all men work in male-intensive occupations, and 48.6% all women work in female-intensive occupations. Overall, about half of the labor force works in occupations numerically dominated by members of their own sex, whereas about 10% of the labor force works in occupations numerically dominated by members of the other sex. The experiences of workers may differ substantially depending on whether they are employed in occupations that are sex-neutral, dominated by members of their own sex, or dominated by members of the other sex. In Chapter 5, we discuss the unique experiences of women in male-intensive groups and men in female-intensive groups in greater depth.[27]

Details about the level of sex segregation in specific occupations are masked by the fact that employment statistics for over 820 different occupations are combined into 22 broad occupational groups in the U.S. government data reported in Table 2.4. For example, although protective service occupations are classified as male-intensive overall (22.8% female), they include female-intensive occupations such as school crossing guards (73.5% female) as well as male-intensive occupations such as fire fighters (4.8% female). Also, although health care practitioner and technical occupations are classified as female-intensive overall (74.6% female), they include male-intensive occupations such as dentists (27.2% female) as well as female-intensive occupations such as dental hygienists (97.7% female); note the large difference in the proportion of women according to occupational status for two types of jobs in the same industry. Finally, although food preparing and serving occupations are classified as sex-neutral overall (56.0% female), they include male-intensive occupations involved in food preparation such as chefs and head cooks (17.0% female) and female-intensive occupations involved in food serving such as waiters and waitresses (73.2% female); note the same type of difference in the proportion of women according to occupational status as for dentists and dental hygienists. We shall examine sex differences in the status of food servers in Chapter 4.[28]

Management occupations, classified as sex-neutral in Table 2.4, deserve special attention because they include workers with power and authority over others. These occupations include managers (also called "supervisors") who work in different types of functions (e.g., marketing, public relations, human resources, operations, purchasing) as well as different types of industries (e.g., lodging, funeral services, medical, construction). Two rules of thumb are used to classify individuals into management occupations or not: (1) Managers of professional and technical workers are usually classified with the workers they manage because they have a shared background with these workers. (2) First-line managers of production, service, and sales workers who spend at least 80% of their time performing management activities are usually classified in management occupations because their work activities are distinct from those of the workers they manage. [29]

As for other occupational groups, the combining of management occupations into one occupational group masks sex segregation within specific types of managerial jobs. For example, some managerial jobs such as computer and information systems managers (27.2% female) are male-intensive, whereas other managerial jobs such as medical and health services managers are female-intensive (69.4% female). However, management occupations as a whole have shifted from once being

Table 2.4   Employment of Women and Men in Occupations

Occupation	Percentage of Female Employees	Occupation Type
1. Management	37.4	
2. Business & financial operations	56.2	
3. Computer & mathematics	24.8	M
4. Architecture & engineering	13.5	M
5. Life, physical, & social sciences	46.1	
6. Community & social services	60.3	
7. Legal	51.9	
8. Education, training, & library	74.0	F
9. Arts, design, entertainment, sports, & media	47.8	
10. Health care practitioner & technical	74.6	F
11. Health care support	88.8	F
12. Protective services	22.8	M
13. Food preparation & serving	56.0	
14. Building & grounds cleaning & maintenance	40.2	
15. Personal care & services	78.4	F
16. Sales	49.5	
17. Office & administrative support	74.8	F
18. Farming, fishing, & forestry	21.1	M
19. Construction & extraction	2.5	M
20. Installation, maintenance, & repair	3.9	M
21. Production	29.7	M
22. Transportation & material moving	14.9	M
TOTAL	46.7	

SOURCE: U.S. Department of Labor, Bureau of Labor Statistics (2009). *Labor force statistics from the Current Population Survey*, table 11. Retrieved December 23, 2009, from http://www.bls.gov/cps.

NOTE: Occupation type equals M for a male-intensive occupation (less than 33.3% female employees) and F for a female-intensive occupation (greater than 66.7% female employees). No symbol indicates a sex-neutral occupation. The table includes both full-time and part-time employees.

male-intensive to now being sex-neutral in composition. In contrast, as the proportion of female executive officers (14%) in *Fortune* 500 corporations suggests, the *top* ranks of management occupations remain male-intensive.[30]

The **racial and ethnic segregation of occupations** also warrants attention. If the U.S. workplace were completely integrated with regard to race and ethnicity, the percentage of the Black labor force in each occupation would about 11%, the percentage of the Asian labor force in each occupation would about 5%, and the percentage of the Hispanic labor force in each occupation would about 14%,. Table 2.5 displays the percentage of Black, Asian, and Hispanic employees in each of the major occupational groups; it does not include percentages for White employees because these percentages are overwhelmingly larger (about 70% or higher) than those for the other groups. The proportion of Black employees is highest in health care support (e.g., nursing, psychiatric, and home health aides), protective services, and community and social services (e.g., counselors, social workers) occupations. The proportion of Asian employees is highest in computer and mathematics; life, physical, and social sciences; and architecture and engineering occupations. The proportion of Hispanic employees is highest in farming, fishing, and forestry; building and grounds cleaning and maintenance; construction and extraction; production; and food preparing and serving occupations. Overall, these statistics suggest that occupations are segregated with regard to race and ethnicity as well as sex.[31]

The Sex Gap in Earnings

Not only do women and men tend to work in different occupations; they also differ in earnings. The ratio of female-to-male earnings (F/M ratio) for full-time U.S. employees across all occupations is 80%. Although this ratio has risen since the 1970s, when it was about 60%, the **sex gap in earnings** remains considerable.[32]

The sex gap in earnings exists across occupations. The wages earned in female-intensive occupations are typically lower than those earned in male-intensive occupations. In fact, the reduction in the earnings gap since the 1970s has been primarily due to the increased employment of women in occupations that were previously male-intensive (e.g., management and law) or are still male-intensive (e.g., architecture and engineering).[33]

The sex gap in earnings also exists within almost all occupations. To cite a few examples, the F/M ratio for full-time workers is 64% for physicians

Table 2.5   Employment of Members of Racial and Ethnic Groups in Occupations

Occupation	Percentage of Employees		
	Black	Asian	Hispanic
1. Management	6.4	4.6	7.3
2. Business & financial operations	9.4	6.5	7.9
3. Computer & mathematics	7.2	16.7	5.1
4. Architecture & engineering	5.1	9.6	6.7
5. Life, physical, & social sciences	7.1	12.0	4.7
6. Community & social services	19.0	2.5	8.9
7. Legal	7.0	2.8	6.6
8. Education, training, & library	9.2	3.8	7.5
9. Arts, design, entertainment, sports, & media	6.1	4.1	8.3
10. Health care practitioner & technical	10.2	8.0	5.9
11. Health care support	25.8	4.2	13.6
12. Protective services	19.1	1.8	10.9
13. Food preparation & serving	12.1	5.4	21.0
14. Building & grounds cleaning & maintenance	15.0	2.8	33.4
15. Personal care & services	14.7	7.4	14.2
16. Sales	9.7	4.7	11.7
17. Office & administrative support	13.0	3.7	12.8
18. Farming, fishing, & forestry	4.5	1.7	39.3
19. Construction & extraction	6.3	1.4	29.6
20. Installation, maintenance, & repair	8.5	2.8	14.5
21. Production	12.2	5.2	21.1
22. Transportation & material moving	16.9	2.5	19.7
TOTAL	11.0	4.8	14.0

SOURCE: U.S. Department of Labor, Bureau of Labor Statistics (2009). *Labor force statistics from the Current Population Survey*, table 11. Retrieved December 23, 2009, from http://www.bls.gov/cps.

NOTE: The table includes both full-time and part-time employees.

and surgeons, 87% for registered nurses, 85% for college and university teachers, 88% for elementary and middle school teachers, 84% for food servers in restaurants (i.e., waiters and waitresses), 82% for bakers, 81% for janitors and building cleaners, 76% for recreation and fitness workers,

87% for cashiers, 94% for customer service representatives, 86% for mail carriers, 83% for laundry and dry-cleaning workers, and 84% for bus drivers. In the managerial occupations, female managers earn 71% as much as male managers. Male and female workers earn exactly the same wages in only one occupation, counselors in community and social services occupations. In rare examples of occupations in which women earn more than men, the F/M ratio is 104% for special education teachers, 109% in construction and extraction occupations, and 101% in installation, maintenance, and repair occupations.[34]

The gap between the earnings of males and females does not diminish with educational attainment. Although education has a strong positive effect on earnings for both women and men, it yields greater economic benefits for men. The earnings gap exists at every educational level—for workers with less than a high school education, a high school diploma, a bachelor's degree, and even an advanced graduate degree. Earnings data suggest that the higher the educational level, the lower the F/M ratio, a depressing thought for women.[35]

The earnings gap exists across racial and ethnic groups. The F/M ratio is 79% for White workers, 89% for Black workers, 78% for Asian workers, and 90% for Hispanic workers. There is an earnings gap between racial and ethnic groups; White workers earn 86%, Black workers earn 68%, and Hispanic workers earn 61% of what Asian workers earn. Overall, Asian men are the most highly paid in the U.S. labor force, followed by White men, Asian women, White women, Black men, Hispanic men, Black women, and Hispanic women in that order.[36]

Finally, the earnings gap exists across national cultures. Although men earn more than women overall, the size of the F/M ratio for employees who perform similar work varies considerably across nations, ranging from 45% for Bolivia to 83% for Uzbekistan. Although U.S. women have higher work qualifications with respect to educational and professional attainment than do women in most other nations, the United States falls at about the average in F/M ratio for employees who perform similar work (67%), ranking 64th out of 125 nations.[37]

Thus, there is a "cost of being female" that prevails within occupations as well as across occupations, educational levels, racial and ethnic groups, and cultures. The gap between male and female earnings is a long-standing attribute of the global economy, and it is not likely that this gap will disappear anytime soon.

In conclusion, women and men tend to play different economic roles in the workplace today. Current employment and compensation patterns send a powerful message to young people entering the labor force such as Hannah Seligson. The message is that although all occupations are theoretically open to all individuals, (1) some occupations are more appropriate for members of one sex than the other sex, (2) the lower-paying occupations are more appropriate for women, (3) the higher-paying occupations are more appropriate for men, (4) work in male-intensive occupations is worth more than work in female-intensive occupations, and (5) work performed by men is worth more than equivalent work performed by women.

Looking Forward

Traditional gender roles have less to do with present-day economic realities than at any previous time. The changes experienced by women in the labor force over the last century have been striking. Women entering male-intensive organizations have gone from being the only woman holding a particular job, to being a member of a small group of women a midst a larger group of men in the job, sometimes to being a member of the majority group, and increasingly more often to being in charge. The changes experienced by men have been less dramatic. However, men have been required to adapt to the presence of more women as their peers, superiors, and subordinates. Both sexes have had to adjust.

Some important differences between the economic roles played by women and men remain. Men continue to hold most top management positions in organizations. Even when organizations consist predominantly of female employees, the leaders are typically male. The gap between male and female wages also persists. Among full-time workers, women consistently earn lower wages than do men. Even with the same job in the same occupation, women's average earnings are typically lower than those of men. The highest-paid occupations are those with predominantly male workers.

Thus, we find ourselves in a period of flux. Even though work and its rewards are not distributed equally between the sexes, enough change has occurred to make traditional gender roles no longer an appropriate guideline for workplace behavior. However, new standards of behavior have not replaced the old standards. Whether consciously or unconsciously, people often are influenced by their own sex and others' sex in their work behavior.

What *does* it mean to be a woman or a man in today's workplace? How *should* women and men take into account their own sex and others' sex in their workplace interactions, if at all? Widely accepted answers to these questions, promoting either a unisex standard of behavior or separate standards of behavior for men and women, have not emerged.

Due to the increase in the proportion of working women, more workplace interactions between people of the opposite sex are occurring than ever before. One of the few advantages of adhering to traditional gender roles was that men and women knew how they were expected to treat each other. That advantage is gone. Instead, women and men need to understand each other better in their work roles. The remainder of the book explores men's and women's work roles, including their experiences as job seekers, recruiters, employees, team members, and leaders.

Notes

1. Seligson, H. (2008, August 31). Girl power at school, but not at the office. *New York Times.* Retrieved September 1, 2008, from www.nytimes.com.

2. Chafe, W. H. (1976). Looking backward in order to look forward: Women, work, and social values in America. In J. M. Kreps (Ed.), *Women and the American economy: A look to the 1980s* (pp. 6–30). Englewood Cliffs, NJ: Prentice Hall; Tilly, L. A., & Scott, J. W. (1978). *Women, work, and family.* New York: Holt, Rinehart & Winston; Smith, B. G. (2000). Industrial revolution. In A. M. Howard & F. M. Kavenik (Eds.), *Handbook of American women's history* (pp. 269–270). Thousand Oaks, CA: Sage.

3. Buenker, J. D. (2000). Nineteenth Amendment to the Constitution—1920. In A. M. Howard & F. M. Kavenik (Eds.), *Handbook of American women's history* (p. 402). Thousand Oaks, CA: Sage; Chafe.

4. Anderson, S. (1935). *Puzzled America.* Mamaroneck, NY: Appel, p. 46, quoted in Dubbert, J. L. (1979). *A man's place: Masculinity in transition.* Englewood Cliffs, NJ: Prentice Hall, p. 210.

5. Fox, M. F., & Hesse-Biber, S. (1984). *Women at work.* Palo Alto, CA: Mayfield; Dubbert; Howard, A. M. (2000). Depression era. In A. M. Howard & F. M. Kavenik (Eds.), *Handbook of American women's history* (p. 146). Thousand Oaks, CA: Sage.

6. U.S. Department of Commerce, Bureau of the Census. (1975). *Historical statistics of the United States: Colonial times to 1970* (p. 133, series D49–62). Washington, DC: Government Printing Office; U.S. Department of Labor, Bureau of Labor Statistics. (1989). *Handbook of labor statistics* (pp. 235–239, table 55). Washington, DC: Government Printing Office; U.S. Department of Commerce, Bureau of the Census. (2000). *Current population survey* (computed from data for October, 2000). Retrieved December 6, 2000, from http://ferret.bls.census.gov.

7. Weiner, L. Y. (1985). *From working girl to working mother: The female labor force in the United States, 1820–1980.* Chapel Hill: University of North Carolina Press; U.S. Department of Commerce. (1975), pp. 131–132, series D29–41, and p. 133, series D49–62; U.S. Department of Commerce. (2000). (computed from data for October, 2000).

8. *The Economist* (1999, December 31). Oral contraceptives: The liberator, p.102; Goldin, C., & Katz, L. F. (2002). The power of the pill: Oral contraceptives and women's career and marriage decisions. *Journal of Political Economy, 110,* 730–770; Huber, J. N. (2008). Reproductive biology, technology, and gender inequality: An autobiographical essay. *Annual Review of Sociology, 34,* 1–13.

9. U. S. Department of Commerce, Bureau of the Census. (1975). *Historical statistics of the United States: Colonial times to 1970* (pp. 139–140, series D182–232). Washington, DC: Government Printing Office; U. S. Department of Labor, Bureau of Labor Statistics. (2002). *Employment and Earnings,* computed from table 9. Retrieved April 24, 2002, from http://www.bls.gov/cps.

10. Friedan, B. (1974). *The feminine mystique* (10th anniversary ed.). New York: Norton, p. 18.

11. Chafe, p. 20.

12. Yelton-Stanley, S. K., & Howard, A. M. (2000). Women's liberation movement. In A. M. Howard & F. M. Kavenik (Eds.), *Handbook of American women's history* (pp. 640–641). Thousand Oaks, CA: Sage.

13. Yelton-Stanley, S. K. (2000). National Organization for Women (NOW). In A. M. Howard & F. M. Kavenik (Eds.), *Handbook of American women's history* (p. 382). Thousand Oaks, CA: Sage; *Ms.* (1979, December). *Special issue: The decade of women.*

14. Sedmak, N. J., & Vidas, C. (1994). *Primer on equal employment opportunity* (6th ed.). Washington, DC: Bureau of National Affairs.

15. Ledvinka, J., & Scarpello, V. G. (1991). *Federal regulation of personnel and human resource management* (2nd ed.). Boston: PWS-Kent, pp. 63–65.

16. Faludi, S. (1999). *Stiffed: The betrayal of the American man.* New York: Morrow; Pleck, J. H., & Sawyer, J. (Eds.). (1974). *Men and masculinity.* Englewood Cliffs, NJ: Prentice Hall.

17. Faludi, S. (1991). *Backlash: The undeclared war against American women.* New York: Crown; Ebeling, K. (1990, November 19). The failure of feminism. *Newsweek,* p. 9; Goodman, E. (1985, March 8). Feminists' mid-life shock. *Hartford Courant,* p. B9.

18. Ricchiardi, S. (2004). Offensive interference. *American Journalism Review, 26* (4), 54–59; Disch, L., & Kane, M. J. (1996). When a looker is really a bitch: Lisa Olson, sport, and the heterosexual matrix. *Signs, 21,* 278–308.

19. Salholz, E. (1992, August 10). Deepening shame. *Newsweek,* pp. 30–36; U.S. Department of Defense, Inspector General. (1993). *Tailhook 91, part 2: Events at the 35th Annual Tailhook Symposium.* Washington, DC: Government Printing Office.

20. Smolowe, J., Gorey, H., Johnson, J., & Traver, N. (1991, October 21). She said, he said. *Time*. Retrieved May 28, 2009, from www.time.com; Abramson, J. (1992, October 5). Reversal of fortune: Image of Anita Hill, brighter in hindsight, galvanizes campaigns. *Wall Street Journal*, pp. A1, A6; Jaschik-Herman, M. L., & Fisk, A. (1995). Women's perceptions and labeling of sexual harassment in academia before and after the Hill-Thomas hearings. *Sex Roles, 33*, 439–446; Fassin, E. (2002). Sexual events: From Clarence Thomas to Monica Lewinsky. *differences, 13*, 127–158.

21. Isikoff, M., & Thomas, E. (1998, February 2). Clinton and the intern. *Newsweek*, pp. 31–46; Powell, G. N. (1998, September 30). How "the affair" would be handled in the private sector. *Hartford Courant*, p. A13.

22. Pollock, E. J. (2000, February 7). In today's workplace, women feel freer to be, well, women. *Wall Street Journal*, pp. A1, A20; Letters to the editor: So now we're sex kittens again? (2000, February 18). *Wall Street Journal*, p. A15.

23. U.S. Department of Labor, Bureau of Labor Statistics. (2009). *Labor force statistics from the Current Population Survey*, table A-19. Retrieved December 22, 2009, from http://www.bls.gov/cps.

24. Seligson.

25. U.S. Department of Labor, Bureau of Labor Statistics. (2009). *Labor force statistics from the Current Population Survey*, tables 3 and 4. Retrieved December 23, 2009, from http://www.bls.gov/cps.

26. England, P. (2006). Toward gender equality: Progress and bottlenecks. In F. D. Blau, M. C. Brinton, & D. B. Grusky (Eds.), *The declining significance of gender?* (pp. 245–264). New York: Russell Sage Foundation; Jacobs, J. A. (1999). The sex segregation of occupations: Prospects for the 21st century. In G. N. Powell (Ed.), *Handbook of gender and work* (pp. 125–141). Thousand Oaks, CA: Sage; Anker, R. (1998). *Gender and jobs: Sex segregation of occupations in the world*. Geneva: International Labour Office; Reskin, B. (1993). Sex segregation in the workplace. In J. Blake & J. Hagan (Eds.), *Annual Review of Sociology, 19*, 241–270.

27. U.S. Department of Labor, Bureau of Labor Statistics (2009). *Labor force statistics from the Current Population Survey*, computed from table 9. Retrieved June 3, 2009, from http://www.bls.gov/cps; Browne, K. R. (2006). Evolved sex differences and occupational segregation. *Journal of Organizational Behavior, 27*, 143–162; Gatta, M. L., & Roos, P. A. (2005). Rethinking occupational integration. *Sociological Forum, 20*, 369–402.

28. U.S. Department of Labor, Bureau of Labor Statistics. (2009). *Labor force statistics from the Current Population Survey*, table 11. Retrieved December 23, 2009, from http://www.bls.gov/cps.

29. U. S. Department of Labor, Bureau of Labor Statistics. (2009). *Standard Occupational Classification (SOC) user guide*. Retrieved June 4, 2009, from http://www.bls.gov/soc.

30. Catalyst. (2009). *2009 Catalyst census:* Fortune *500 women executive officers and top earners*. New York: Author. Retrieved January 18, 2010, from http://www.catalyst.org.

31. Tomaskovic-Devey, D., Stainback, K., Taylor, T., Zimmer, C., Robinson, C., & McTague, T. (2006). Documenting desegregation: Segregation in American workplaces by race, ethnicity, and sex, 1966–2003. *American Sociological Review, 71,* 565–588; Reskin, B. F., & Padavic, I. (1999). Sex, race, and ethnic inequality in United States workplaces. In J. S. Chafetz (Ed.), *Handbook of the sociology of gender* (pp. 343–374). New York: Kluwer Academic/Plenum.

32. U.S. Department of Labor, Bureau of Labor Statistics. (2009). *Labor force statistics from the Current Population Survey,* table 39. Retrieved June 4, 2009, from http://www.bls.gov/cps; Blau, F. D., & Kahn, L. M. (2007). The gender pay gap: Have women gone as far as they can? *Academy of Management Perspectives, 27*(1), 7–23; Blau, F. D., & Kahn, L. M. (2006). The gender pay gap: Going, going . . . but not gone. In F. D. Blau, M. C. Brinton, & D. B. Grusky (Eds.), *The declining significance of gender?* (pp. 37–66). New York: Russell Sage Foundation.

33. England, P., Allison, P., & Wu, Y. (2007). Does bad pay cause occupations to feminize, does feminization reduce pay, and how can we tell with longitudinal data? *Social Science Research, 36,* 1237–1256.

34. U.S. Department of Labor. (2009), table 39.

35. Roos, P. A., & Gatta, M. L. (1999). The gender gap in earnings: Trends, explanations, and prospects. In G. N. Powell (Ed.), *Handbook of gender and work* (pp. 95–123). Thousand Oaks, CA: Sage.

36. U.S. Department of Labor, Bureau of Labor Statistics. (2009). Labor force statistics from the Current Population Survey, table 37. Retrieved June 4, 2009, from http://www.bls.gov/cps.

37. Hausmann, R., Tyson, L. D., & Zahidi, S. (2009). *The global gender gap report 2009.* Geneva, Switzerland: World Economic Forum. Retrieved October 27, 2009, from http://www.weforum.org.

CHAPTER 3

Becoming Women and Men

Boys Mow Lawns, Girls Do Dishes

I've always considered myself tuned-in to the gender politics of the Chore Wars—the household battles between husbands and wives over who does what at home. Imagine my surprise when I realized I'm guilty of perpetuating this conflict into the next generation. While reporting on the topic, I saw that I myself expect different things of my son, 16, and my daughter, 18: I want him to handle more fix-it jobs, while my daughter does more cleaning.

The latest research suggests I'm not alone. The way parents are divvying up and paying kids for chores suggests that this is one family battle that will extend well into the next generation and beyond. A nationwide study by the University of Michigan's Institute for Social Research shows boys ages 10 through 18 are more likely than girls to be getting paid for doing housework—even though boys spend an average 30% less time doing chores. Boys are as much as 10 to 15 percentage points more likely than girls at various ages to be receiving an allowance for doing housework . . .

Boys may be handling more of the kinds of chores that are regarded as a job that should be paid, such as lawn mowing, speculates Frank Stafford, the University of Michigan economics professor heading the research. Chores such as dishwashing or cooking, often regarded as routine and done free, may fall more often to girls.[1]

A re there sex differences beyond the obvious ones? What do people believe sex differences to be? How are beliefs about sex differences conveyed? What causes sex differences, and what effects do they have on individuals' well-being?

Sex differences influence how people are disposed to behave in work settings. Females and males are similar in some ways and different in others. Despite thousands of studies, however, researchers do not agree about the scope, magnitude, or cause of sex differences. As noted in Chapter 1, this may be due to researchers' inclinations to engage in either alpha bias, magnifying existing differences, or beta bias, downplaying existing differences. It is also due to the imperfect nature of the research evidence.

Gender differences influence how people react to others' behavior in work settings. In this book, we are particularly interested in gender stereotypes and roles. **Gender stereotypes** represent beliefs about the psychological traits that are characteristic of members of each sex. According to gender stereotypes, males are high in "masculine" traits such as independence, aggressiveness, and dominance, and females are high in "feminine" traits such as gentleness, sensitivity to the feelings of others, and tactfulness. Gender stereotypes have been generally stable over time. **Gender roles** represent beliefs about the behaviors that are appropriate for members of each sex. According to gender roles, men's proper place is at work and women's proper place is at home. However, both men and women have been less likely to endorse gender roles in recent years. The drop-off has been especially pronounced among men, such that the sex difference in attitudes toward gender roles has essentially disappeared. Also, younger people are the least likely to endorse gender roles, suggesting that further societal changes in norms regarding the proper roles of men vis-à-vis women are likely to come.[2]

This chapter examines sex and gender differences in society that influence male–female interactions in the workplace. First, selected research evidence about sex differences is presented. Next, gender stereotypes are examined and concepts such as gender identity and psychological androgyny are introduced. Different types of sexist attitudes, representing prejudice on the basis of sex, are examined. The influence of nature and nurture on individuals' behavior is considered, and the ways in which gender role expectations are conveyed to children by parents, schools, and the mass media are examined. Finally, the chapter considers how gender stereotypes and roles influence adult health and well-being and unduly restrict adult behavior.

Sex Differences

The study of sex differences is an international preoccupation. Thousands of research studies on the topic have been published by scholars. This topic is not simply "hot" in the sense of being fashionable; it is also inflammatory. Many people have strong beliefs about male and female similarities and differences in basic interests, abilities, attitudes, and behaviors.[3]

Research methods used in reviews of studies of sex differences have evolved over time. Early reviews used what may be called a **vote counting** technique. That is, they simply tallied the number of studies on a given topic that found significant differences favoring females, significant differences favoring males, or no significant sex differences and then reached conclusions based on the "vote." A statistical method called **meta-analysis** is commonly used now. Meta-analysis uses sophisticated quantitative methods to synthesize statistical evidence from numerous studies. It yields results that are typically more complex and often different from those yielded by vote counting. Sex differences have been examined in many types of psychological traits and behavior using the meta-analysis technique.[4]

In this section of the chapter, we consider sex differences in children's interests and activities and in adults' social behavior.

Children's Interests and Activities

Starting at an early age, the interests and activities of boys and girls differ greatly. A sex difference in toy preferences emerges at about 2 years of age. Boys are more likely than girls to prefer action figures, blocks, mock aggression toys such as guns and swords, transportation toys such as toy trucks and trains, construction toys, and sports collectibles. For example, the G.I. Joe product line, introduced by Hasbro in 1964, is marketed particularly to boys. They may choose from action figures representing soldiers, intergalactic warriors, generals, astronauts, football players, and wrestlers; vehicles such as tanks, land assault vehicles, and motorcycles; accessories such as rifles, bomber jackets, and emergency ration kits; books; and movies. Until 1997, when a female helicopter pilot was introduced, the only female action figure in the G.I. Joe line was (of course) a nurse. Over time, G.I. Joe's physical appearance has conveyed what may be called **emphatic masculinity** in the form of extreme muscularity backed up by huge guns.[5]

In contrast, girls are more likely than boys to prefer dolls, dollhouses, jewelry, play kitchens, and domestic toys such as tea sets and playhouses sold in product lines such as Mattel's Barbie. In the book *Barbie Culture,* Mary Rogers observed, "Barbie's style might be called **emphatic femininity.** It takes feminine appearances and demeanor to unattainable extremes. Nothing about Barbie ever looks masculine, even when she is on the police force. Police Officer Barbie comes with a night stick and walkie-talkie but no gun and no handcuffs. She also comes with a 'glittery evening dress' to wear to the awards dance when she will get the 'Best Police Officer Award for her courageous acts in the community,' yet Police Officer Barbie is pictured on the box 'lov(ing) to teach safety tips to children.' Barbie thus feminizes, even maternalizes, law enforcement." Introduced in 1959, more than 1 billion Barbie dolls have been sold in 150 countries. Ninety percent of 3- to 10 year-old U.S. girls own at least one Barbie doll. Although other product lines of dolls have emerged, Barbie remains the best-selling doll in the world.[6]

Of course, the difference between action figures, preferred by boys, and dolls, preferred by girls, may be semantic. The following exchange that actually occurred between two children is instructive: Elise, a 5-year-old girl, was speaking with a 5-year-old boy who said that he didn't play with dolls, Elise replied, "Yes, you do. They just call them action figures so you don't know you're playing with dolls!" Her tone of voice came across as, "You moron, can't you see what they are putting over you?"[7]

Boys prefer a more physically aggressive rough-and-tumble style of play than do girls, including both fighting and mock fighting. They welcome a physically active style of play with both parents. However, due to a sex difference in parental preferences for this style of play, boys engage in it more with their fathers than with their mothers. Boys spend more time watching television and participating in sports, whereas girls spend more time reading. The sex difference in play interests is seen on doorsteps on Halloween. Boys are more likely to dress as villainous characters, monsters, or symbols of death, whereas girls are more likely to dress as princesses, beauty queens, and other examples of traditional femininity.[8]

Sex differences are also manifested in what may be called a "digital divide." Overall, girls are less comfortable using computers and suffer greater computer anxiety than boys, resulting in their spending less time working and playing with computers, taking fewer computer courses in school, and being less likely to major in computer science in college. Girls are more likely to view computers as a way to accomplish tasks (e.g., writing papers and communicating with friends), whereas boys are more likely to view computers as a way to achieve mastery (e.g., scoring highly in video games). Compared with girls, boys are much more involved with the many possible uses of computers. [9]

The source of girls' greater anxiety in using computers may be due to the emphatic masculinity of most computer games and educational software packages. A study compared reactions of sixth-grade to eighth-grade girls and boys to two software programs used to teach arithmetic skills. In *Demolition Division,* tanks with division problems moved toward the student's blaster, with possible answers to the problems appearing below the blaster. If the student fired the blaster at the tank with the correct problem before the tank hit the wall, the tank exploded; otherwise, the blaster was destroyed. In contrast, in *American Classroom Fractions,* problems were presented less aggressively in words and verbal feedback on performance was provided. After the student completed the problems, he or she received an assessment of mastery and areas for further practice. Girls experienced more anxiety than boys when playing *Demolition Division,* whereas boys experienced more anxiety than girls when playing *American Classroom Fractions.* Most computer games and educational software are more like *Demolition Division* than *American Classroom Fractions,* which may help to explain why girls are more anxious than boys when using computers.[10]

Mattel, the maker of Barbie dolls and related products, sensed an opportunity to take advantage of this sex difference in reactions to and usage of computers in the 1990s. It marketed a pink-flowered Barbie computer and several interactive video games for girls, including Barbie Fashion Designer, Barbie Magic Hair Styler, Barbie Nail Designer, Barbie Digital Makeover, Barbie Pet Rescue, Detective Barbie, Barbie Magic Genie, Barbie as Sleeping Beauty, and Barbie as Princess Bride. (Note the emphatic femininity of most of the activities in which the software Barbie was engaged.) Mattel quickly captured the lioness's share of the girls' computer game market, thereby promoting computer usage by girls. Video game makers are still trying to expand the largely untapped female market with games focusing on television stars who appeal particularly to girls, pets, dancing, fashion, and personal training. [11]

Video games are marketed primarily to boys, with images of the sexes that largely reinforce gender stereotypes. Male characters tend to be high in emphatic masculinity (e.g., extremely muscular, aggressive, and violent), whereas female characters are high in emphatic femininity (e.g., voluptuous, thin, and wearing much less clothing than male characters). Although girls find these images more troublesome than boys do, their negative reactions have little influence on video game sales since they are not the intended audience.[12]

Although there is variation across cultures, boys and girls exhibit considerable differences in how they spend their time. In Western cultures, it is believed that play is the work of children; play is culturally sanctioned. However, boys have more time to play than do girls because they do not have to devote as much time to household chores. Boys and girls also differ in the types of household chores they perform. As the opening passage for this chapter suggests, boys perform more tasks outside the home for which they get paid, including yard work and outdoor errands. Girls perform more tasks inside the home for which they do not get paid, including taking care of younger children, cleaning, and preparing food.[13]

As they move into adolescence, girls and boys in Western cultures devote similar amounts of time to paid labor. Adolescent employment is particularly encouraged in the United States as a way to learn self-sufficiency and responsibility. However, girls and boys are employed in different kinds of activities. Girls are likely to be babysitters, waitresses, and food counter workers, whereas boys are likely to be gardeners, busboys, and manual laborers.[14]

Overall, girls show more interest in activities associated with boys than vice versa. Toy retailers assume that they can sell a "boy" product to a girl but not the reverse. Although boys as well as girls might enjoy playing at rescuing pets, no boy would want to be caught by his peers using Barbie-oriented computer games to do so. Girls who are interested in activities that are considered more typical of boys than of girls are labeled "tomboys," whereas boys who are interested in activities associated with girls are labeled "sissies." Sissies are more negatively evaluated than tomboys, especially by males. Tomboys are seldom rejected by their peers because of their interest in activities associated with boys; they can always return to playing with other girls. However, boys have less freedom of choice and run a greater risk of being taunted by other boys for showing any interest in girls' activities. Most tomboy activity stops at puberty, when pressures on girls to adhere to the female gender role become particularly intense. However, former or would-be tomboys now have more outlets for their interests, such as female athletic teams at all levels of education. In fact, female undergraduates who participate in varsity athletics are more likely than nonathletes to describe themselves as having been tomboys.[15]

As children grow up and progress through adolescence, they exhibit considerable sex differences in activities and interests. Girls, however, engage more in activities typically associated with boys than the opposite.

As discussed later in the chapter, the ways parents socialize girls and boys contribute greatly to sex differences in children's activities.

Adults' Social Behavior

Sex differences have been examined in many types of social behavior exhibited by adults, including aggression, altruism, and nonverbal communications. **Aggression,** or behavior that is intended to hurt someone else, may be physical, verbal, or indirect. Males are more likely to engage in physical aggression that produces pain or physical injury than are females, especially when their emotions are aroused. However, this does not necessarily mean that males are the more aggressive sex. Because females are on average physically weaker than males, they may learn to avoid physical aggression and to adopt other ways to bring about harm. For instance, they may use their superior verbal skills for aggressive purposes; the sex difference in aggression favoring males is less pronounced for verbal than for physical aggression.[16]

Females may also engage in indirect aggression by trying to hurt others without being identified by their victims. For example, on Bellona, an island in the Pacific Ocean, the society was characterized until recent times by extreme male violence and physical dominance. Women were to respond quickly and unquestioningly to the demands of men, especially their husbands, or expect to be beaten. However, women found creative ways to get back at men. One approach was to compose a "mocking song" to humiliate the offending man. As the song was circulated around the island, the subject was stigmatized in the eyes of his fellow men. The mocking song is a form of indirect aggression.[17]

Women and men exhibit similarities and differences in **altruism,** or behavior that is intended to help someone else. Although both females and males behave altruistically, they do so differently. Males are more likely to offer heroic or chivalrous help in areas where they feel most competent, such as helping a motorist with a flat tire at the side of a dangerous highway. In contrast, females are more likely to offer nurturant or caring help in areas where they feel most competent, such as volunteering to spend time with a sick child. These differences are also seen in occupational roles: Women are particularly well represented in occupations that involve some type of personal service, such as nurse and teacher, whereas men are especially well represented in occupations that call for placing one's life in jeopardy to help others, such as firefighter and law enforcement officer.[18]

Status differences between women and men play an important role in **nonverbal communications.** Nonverbal communication skills include the ability to express oneself accurately using the face, body, and voice; to assess the meaning of nonverbal cues from others; and to recall having met or seen people. Females have higher skills than do males in all three areas, perhaps because they tend to have lower status in organizations and society. They also tend to smile more than males, especially when they are aware that they are being observed. Overall, compared to males, females may be better able to interpret others' nonverbal cues and more inclined to offer positive nonverbal cues themselves because they are in weaker status positions and constantly have to monitor others' reactions to themselves.[19]

In summary, this is a selective review of some of the major findings about sex similarities and differences obtained from psychological research. It suggests that there are both sex differences and sex similarities. Sex similarities prevail, for example, in altruism, but sex differences exist in how it is expressed. Some sex differences, such as those in nonverbal communications, may be attributable to factors other than sex such as status. Other sex differences, such as those in children's interests and activities, remain strong. However, as for adults' interests as indicated by the occupations they pursue, girls are more interested in activities associated with boys than boys are interested in activities associated with girls.

Gender Stereotypes

Before we discuss gender stereotypes, try the following exercise. Create a mental image of the "typical woman"; then create a mental image of what most people would consider the typical woman. Next, complete these two sentences with five different adjectives or phrases: (1) I think the typical woman is _____. (2) Most other people think the typical woman is _____. Now repeat the exercise, this time thinking about the "typical man."[20]

Now consider your responses. You probably feel that most people would answer in a more biased manner than you, invoking gender stereotypes of the two sexes. But, have you noticed the bias of the exercise itself? It is likely to have led you to focus on the differences between the sexes, when, in fact, there is considerable overlap and similarity between their characteristics.

One of the earliest studies of gender stereotypes, defined as shared beliefs about the psychological traits that are characteristic of each sex, was conducted in this manner. Inge Broverman and her colleagues asked a group of college students to list characteristics, attitudes, and behaviors in which they believed women and men differ; these students compiled a list of 122 items. A second group of college students rated the extent to which they agreed that these 122 items were typical of an adult man or an adult woman. Analysis of these results yielded 41 items that were believed to differentiate men and women. The men and women who responded to the survey were in almost complete agreement on the items, which fell into two clusters. Men were seen as more **competent** (i.e., instrumental or "agentic") than women, rating higher on items such as "very skilled in business," "can make decisions easily," and "almost always acts as a leader." In contrast, women were seen as more **warm** (i.e., expressive or "communal") than men, rating higher on items such as "very aware of feelings of others," "very talkative," and "easily expresses tender feelings." Competence was labeled as **masculine** because it was associated with males, whereas warmth was labeled as **feminine** because it was associated with females. Subsequent research has found little change in these stereotypes over time. Moreover, there is consensus in gender stereotypes across national cultures.[21]

In general, stereotypes of people are represented by two dimensions, competence and warmth. Individuals and groups may be seen as high or low in each dimension. As individuals' life situations change, stereotypes of them change as well. For example, childless working women and men are stereotyped as significantly more competent than warm. When working women become mothers, they are perceived as losing competence but gaining warmth. In contrast, when working men become fathers, they are perceived as maintaining their competence and gaining warmth. Given that decision makers are more likely to hire, promote, and develop individuals whom they see as more competent, these stereotypes suggest that becoming a parent leads to discrimination on the basis of sex that hurts women professionally but not men.[22]

Why have gender stereotypes appeared to remain stable over time? Stereotypes of all kinds tend to be durable. People like to categorize themselves and others into groups along primary and secondary dimensions of diversity and then identify ways in which their own group is better than and different from other groups. When these beliefs act as self-fulfilling prophecies, there is little reason for them to change. Also, girls and boys tend to learn stereotypes of different groups in their formative years from parents, teachers, other adults, and the media. By the time they become adults themselves, their stereotypes of various groups are mostly fixed. People are reluctant to give up a long-held stereotype unless it is thoroughly discredited, and even then they may still hold onto it. After all, using stereotypes saves us mental work in identifying and categorizing others.[23]

However, stereotypes of groups can evolve in respond to overwhelming evidence of change in their social roles. A provocative study asked participants to describe the average man or woman either 50 years in the past, in the present, or 50 years in the future. Women of the future were described as more masculine than women of the present, who in turn were described as more masculine than women of the past. Relatively little change was seen in descriptions of women's femininity or men's masculinity or femininity over time. Stereotypes of women, especially regarding their possession of masculine traits traditionally associated with men, may be particularly dynamic as a result of considerable change in their societal roles over time (e.g., increased educational attainment, increased labor force participation, and increased pursuit of careers in male-intensive occupations). In comparison, stereotypes of men, who have exhibited less change in their societal roles over time, may be more static.[24]

Gender Identity

At one time, psychologists regarded masculinity and femininity as opposites. If a person was high in masculinity, he or she was regarded as low in femininity, and vice versa. It was considered appropriate for an individual to conform to his or her gender stereotype. Males were supposed to be masculine, females were supposed to be feminine, and anyone who fell in the middle or at the "wrong" end of the scale was considered to be maladjusted and in need of intensive therapy.[25]

Sandra Bem challenged these assumptions and beliefs in a series of studies beginning in the 1970s. As others had done, she labeled traits as masculine or feminine based on whether they were typically seen as desirable for men or for women. However, unlike earlier researchers, Bem defined masculinity and femininity as independent dimensions rather than opposite ends of a single dimension. Instead of classifying each trait on a single scale ranging from masculine at one end to feminine at the other end, she classified masculine and feminine traits on two separate scales. Masculine items were evaluated on a scale ranging from "high in masculinity" at one end to "low in masculinity" at the other end, and feminine items were evaluated on a scale ranging from "high in femininity" at one end to "low in femininity" at the other. Bem used data from this procedure to choose items for a new survey instrument to be used in research studies, the Bem Sex-Role Inventory (BSRI).[26]

The BSRI contained 20 masculine items, 20 feminine items, and 20 filler items to disguise the purpose of the instrument. Individuals were asked to rate the extent to which they thought each item was characteristic of themselves. Masculinity and femininity scores were calculated by averaging individuals' self-ratings for the respective items. Thus, rather than measuring beliefs about others, the BSRI measured beliefs about oneself in relation to traditional concepts of masculinity and femininity. Although Bem called these beliefs an individual's "sex role identity," we use the term **gender identity** to refer to beliefs about the extent to which one possesses masculine traits and the extent to which one possesses feminine traits. She adopted the four-quadrant classification scheme for gender identity as shown in Figure 3.1. According to this scheme, individuals' gender identity may be classified as androgynous (high in masculinity and femininity), masculine (high in masculinity and low in femininity), feminine (low in masculinity and high in femininity), or undifferentiated (low in masculinity and femininity).[27]

Gender identity also refers to beliefs about oneself in social relationships. Individuals' self-construals capture their sense of self in relation to others. People who are classified as feminine according to the BSRI are more likely to display an **interdependent self-construal,** in which people who are important in their lives are included in their representations of themselves (e.g., "I am a loving parent"; "I am a valuable team member"). In contrast, people who are classified as masculine are more likely

Figure 3.1   Classification of Gender Identity

		Femininity Score	
		High	**Low**
Masculinity Score	**High**	Androgynous	Masculine
	Low	Feminine	Undifferentiated

SOURCE: Bem, S. L. (1977). On the utility of alternative procedures for assessing psychological androgyny. *Journal of Consulting and Clinical Psychology, 45,* 196–205.

to display an **independent self-construal,** in which others are seen as separate and distinct from themselves (e.g., "I am a strong-willed individual"; "I value my autonomy"). The nature of self-construals for androgynous and undifferentiated individuals is less clear. [28]

In advocating her own notions of gender identity, Bem introduced the concept of **psychological androgyny,** representing high amounts of both masculinity and femininity, and a means of measuring it. The term *androgyny* comes from the Greek words "andr" (man) and "gyne" (woman), meaning both masculine and feminine. An androgynous gender identity was found by Bem and others to be associated with higher self-esteem, a more flexible response to situations that seemed to call for either feminine or masculine behaviors, and a host of other positive factors. The individual who adheres to gender stereotypes no longer seemed the ideal of psychological health. Instead, the androgynous individual, whose self-image and behavior are less narrowly restricted, was seen as more ready to meet the complex demands of society. In short, androgyny was proposed as an ideal combination of the "best of both worlds."[29]

The revolutionary nature of the concept of androgyny in the field of psychology matched the feminist spirit of the women's movement that prevailed at the time the concept was developed. However, not surprisingly given the emotions stirred by the same spirit, the concept of androgyny came under severe attack almost as quickly as it was idealized. Some criticized Bem for poor science because her beliefs in what is "right" for individuals were made so obvious. This is not a valid argument. Although *all* scientific research is value-laden, most researchers are not as explicit as Bem in stating their values. More meaningful criticism was made of the items that composed the BSRI. Here, Bem appears to have been victimized by her original methodology. The average desirability of the masculine items in the BSRI for a man was similar to the average desirability of the feminine items for a woman, but the desirability of the various items had not been assessed for an adult in general. Other researchers found that masculine characteristics were more desirable overall than feminine characteristics when rated for an adult of unspecified sex. Bem accepted this criticism, and developed an alternative instrument, the Short BSRI, with 10 masculine items, 10 feminine items, and 10 filler items that eliminated most of the items regarded as undesirable for adults.[30]

The BSRI and other inventories of masculine and feminine characteristics do not acknowledge possible differences on the basis of race or ethnicity in definitions of desirable male and female behavior. The BSRI does a good job of capturing definitions of masculinity and femininity held by Whites and Hispanics, even though emphatic masculinity and femininity have historically been associated with Hispanic cultures. However, it does not do as good a job of capturing Blacks' definitions of masculinity and femininity.[31]

The debate over the merits of androgyny has died down somewhat but has never been fully settled. Several conceptions of what females and males should be like have been proposed. One view argues for conformity with gender stereotypes. A second view argues that people should break free from gender stereotypes and pursue an androgynous ideal. However, both of these views are limited. A more reasonable view is that there should be no conception of ideal behavior for females and males. Instead, the goal should be development of an environment in which everyone is free to be themselves rather than expected to live up to any standard of psychological health. As Sandra Bem later put it, "if there is a moral to the concept of psychological androgyny, it is that *behavior* should have no gender."[32]

Sexism

The term **sexism** refers to prejudice displayed toward members of one sex.[33] Sexism, like prejudice in general, is usually assumed to represent a negative attitude. However, some researchers have distinguished between hostile sexism and benevolent sexism (also known as "subtle sexism"). **Hostile sexism** toward women as a group entails antagonism toward women who are viewed as challenging or usurping men's power (e.g., feminists, career women, seductresses). In contrast, **benevolent sexism** puts women on pedestals; it characterizes women as "pure creatures who ought to be protected, supported, and adored and whose love is necessary to make a man complete." Benevolent sexism implies that women are weak and best suited to conventional feminine roles, and offers protection, affection, and rewards to women who endorse these roles (e.g., wives, mothers, romantic objects). Benevolent sexism is not benign; it assumes women's inferiority and is used to justify women's subordination to men.[34]

A research study examined sex differences in hostile sexism and benevolent sexism toward women in 19 countries. Men scored significantly higher in hostile sexism than did women in all countries. The sex difference in benevolent sexism was much less than the sex difference in hostile sexism. Overall, women rejected hostile sexism outright but often accepted benevolent sexism, believing that they needed to be protected by men.[35]

Similarly, people may display hostile and benevolent sexism toward men as a group. For example, women may exhibit hostile attitudes by criticizing men's greater power and status in society, sexist attitudes, and manner of asserting control. Women also may display the benevolent attitudes of protective maternalism, admiration for men's competence, and appreciation of men's roles in making women's lives complete. Women score higher than men on hostile sexism toward men and lower on benevolent sexism toward men.[36]

A distinction may also be made between old-fashioned sexism and modern sexism. **Old-fashioned sexism,** like hostile sexism, is blatant; it is associated with endorsement of traditional gender roles in the workplace, differential treatment of women and men, and endorsement of laws and societal norms that promote adherence to gender roles. In contrast, **modern sexism** is associated with denial of the existence of sex discrimination, antagonism toward women's demands that alleged sex discrimination be discontinued, and lack of support for programs designed to help women in the workplace. The old-fashioned sexist says, "Women cause problems in the workplace when they don't stick to their proper roles." The modern sexist says, "Women cause problems in the workplace when they complain too much about alleged problems they face." Both statements reflect sexist attitudes, but in different ways. The old-fashioned sexist is prejudiced against women who seek to play nontraditional roles in the workplace, whereas the modern sexist is prejudiced against women who claim that there are barriers to their performing such roles.[37]

Sexism leads to negative outcomes for women in organizations, particularly those who pursue occupations that are associated with men. For instance, modern sexists exaggerate women's representation in male-intensive occupations, reject sex discrimination as a cause of the sex segregation of occupations, and have negative attitudes toward programs designed to assist women. Ironically, modern sexists seem to personally benefit from their sexist attitudes; they rely more on men for work-related advice, and, in turn, may gain more access to resources and receive more promotions. Both hostile and benevolent sexism among men pose barriers to women's status in the workplace, particularly in nontraditional roles. Hostile sexists of both sexes prefer male authority figures over female authority figures, evaluate male candidates for managerial positions more highly than female candidates, and are more tolerant of sexual harassment toward women.[38]

The distinction between old-fashioned and modern sexism is similar to one that has been made between old-fashioned and modern racism. **Old-fashioned racism** entails overt expressions of hostility and antagonism. **Modern racism,** which is also called "aversive" or "symbolic" racism, is a more subtle form of prejudice. Modern racists endorse racial equality and avoid obvious acts of discrimination to maintain their self-images as fair and just individuals. However, they still harbor unconscious negative feelings and beliefs about low-status racial groups. These feelings and beliefs result in subtle bias, particularly when such bias is not obvious or can be rationalized based on factors other than race. Like modern sexists, some modern racists deny the existence of racial discrimination, express antagonism toward the demands of people of color and resent programs that support people of color. Despite its subtle nature, modern racism is extremely detrimental to people of color. It may lead Whites to display acts of "microaggression" toward people of color, including avoidance, closed and unfriendly verbal and nonverbal communication, and failure to help, all of which lead people of color to feel devalued and discriminated against.[39]

In Chapter 1, we discussed comparisons of which type of "ism" was more severe during the 2008 U.S. presidential campaign, sexism directed toward Hillary Clinton or racism directed toward Barack Obama. This type of comparison is not particularly useful, because both sexism and racism hurt the intended targets. However, sexism and racism differ in basic ways in how they are learned and experienced. Women are not statistically in the minority in most cultures, whereas members of many racial and ethnic groups are in the minority depending on the culture. The socialization of males and females takes place in the presence of the other, whereas races are far more separate in society. Thus, White males may view racism as a problem affecting a small group of "outsiders" (i.e., non-Whites), whereas they may be more concerned with sexism, especially the hostile or old-fashioned kind, because they can directly observe its effects on their mothers, wives, sisters, and daughters.[40]

Open displays of negative sexist as well as racist attitudes, at least in public settings, have diminished over the years. It is now less fashionable to be a hostile or old-fashioned sexist than it is to be a benevolent or modern sexist. However, old-fashioned sexism has not completely disappeared.

Nature and Nurture

Numerous theories have been offered for why sex differences occur in the first place. These theories focus on two competing explanations: biological forces (nature) and social-environmental forces (nurture). What ultimately determines individual behavior, nature or nurture or both? To understand the effects of nature and nurture, we need to consider the basic arguments concerning how biological and social-environmental factors lead to sex differences.[41]

Those who focus on the effects of **biological forces** argue that sex differences in adults and children are mostly innate, such that individuals are born masculine or feminine. According to this argument, boys behave the way they do simply because they are male and girls behave as they do because they are female, although the underlying reasons proposed for biological effects differ. Sex differences in cognitive abilities, social behavior, gender identity, and other psychological variables have been attributed to sex differences in physiological properties such as genes, prenatal and current hormone levels, nerve cell activity, and brain structure. The creationist perspective attributes male–female differences to distinct acts of creation by God.[42]

A prominent biological view focuses on the effects of **evolutionary processes** on men's and women's genes and subsequent behavior. Evolutionary psychologists, following the famed 19th-century scientist Charles Darwin, suggest that sex differences in behavior reflect adaptations to the differential demands of the environment on males and females during prehistoric times. According to evolutionary theory, men and women coexisted in hunting-and-gathering groups at the beginning of civilization, with men doing most of the hunting of food, being the physically stronger sex, and women doing most of the food gathering. This ancestral division of labor between the sexes favored men and women who were the most psychologically prepared for their assigned roles. Effective adaptations to these environmental demands were then incorporated into the genetic makeup of humans and inherited by future generations. Thus, different psychological mechanisms evolved in males and females over time, leading to the sex differences in behavior that we observe today.[43]

Others argue that **social-environmental forces** such as family, peers, media, schools, employers, and pressures to conform in social settings cause sex differences in interests, abilities, gender identity, and behavior to be learned in childhood and reinforced in adulthood. According to this view, the present-day environment influences the behavior of girls and boys by rewarding them for engaging in the "right" behaviors (i.e., behaviors consistent with gender stereotypes and roles) and by punishing them for engaging in the "wrong" behaviors. The modern division of labor between the sexes, as reflected in differences in women's and men's domestic and occupational roles (see Chapter 2), leads to the formation of gender roles that dictate the behaviors appropriate for each sex. Children are expected to behave in accordance with these gender roles, with boys socialized to behave in a masculine manner and girls in a feminine manner. Parents play a large role in shaping their sons' and daughters' behavior, but other people and institutions have a considerable effect as well. Children's contacts with their peers, especially same-sex peers, are important in the development of gender roles. Children actively exchange knowledge about gender roles and reinforce each other's adherence to these roles. [44]

In summary, arguments may be made for the influence of both biological forces (nature) and social-environmental forces (nurture) on the development of children and subsequent behavior of adults. No agreement has been reached as to whether nature or nurture is more important, but both have some effect. In fact, their effects are so intertwined that it is difficult to separate them. The combined effects of nature and nurture may be summarized as follows:

People are hard-wired—due to physiological properties that are the result of biological forces, evolutionary processes, or acts of creation—to think and act in certain ways, some of which differ for males and females and others of which do not differ. Whether sex similarities or differences are learned or exhibited in a particular setting is influenced by the nature of the social-environmental forces operating in the setting.

Because biological forces are less amenable to change, we focus in the next section of the chapter on the influence of social-environmental forces.

Gender Socialization

Although the concept of androgyny offers a vision of a society free of the influence of gender roles and stereotypes, that society has not materialized. Boys grow up under the heavy influence of the male gender role and girls under the influence of the female gender role. To explain the effects of these influences, we need to examine how young males and females are socialized to live up to the expectations of the appropriate gender role. Although many social-environmental forces contribute to children's socialization into gender roles, we will focus on the influence of parents, schools, and the mass media.

Parents

Parents are in a position to have a special effect on child development. They provide the opportunity for imitation of their own behavior and reinforcements for their children's behavior. Children imitate same-sex models more than opposite-sex models, although they could imitate any adult to whom they were exposed. Because parents are highly available and powerful, they are the role models children are most likely to copy, particularly during the preschool years. Boys spend more time with their fathers than girls do, and girls spend more time with their mothers than boys do. Parents who are absent, however, are unavailable to serve as role models. Overall, 70% of U.S. children live with both parents, a proportion that has been decreasing over time; 23% live with their mother only; 3% with their father only; and 4% with neither parent.[45]

A meta-analysis of studies on childhood socialization found few differences in parents' actual treatment of boys and girls. There are minimal differences in amounts of interaction, encouragement of achievement, warmth and nurturance, encouragement of dependency or independence, and disciplinary strictness displayed toward sons and daughters of all ages. However, parents display a strong tendency to emphasize gender stereotypes in their children's household chores and play activities. The opening passage of this chapter describes differences in children's household responsibilities according to the sex of the child; in short, boys are assigned different activities and are paid more to perform these activities than girls. Parents also offer their sons and daughters different types of toys. Boys are provided with more sports equipment, tools, and vehicles (including, of course, G.I. Joe tanks and other assault vehicles). Girls are provided with more dolls (including, of course, Barbie), jewelry, and children's furniture. Moreover, this tendency spills over into how children are dressed and how their rooms are decorated. Girls wear more pink and less blue clothing than boys, and more pink and less blue is seen in girls' rooms than in boys' rooms.[46]

Parents' beliefs about gender stereotypes and roles affect how they raise their children. Parents who endorse gender stereotypes are more likely to treat girls and boys differently. However, parents who believe that opportunities for both sexes should be equal are more likely to encourage their children to deviate from gender stereotypes than parents who advocate distinct roles for women and men.[47]

Parents' employment also affects how they raise their children. The effects of **maternal employment** on children's development have been hotly debated. (In comparison, because **paternal employment** is expected according to gender roles, its effects on children's development receive far less attention.) Defenders of gender roles perceive a backlash against stay-at-home mothers in favor of working mothers. Myths perpetuated about maternal employment include that working mothers work only for the money, care only about their own needs, and neglect their children, thereby contributing to antisocial behavior.[48]

Research suggests that all children benefit from the income that their mothers as well as fathers earn, as increased family income has a positive effect on children's academic performance and reduces behavioral problems. In addition, daughters of mothers who work outside of the home have more egalitarian attitudes toward gender roles, and score higher on measures of achievement such as grades and formal test scores, than daughters of mothers who are not employed outside of the home. This may be because employed mothers play a less stereotypical role than do stay-at-home mothers. Husbands of employed mothers devote more time to household labor and child care than do husbands of stay-at-home mothers, giving their daughters another example of deviation from traditional gender roles. Further, mothers who work provide positive role models for their daughters' aspirations and achievement.[49]

Maternal employment has less influence on sons' attitudes toward gender roles or achievement, primarily because sons are less likely than daughters to use their mothers as role models. However, sons of employed mothers, when their father was present during their growing-up years, devote more time to housework when married than sons whose mothers were not employed. This suggests a long-term effect of mothers' employment, combined with fathers' greater time spent on housework, on their sons' future domestic roles.[50]

In addition, parents' workplace experiences influence their moods and parenting behaviors, which in turn influence how their children behave. Mothers and fathers whose jobs put them in a bad mood are more likely to punish their children, which negatively influences their children's motivation and academic performance and increases their behavioral problems at school. However, stay-at-home mothers whose family roles put them in a bad mood also are more likely to engage in punishing behavior, thereby contributing to their children's behavioral problems. Happier parents, no matter what roles they play in the household and workplace, tend to raise happier, better-adjusted sons and daughters.[51]

In conclusion, in parents' encouragement or discouragement of activities, creation of household environments, and general parenting behavior, they contribute to the arousal of different interests and development of different behaviors in their children that last into adulthood. In so doing, they both convey and reinforce the message that girls and boys are different. The same theme emerges as we consider children's experiences in schools.

Schools

Once they enter school systems, children are subject to the influence of additional authority figures other than their parents. They have more adult role models from which to choose, and they have more occasion to be rewarded or punished for their behavior. One of the first messages that children receive at school is the sex segregation of positions in the school system itself: Men typically run the schools in which women teach. Women are not represented in educational administration in equal proportion to their representation in teaching. The older the child and the higher the grade, the fewer women administrators and teachers. When women become school administrators, it is more likely to be in primary schools than at higher levels.[52]

Both women and men are more likely to graduate from high school and college than ever before. Also, average test scores at all levels, from standardized tests administered in elementary and secondary school to college entrance exams, have risen or remained stable for both girls and boys. These results testify to the success of school systems in educating children of both sexes.[53]

However, when children's academic performance is graded, there is a consistent sex difference: Girls get better grades than do boys across all ethnic groups, subject areas, ages, and levels of education beginning with the earliest school years and extending through college. This does not necessarily mean that girls are smarter than boys. Nor does it mean that girls' successes come at boys' expense. Instead, better grades are earned by students with better study habits and skills. Female students tend to be more disciplined in their approach to schoolwork, organized, orderly, and respectful of rules and regulations than male students, all of which contribute to their getting good grades. These study habits and skills are more associated with the feminine than with the masculine gender role. In addition, boys are more likely than girls to exhibit seriously dysfunctional school behaviors, including cutting classes, disobeying rules, and being suspended or transferred to other schools for disciplinary reasons, all of which interfere with their getting good grades.[54]

Even though girls get better grades, boys get more classroom attention. Teachers seldom see themselves as feeling differently toward girls and boys or treating them differently. However, classroom observations at all grade levels reveal considerable differences in both male and female teachers' interactions with students. Boys receive more positive and negative attention than do girls. Boys are questioned more, criticized more, and have more ideas accepted and rejected. Girls volunteer more often but are not called upon as often and are given less time to answer. When teachers give more attention and "air time" to boys than to girls, whether consciously or unconsciously, they convey a message that boys as a group deserve more attention. This message may suppress self-esteem in girls.[55]

Self-esteem may come from two sources, others' beliefs and perceptions and one's own accomplishments. According to the **reflected appraisals model of self-esteem,** sex differences occur in areas where societal expectations differ for men and women; people base their self-esteem on what others think of them. According to the **competencies model of self-esteem,** sex differences occur in areas where actual performance differs for men and women; people base their self-esteem on competency tests or other objective measures. A meta-analysis found no sex differences in self-esteem regarding academics across all educational levels. Given that females demonstrate higher academic performance in the form of better grades across all levels, the results of this meta-analysis support the reflected appraisals model over the competencies model. Females may discount their own academic abilities, even in areas where they excel, resulting in their academic self-esteem being lower than their performance warrants. In contrast, males may inflate their own academic abilities, even in areas where they trail, resulting in their academic self-esteem being higher than their performance warrants.[56]

Girls' self-esteem influences their choice of courses, fields of study, and eventual employment. In high school, girls tend to avoid advanced mathematics and science courses, even though girls earn higher grades in such courses than do boys. Even when girls are personally identified as being highly gifted in math and science, they have lower academic self-esteem and show less interest in pursuing math and science careers than do their male peers. As a result, although women have more access to college education than ever before, female undergraduates are less likely than male undergraduates to major in math and science fields. After their undergraduate schooling, women are less likely to pursue graduate degrees and seek employment in these areas.[57]

In summary, despite getting better grades, girls emerge from their school years with no greater academic self-esteem than boys, in this case a sex similarity with lasting consequences. Girls may be both rewarded with good grades in the short run and punished in the long run by their experiences in schools.

The Mass Media

The mass media, particularly television, influence children's development by providing a view, whether real or distorted, of the outside world. Television is the most popular source of information and entertainment worldwide, partly because it is so accessible and easy to use. Unlike print media such as magazines and newspapers, TV watching does not require literacy. Unlike the movies, theater, and concerts, TV is always running and available; it comes directly into the home. Television is the first centralized cultural influence in the earliest years of life. Children begin to watch TV before they can walk or talk. By the time they begin school, they will have spent more time watching TV than they will ever spend in a college classroom.[58]

TV can have beneficial effects for children. For example, educational programming, although not a major part of most children's TV viewing, has a positive effect on their academic performance. However, TV watching in general is characterized by mental and physical passivity. Children who watch more than 3 hours per day of TV are more likely to experience negative side effects such as obesity and poor academic performance. Furthermore, children who watch more hours of TV violence, especially boys, are more likely to exhibit aggressive behavior. Thus, TV watching has a strong influence on children's development.[59]

TV has been described as the great socializer. It teaches children what is important and how to behave. It also teaches gender stereotypes and roles. Stereotypical portrayals of females and males have been the norm in most television programming. In prime-time TV programs, despite the fact that women comprise more than half the population, male characters outnumber female characters. Also, despite the fact that the average woman is older than the average man, female characters are younger than male characters, conveying the message that a woman's value is in her youthfulness. More women are depicted working outside the home than in the past, and the jobs they hold are more likely to be in male-intensive occupations such as law and medicine. However, prime-time TV programs focus on male-intensive occupations more than sex-neutral or female-intensive occupations. As a result, television is still primarily a man's world, and secondarily a young woman's world.[60]

Depictions of female and male characters differ in TV commercials. Although women make the bulk of household purchases, there are relatively few female characters in TV commercials, and they are more likely to be shown in families, less likely to hold jobs, and less likely to exercise authority. On the rare occasions when men are shown in family situations, they are less likely than women to cook, clean, wash dishes, shop, change a diaper, or care for a sick child. Instead, men are more often shown reading, talking, eating, and playing with children.[61]

Male and female characters in TV commercials differ in the kinds of products they sell. Females are more likely to promote products used on themselves, such as health and beauty products, or in the home, such as foods and cleaning products. In contrast, males are more likely to promote products used outside the home, such as cars, trucks, and cameras. Commercials often make different types of appeals to women and men. For example, in commercials for jeans, the emphasis for men is on being an individual and doing your own thing, whereas the emphasis for women is on enhancing one's appearance to get a man. In beer commercials, the goal is to appeal to men's masculinity. Men are promised sex and fun if they drink the right brand of beer. In these ads, male characters are physically active and spend their time either outdoors or in bars. If women are pictured, they are admiring onlookers. Some beer commercials portray mixed-sex bar scenes where the focus is on women's bodies (for male viewers to admire) and men's faces (as they admire the women's bodies).[62]

TV commercials also differ in their portrayals of different racial and ethnic groups. Black characters appear most often in commercials for financial services and food, Asian characters in commercials for technology, Hispanic characters in commercials for soap and deodorants, and White characters in commercials for technology and food. White men are depicted as powerful, White women as sex objects, Black men as aggressive, and Black women as having no distinctive presence. White infants and small children are depicted as go-getters, whereas Black children are more likely to be passive observers. White children may be pictured with Black children playing in public settings, such as schools, but family scenes are totally segregated by race. Overall, Whites are overrepresented in TV commercials compared with their proportion in the U.S. population, Blacks appear at a rate commensurate with their proportion, and Hispanics and Asians are underrepresented.[63]

What is the ultimate impact on children of TV portrayals of gender roles? Many studies suggest that television viewing affects perceptions of social reality. The more time people spend watching TV, the more likely they are to perceive the real world in ways that reflect what they have seen on TV. Children and adolescents who watch more TV are more aware of gender stereotypes and hold more traditional attitudes toward gender roles. For example, children who watch more TV are more likely to say that only girls should do household chores tradition-ally associated with women and only boys should do chores traditionally associated with men.[64]

However, television viewing does not always reinforce gender stereo-types. One study found that public perceptions of the proportion of women in nine different occupations, including physician, nurse, lawyer, college teacher, and grade school teacher, differed from U.S. cen-sus data and also from the proportion of women seen in these occupa-tions in prime-time television programming. Respondents erred consistently in the direction of sex neutrality in the chosen professions. That is, their estimates were closer to a 50–50 split of women and men in occupations than was really the case. They may have learned from TV news shows about trends toward a more equal distribution of men and women in different types of jobs, and then confused those trends with the status quo.[65]

Moreover, television and other forms of media occasionally celebrate diversity. For a good example, we need only turn to the world of *Star Trek,* depicted in the original television series and its successors (*The Next Generation, Deep Space Nine, Voyager, Enterprise*) as well as several movies. *Star Trek* is set in a universe full of races of different kinds of beings. It assumes not only the existence of other life in this universe, but also the existence of compatible life. Thus, other kinds of beings are never viewed as completely alien. The challenge then becomes to under-stand, communicate, and get along with other races. The original crew of the *U.S.S. Enterprise* was all-inclusive. Although the crew had a White male captain, it had Black, Asian, Russian, Scottish, Anglo-Saxon, and Vulcan members. *Star Trek*'s portrayal of members of different races as well as members of both sexes in key positions of responsibility was rare in television at the time (the 1960s). According to George Takei, the Japanese American actor who played Mr. Sulu in the original *Star Trek* series, "True Trekkies embrace diversity."[66]

In conclusion, television and other mass media now portray women and men in roles that are somewhat less stereotypical than they have in the past. However, their overall depiction of men and women in and out-side the workplace largely conveys and reinforces gender stereotypes and roles. Given how much time children spend watching TV, it has enormous potential to influence their perceptions of reality.

Beyond Gender Stereotypes and Roles

With the assistance of their peers, parents, schools, and the mass media, children learn about gender stereotypes and roles. However, children eventually face hazards as adults if they learn these lessons too well. In this section, we consider the limitations associated with strict belief in gender stereotypes and strict adherence to gender roles.

Limitations of Gender Stereotypes

Stereotyping, or the cognitive activity of sorting people into different groups based on some personal characteristic or characteristics and then assigning traits to members of each group, is a pervasive human phenomenon that may seem harmless at first glance. Several types of problems may result from an overreliance on stereotypes, in this case, gender stereotypes. First, without stereotyping, prejudice and discrimination would be less likely to take place. If people did not stereotype one another, perhaps they would exhibit less prejudice and discrimination toward each other.[67]

Second, although a given stereotype may accurately describe the average member of a group, it rarely applies to all group members. For example, when the BSRI is administered to undergraduate college students, males as a group are more likely than females as a group to be classified as masculine and less likely to be classified as feminine.[68] Thus, gender stereotypes of men as masculine and women as feminine hold for the average male and female undergraduate respectively. This does not mean that every male undergraduate is masculine and every female undergraduate is feminine. Male undergraduates may be androgynous, undifferentiated, or feminine as well as masculine in gender identity. Similarly, female undergraduates may be androgynous, undifferentiated, or masculine as well as feminine in gender identity. When people are stereotyped on the basis of sex (or any other dimension of diversity), who they are as individuals may be overlooked.

Third, stereotypes imply that differences between members of different groups are a result of their group membership. This is virtually impossible to prove. When we examine whether a sex difference is present in some type of ability, attitude, or behavior, we need to distinguish between two questions: "Is there a difference *between* the sexes?" and "Is there a difference *on account of* sex?"[69] Answering the first question is relatively simple; it involves only testing and comparing male and female populations. Answering the second question is much more difficult. It requires demonstrating that a difference is innate and due to biological sex alone, which involves testing and comparing male and female populations who have been living under identical environmental conditions. Due to differences in the gender socialization of girls and boys, these conditions are not present in any culture. Thus, people need to be cautious in what they conclude about the causes of sex differences in individuals' interests, abilities, attitudes, and behavior.

Limitations of Gender Roles

Different types of problems result from strict adherence to gender roles. Neither the female nor the male gender role offers an ideal prescription for an emotionally satisfying and rewarding life. A rigid adherence to either role may be hazardous to one's mental and physical health.

The female gender role encourages dependence and surrender of control over many aspects of one's life to others. Reactions to this lack of control may be manifested in depression and other forms of illness. However, the female gender role places an emphasis on self-awareness, which could lead women to be more aware than men of symptoms of ill health, even if they were no less healthy. This role also encourages expression of feelings, including admission of difficulties, which can lead people to seek help from others.[70]

In contrast, the male gender role encourages aggressiveness and competitiveness, which can lead men to put themselves in risky situations. This role is also associated with emotional inexpressiveness, which may cause psychosomatic and other health problems. Lack of self-awareness keeps men from being sensitive to signals that all is not well with them. Adherence to the male gender role means suppressing one's feelings and always striving (or pretending) to be in control of one's own life. The effects of this unbridled push for dominance may take a toll on men, even though it may seem better to dominate than to be dominated.[71]

One way to shed light on the effects of the toll of gender roles is to examine sex differences in indicators of mental and physical health. We need to proceed with caution in using this approach because pressure to conform to gender roles is only one of many factors that could influence behavior and health.

Mortality statistics are striking. In 1900, the expectation of longevity at birth for the U.S. population was 48 years for women and 46 years for men. Since then, these expectations have risen to 80 years for women and 75 years for men. The sex difference in mortality favoring women is present in every country for which data are reported and for individuals of all races and ethnic groups. Males die at a higher rate than females at all ages, ranging from 1 year or less to 85 years and older. Life expectancy has increased substantially for women and men, but the difference favoring women has also increased.[72]

Health statistics vary considerably for women and men. Overall, women experience more frequent illnesses and short-term disability than men. For example, women report higher rates of mood disorders such as depression and anxiety, eating disorders such as anorexia and bulimia, and minor physical ailments such as headaches and stomach upsets. However, women's health problems typically do not endanger their lives, and they take more actions to address their problems. They report more visits to physicians, use more prescription medicines and over-the-counter drugs, and restrict their activities due to health problems more.[73]

In contrast, men suffer from more life-threatening diseases that cause permanent disability and earlier death than women. They suffer more from substance abuse involving alcohol or drugs and from antisocial disorders such as aggression. They are more likely to be murdered or to die in an accident while driving or participating in a dangerous sport. Men are also less likely to take health promotion messages seriously or to consult a doctor when health problems arise.

In summary, mortality and health statistics suggest that women are "sicker" in the short run and men are "sicker" in the long run. At least part of the reason for these sex differences may be the adherence of women and men to gender roles.

What's Next?

This chapter began by posing several questions about the existence of sex differences, gender differences, and their causes and effects. Although there are both similarities and differences between the sexes, most people believe that there are substantial differences. These beliefs are reflected in gender stereotypes (although stereotypes of women may be more dynamic than those of men) and sometimes in sexist attitudes. Women and men are expected to adopt roles that are consistent with gender stereotypes. However, individuals develop their own gender identities, or beliefs about themselves in relation to traditional definitions of masculinity and femininity. Individual behavior is influenced by a combination of biological and social-environmental forces. Parents, schools, and the mass media shape children's behavior in a manner consistent with traditional notions of masculinity and femininity. Strict adherence to traditional gender roles escalates stereotyping and prejudice and can be hazardous to the mental and physical health of adults.

Given the persistence of gender stereotypes and roles, is it possible to create settings in which behavior is not linked to gender? I believe that change is possible and existing influences do not have to be taken for granted. Parents, teachers, the mass media, and society at large may change the way they view gender-related issues. Parents and teachers may be made aware of the powerful effect of their expectations on children's learning. Institutions that train teachers can ensure that teachers are made aware of how their own expectations and interactions with students affect student performance. The media can do a better job of informing the public accurately about gender-related issues and may offer a more realistic depiction of the roles that males and females actually play in society.

What societal changes would it take to reduce adherence to gender roles that is only for the sake of conforming to others' expectations? Parents requiring their daughters to mow the lawn and their sons to wash the dishes? Teachers paying similar attention to boys and girls in classrooms? More boys as well as girls pursuing careers in occupations numerically dominated by the other sex? Video games in which males are less emphatically masculine and females less emphatically feminine, or in which women are warriors who rescue men in peril? Television programs and movies that embrace diversity more and gender roles less? I hope to get the chance to find out.

Notes

1. Shellenbarger, S. (2006, December 7). Boys mow lawns, girls do dishes: Are parents perpetuating the chore wars? *Wall Street Journal.* Wall Street Journal Online Edition (Only Staff-Produced Materials May Be Used) by S. Shellenbarger. Copyright 2006 by DOW JONES & COMPANY, INC. Reproduced with permission of DOW JONES & COMPANY, INC. in the format Textbook via Copyright Clearance Center.

2. Kite, M. E., Deaux, K., & Haines, E. L. (2008). Gender stereotypes. In F. L. Denmark & M. A. Paludi (Eds.), *Psychology of women: A handbook of issues*

and theories (2nd ed., pp. 205–236). Westport, CT: Praeger; Kite, M. E. (2001). Changing times, changing gender roles: Who do we want women and men to be? In R. K. Unger (Ed.), *Handbook of the psychology of women and gender* (pp. 215–227). New York: Wiley; Eagly, A. H., Wood, W., & Diekman, A. B. (2000). Social role theory of sex differences and similarities: A current appraisal. In T. Eckes & H. M. Trautner (Eds.), *The developmental social psychology of gender* (pp. 123–174). Mahwah, NJ: Erlbaum; Galinsky, E., Aumann, K., & Bond, J. T. (2009). *Times are changing: Gender and generation at work and at home.* New York: Families and Work Institute. Retrieved March 26, 2009, from http://familiesandwork.org.

3. Lippa, R. A. (2005). *Gender, nature, and nurture* (2nd ed.). Mahwah, NJ: Erlbaum; Archer, J., & Lloyd, B. (2002). *Sex and gender* (2nd ed.). Cambridge, UK: Cambridge University Press; Maccoby, E. E., & Jacklin, C. N. (1974). *The psychology of sex differences.* Stanford, CA: Stanford University Press.

4. Hyde, J. S., & Grabe, S. (2008). Meta-analysis in the psychology of women. In F. L. Denmark & M. A. Paludi (Eds.), *Psychology of women: A handbook of issues and theories* (2nd ed., pp. 142–173). Westport, CT: Praeger.

5. Lippa, pp. 158–159; Hasbro, Inc. (2002). *History of G.I. Joe.* Retrieved April 30, 2002, from http://www.gijoe.com; Sobieraj, S. (2004). G.I. Joe. In M. Kimmel & A. Aronson (Eds.), *Men and masculinities: A social, cultural, and historical encyclopedia* (pp. 354–355). Santa Barbara, CA: ABC-CLIO; Hall, K. J. (2004). A soldier's body: GI Joe, Hasbro's great American hero, and the symptoms of empire. *Journal of Popular Culture, 38,* 34–54.

6. Mattel, Inc. (2009). *Barbie.com: Official site.* Retrieved July 2, 2009, from http://barbie.everythinggirl.com; Mattel, Inc. *By the numbers.* Retrieved December 26, 2009, from http://www.barbiemedia.com; Rogers, M. F. (1999). *Barbie culture.* London: Sage, p. 14; Frey, J. (2002, April 30). The doll with a life of its own. *Washington Post.* Retrieved April 30, 2002, from http://www.washingtonpost.com.

7. Bowes-Sperry, L. (2006, December 19). Personal correspondence with the author.

8. Larson, R. W., & Verma, S. (1999). How children and adolescents spend time across the world: Work, play, and developmental opportunities. *Psychological Bulletin, 125,* 701–736; Archer & Lloyd, pp. 73–74; Lippa, pp. 158–159; Roos, H., & Taylor, H. (1989). Do boys prefer Daddy or his physical style of play? *Sex Roles, 20,* 23–33; Goldstein; Nelson, A. (2000). The pink dragon is female: Halloween costumes and gender markers. *Psychology of Women Quarterly, 24,* 137–144.

9. Lippa, pp. 241–243; Markoff, J. (1989, February 13). Computing in America: A masculine mystique. *New York Times,* pp. A1, B10.

10. Cooper, J., Hall, J., & Huff, C. (1990). Situational stress as a consequence of sex-stereotyped software. *Personality and Social Psychology Bulletin, 16,* 419–429; Academic Skill Builders. (2009). *Demolition Division.* Retrieved July 17, 2009, from http://arcademicskillbuilders.com.

11. Gahr, E. (1998, October 30). Computers are for girls. *Wall Street Journal,* p. W11; Mattel, Inc. (2001). *Barbie.com: Activities and games for girls online!* Retrieved June 28, 2001, from http://www.barbie.com; Kane, Y. I. (2009, October 13) Videogame firms make a play for women. *Wall Street Journal.* Retrieved October 21, 2009, from http://online.wsj.com.

12. Brenick, A., Henning, A., Killen, M., O'Connor, A., & Collins, M. (2007). Social evaluations of stereotypic images in video games: Unfair, legitimate, or "just entertainment?" *Youth & Society, 38,* 395–419; Beasley, B., & Standley, T. C. (2002). Shirts vs. skins: Clothing as an indicator of gender role stereotyping in video games. *Mass Communication & Society, 5,* 279–293; Dietz, T. L. (1998). An examination of violence and gender role portrayals in video games: Implications for gender socialization and aggressive behavior. *Sex Roles, 38,* 425–442.

13. Larson & Verma; Shellenbarger.

14. Larson & Verma.

15. Archer & Lloyd, pp. 80–81; Burn, S. M., O'Neil, A. K., & Nederend, S. (1996). Childhood tomboyism and adult androgyny. *Sex Roles, 34,* 419–428; Martin, C. L. (1990). Attitudes and expectations about children with nontraditional and traditional gender roles. *Sex Roles, 22,* 151–165; Giuliano, T. A., Popp, K. E., & Knight, J. L. (2000). Footballs versus Barbies: Childhood play activities as predictors of sport participation by women. *Sex Roles, 42,* 159–181.

16. Archer, J. (2004). Sex differences in aggression in real-world settings: A meta-analytic review. *Review of General Psychology, 8,* 291–322; Knight, G. P., Guthrie, I. K., Page, M. C., & Fabes, R. A. (2002). Emotional arousal and gender differences in aggression: A meta-analysis. *Aggressive Behavior, 28,* 366–393; Eagly, A. H., & Steffan, V. J. (1986). Gender and aggressive behavior: A meta-analytic review of the social psychological literature. *Psychological Bulletin, 100,* 309–330.

17. Kuschel, R. (1992). "Women are women and men are men": How Bellonese women get even. In K. Björkqvist & P. Niemelä (Eds.), *Of mice and women: Aspects of female aggression* (pp. 173–185). San Diego, CA: Academic Press.

18. Howard, J. A., & Hollander, J. (1997). Altruism and aggression: Gendered dynamics of helping and harming others. In *Gendered situations, gendered selves: A gender lens on social psychology* (pp. 117–148). Thousand Oaks, CA: Sage; Eagly, A. H., & Crowley, M. (1986). Gender and helping behavior: A meta-analytic review of the social psychological literature. *Psychological Bulletin, 100,* 283–308; Piliavin, J. A., & Unger, R. K. (1985). The helpful but helpless female: Myth or reality? In V. E. O'Leary, R. K. Unger, & B. S. Wallston (Eds.), *Women, gender, and social psychology* (pp. 149–189). Hillsdale, NJ: Erlbaum.

19. Hall, J. A. (2006). How big are nonverbal sex differences? The case of smiling and nonverbal sensitivity. In K. Dindia & D. J. Canary (Eds.), *Sex differences and similarities in communication* (2nd ed., pp. 59–81). Mahwah, NJ: Erlbaum; LaFrance, M., Hecht, M. A., & Paluck, E. L. (2003). The contingent

smile: A meta-analysis of sex differences in smiling. *Psychological Bulletin, 129,* 305–334.

20. Larwood, L., & Wood, M. M. (1977). *Women in management.* Lexington, MA: Lexington Books, p. 33.

21. Broverman, I. K., Vogel, S. R., Broverman, D. M., Clarkson, F. E., & Rosenkrantz, P. S. (1972). Sex role stereotypes: A current appraisal. *Journal of Social Issues, 28* (2), 59–78; Kite, Deaux, & Haines; Williams, J. E., & Best, D. L. (1990). Pancultural similarities. In *Measuring sex stereotypes: A multination study* (Rev. ed., pp. 225–245). Newbury Park, CA: Sage.

22. Fiske, S. T., Cuddy, A. J. C., Glick, P., & Xu, J. (2002). A model of (often mixed) stereotype content: Competence and warmth respectively follow from perceived status and competition. *Journal of Personality and Social Psychology, 82,* 878–902; Cuddy, A. J. C., Fiske, S. T., & Glick, P. (2004). When professionals become mothers, warmth doesn't cut the ice. *Journal of Social Issues, 60,* 701–718.

23. Fiske, S. T. (1998). Stereotyping, prejudice, and discrimination. In D. T. Gilbert, S. T. Fiske, & G. Lindzey (Eds.), *The handbook of social psychology* (4th ed., Vol. 2, pp. 357–411). Boston: McGraw-Hill.

24. Diekman, A. B., & Eagly, A. H. (2000). Stereotypes as dynamic constructs: Women and men of the past, present, and future. *Personality and Social Psychology Bulletin, 26,* 1171–1188; Eagly, A. H., & Diekman, A. B. (2003). The malleability of sex differences in response to changing social roles. In L. G. Aspinwall & U. M. Staudinger (Eds.), *The psychology of human strengths: Fundamental questions and future directions for a positive psychology* (pp. 103–115). Washington, DC: American Psychological Association.

25. Constantinople, A. (1973). Masculinity-femininity: An exception to a famous dictum? *Psychological Bulletin, 80,* 389–407.

26. Bem, S. L. (1974). The measurement of psychological androgyny. *Journal of Consulting and Clinical Psychology, 42,* 155–162.

27. Bem, S. L. (1977). On the utility of alternative procedures for assessing psychological androgyny. *Journal of Consulting and Clinical Psychology, 45,* 196–205.

28. Cross, S. E., & Madson, L. (1997). Models of the self: Self-construals and gender. *Psychological Bulletin, 122,* 5–37; Wood, W., & Eagly, A. H. (2009). Gender identity. In M. R. Leary & R. H. Hoyle (Eds.), *Handbook of individual differences in social behavior* (pp. 109–125). New York: Guilford.

29. Korabik, K. (1999). Sex and gender in the new millennium. In G. N. Powell (Ed.), *Handbook of gender and work* (pp. 3–16). Thousand Oaks, CA: Sage; Lenney, E. (1979). Androgyny: Some audacious assertions toward its coming of age. *Sex Roles, 5,* 703–719.

30. Pedhazur, E. J., & Tetenbaum, T. J. (1979). Bem Sex Role Inventory: A theoretical and methodological critique. *Journal of Personality and Social Psychology, 37,* 996–1016; Bem, S. L. (1981). *Bem Sex-Role Inventory: Professional manual.* Palo Alto, CA: Consulting Psychologists Press.

31. Harris, A. C. (1994). Ethnicity as a determinant of sex role identity: A replication study of item selection for the Bem Sex Role Inventory. *Sex Roles, 31,* 241–273.

32. Bem, S. L. (1978). Beyond androgyny: Some presumptuous prescriptions for a liberated sexual identity. In J. A. Sherman & F. L. Denmark (Ed.), *The psychology of women: Future direction in research* (pp. 1–23). New York: Psychological Dimensions, p. 19.

33. This section of the chapter is based on portions of Graves, L. M., & Powell, G. N. (2008). Sex and race discrimination in personnel decisions. In S. Cartwright & Cary L. Cooper (Eds.), *The Oxford handbook of personnel psychology* (pp. 438–463). Oxford, UK: Oxford University Press.

34. Glick, P., & Fiske, S. T. (2001). An ambivalent alliance: Hostile and benevolent sexism as complementary justifications for gender inequality. *American Psychologist, 56,* 109–118 (quotation from p. 109); Glick, P., & Fiske, S. T. (1996). The Ambivalent Sexism Inventory: Differentiating hostile and benevolent sexism. *Journal of Personality and Social Psychology, 70,* 491–512.

35. Glick, P., Fiske, S. T., Mladinic, A., Saiz, J. L., Abrams, D., Masser, B., et al. (2000). Beyond prejudice as simple antipathy: Hostile and benevolent sexism across cultures. *Journal of Personality and Social Psychology, 79,* 763–775.

36. Glick, P., & Fiske, S. T. (1999). The Ambivalence toward Men Inventory: Differentiating hostile and benevolent beliefs about men. *Psychology of Women Quarterly, 23,* 519–536.

37. Swim, J. K., Aikin, K. J., Hall, W. S., & Hunter, B. A. (1995). Sexism and racism: Old-fashioned and modern prejudices. *Journal of Personality and Social Psychology, 68,* 199–214.

38. Swim, Aikin, Hall, & Hunter; Watkins, M. B., Kaplan, S., Brief, A. P., Shull, A., Dietz, J., Mansfield, M., et al. (2006). Does it pay to be a sexist? The relationship between modern sexism and career outcomes. *Journal of Vocational Behavior, 69,* 524–537; Glick et al. (2000); Glick, P., Diebold, J., Bailey-Werner, B., & Zhu, L. (1997). The two faces of Adam: Ambivalent sexism and polarized attitudes toward women. *Personality and Social Psychology Bulletin, 23,* 1323–1334; Masser, B. M., & Abrams, D. (2004). Reinforcing the glass ceiling: The consequences of hostile sexism for female managerial candidates. *Sex Roles, 51,* 609–615; Rudman, L. A., & Kilianski, S. E. (2000). Implicit and explicit attitudes toward female authority. *Personality and Social Psychology Bulletin, 26,* 1315–1328; Russell, B. L., & Trigg, K. Y. (2004). Tolerance of sexual harassment: An examination of gender differences, ambivalent sexism, social dominance, and gender roles. *Sex Roles, 50,* 565–573.

39. McConahay, J. B. (1986). Modern racism, ambivalence, and the Modern Racism Scale. In J. F. Dovidio & S. L. Gaertner (Eds.), *Prejudice, discrimination, and racism* (pp. 91–125). Orlando, FL: Academic; Gaertner, S. L., & Dovidio, J. F. (1986). The aversive form of racism. In J. F. Dovidio & S. L. Gaertner (Eds.), *Prejudice, discrimination, and racism* (pp. 61–89). Orlando, FL: Academic;

Sears, D. O. (1988). Symbolic racism. In P. A. Katz & D. A. Taylor (Eds.), *Eliminating racism: Profiles in controversy* (pp. 53–84). New York: Plenum; Deitch, E. A., Barsky, A., Butz, R. M., Chan, S., Brief, A. P., & Bradley, J. C. (2003). Subtle yet significant: The existence and impact of everyday racial discrimination in the workplace. *Human Relations, 56,* 1299–1324.

40. Crary, D. (2008, January 14). Presidential campaign fuels debate over sexism, racism: Is one more taboo than the other? *Associated Press.* Retrieved January 14, 2008, from http://www.ap.org; Reid, P. T. (1988). Racism and sexism: Comparisons and conflicts. In P. A. Katz and D. A. Taylor (Eds.), *Eliminating racism: Profiles in controversy* (pp. 203–221). New York: Plenum.

41. Lippa; Archer & Lloyd; Jacklin, C. N. (1989). Female and male: Issues of gender. *American Psychologist, 44,* 127–133.

42. Lippa; Archer & Lloyd; Browne, K. R. (2002). *Biology at work: Rethinking sexual equality.* New Brunswick, NJ: Rutgers University Press; Udry, J. R. (2000). Biological limits of gender construction. *American Sociological Review, 65,* 443–457.

43. Darwin, C. (1871). *The descent of man, and selection in relation to sex.* New York: Murray; Lippa; Archer, J. (1996). Sex differences in social behavior: Are the social role and evolutionary explanations compatible? *American Psychologist, 51,* 909–917; Buss, D. M. (1995). Evolutionary psychology: A new paradigm for psychological science. *Psychological Inquiry, 6,* 1–30; Buss, D. M. (1995). Psychological sex differences: Origins through sexual selection. *American Psychologist, 50,* 164–168.

44. Wood, W., & Eagly, A. H. (2002). A cross-cultural analysis of the behavior of women and men: Implications for the origins of sex differences. *Psychological Bulletin, 128,* 699–727; Eagly, A. H., & Wood, W. (1999). The origins of sex differences in human behavior: Evolved dispositions versus social roles. *American Psychologist, 54,* 408–423; Maccoby, E. E. (1990). Gender and relationships: A developmental account. *American Psychologist, 45,* 513–520; Harris, J. R. (1995). Where is the child's environment? A group socialization theory of development. *Psychological Review, 102,* 458–489; Stockard, J. (1990). Gender socialization. In J. S. Chafetz (Ed.), *Handbook of the Sociology of Gender* (pp. 215–227). New York: Kluwer Academic/Plenum; Larson & Verma; Lippa.

45. U.S. Census Bureau. (2009). *Families and living arrangements,* table CH-1. Retrieved July 23, 2009, from http://www.census.gov.

46. Lytton, H., & Romney, D. M. (1991). Parents' differential socialization of boys and girls: A meta-analysis. *Psychological Bulletin, 109,* 267–296; Pomerleau, A., Boldue, D., Malcuit, G., & Cossette, L. (1990). Pink or blue: Environmental gender stereotypes in the first two years of life. *Sex Roles, 22,* 359–367.

47. Pomerantz, E. M., Ng, F. F.-Y., & Wang, Q. (2004). Gender socialization: A parent x child model. In A. H. Eagly, A. E. Beall, & R. J. Sternberg (Eds.), *The psychology of gender* (2nd ed., pp. 120–144). New York: Guilford; Antill, J. K. (1987). Parents' beliefs and values about sex roles, sex differences, and sexuality: Their sources and implications. In P. Shaver & C. Hendrick (Eds.), *Sex and*

gender: Review of personality and social psychology (Vol. 7, pp. 294–328). Newbury Park, CA: Sage.

48. Tan, S. J. (2008). The myths and realities of female employment. In A. Marcus-Newhall, D. F. Halpern, & S. J. Tan (Eds.). *The changing realities of work and family: A multidisciplinary approach* (pp. 9–24). Chichester, UK: Wiley-Blackwell.

49. Harvey, E. (1999). Short-term and long-term effects of early parental employment on children of the National Longitudinal Survey of Youth. *Developmental Psychology, 35,* 445–459; Goldberg, W. A., Prause, J., Lucas-Thompson, R., & Himsel, A. (2008). Maternal employment and children's achievement in context: A meta-analysis of four decades of research. *Psychological Bulletin, 134,* 77–108; Hoffman, L. W., & Youngblade, L. M. (1999). *Mothers at work: Effects on children's well-being.* Cambridge, UK: Cambridge University Press.

50. Gupta, S. (2006). The consequences of maternal employment during men's childhood for their adult housework performance. *Gender & Society, 20,* 60–86.

51. Stewart, W., & Barling, J. (1996). Fathers' work experiences effect children's behaviors via job-related affect and parenting behaviors. *Journal of Organizational Behavior, 17,* 221–232; MacEwen, K. E., & Barling, J. (1991). Effects of maternal employment experiences on children's behavior via mood, cognitive difficulties, and parenting behavior. *Journal of Marriage and the Family, 53,* 635–644; Barling, J., MacEwen, K. E., & Nolte, M-L. (1993). Homemaker role experiences affect toddler behaviors via maternal well-being and parenting behavior. *Journal of Abnormal Child Psychology, 21,* 213–229.

52. Shakeshaft, C. (1999). The struggle to create a more gender-inclusive profession. In J. Murphy & K. S. Louis (Eds.), *Handbook of research on educational administration* (2nd ed. pp. 99–118). San Francisco: Jossey-Bass.

53. Corbett, C., Hill, C., & St. Rose, A. (2008). *Where the girls are: The facts about gender equity in education.* Washington, DC: American Association of University Women Educational Foundation. Retrieved May 20, 2008, from http://www.aauw.org.

54. Dwyer, C. A., & Johnson, L. M. (1997). Grades, accomplishments, and correlates. In W. W. Willingham & N. S. Cole (Eds.), *Gender and fair assessment* (pp. 127–156). Mahwah, NJ: Erlbaum; Kenney-Benson, G. A., Pomerantz, E. M., Ryan, A. M., & Patrick, H. (2006). Sex differences in math performance: The role of children's approach to schoolwork. *Developmental Psychology, 42,* 11–26.

55. Golombok, S., & Fivush, R. (1994). *Gender development.* Cambridge, UK: Cambridge University Press; American Association of University Women. (1998). *Gender gaps: Where schools still fail our children.* Washington, DC: Author; American Association of University Women. (1992). *How schools short-change girls.* Washington, DC: Author; Guttentag, M., & Bray, H. (1977). Teachers as mediators of sex-role standards. In A. G. Sargent (Ed.), *Beyond sex roles,* (pp. 395–411). St. Paul, MN: West.

56. Gentile, B., Grabe, S., Dolan-Pascoe, B., Twenge, J. M., Wells, B. E., & Maitano, A. (2009). Gender differences in domain-specific self-esteem: A meta-analysis. *Review of General Psychology, 13*, 34–45.

57. Dwyer & Johnson; Lubinski, D., & Benbow, C. P. (1994). The Study of Mathematically Precocious Youth: The first three decades of a planned 50-year study of intellectual talent. In R. F. Subotnik & K. D. Arnold (Eds.), *Beyond Terman: Contemporary longitudinal studies of giftedness and talent* (pp. 255–281). Norwood, NJ: Ablex; Arnold, K. D. (1994). The Illinois Valedictorian Project: Early adult careers of academically talented male high school students. In R. F. Subotnik & K. D. Arnold (Eds.), *Beyond Terman: Contemporary longitudinal studies of giftedness and talent* (pp. 24–51). Norwood, NJ: Ablex; Jacobs, J. A. (1996). Gender inequality and higher education. In J. Hagan & K. S. Cook (Eds.), *Annual review of sociology* (Vol. 22, pp. 153–185). Palo Alto, CA: Annual Reviews.

58. Gerbner, G., & Gross, L. (1976). Living with television: The violence profile. *Journal of Communications, 26* (2), 172–199; Larson & Verma.

59. Davis, D. M. (1990). Portrayals of women in prime-time network television: Some demographic characteristics. *Sex Roles, 23*, 325–332; Larson & Verma.

60. Signorielli, N., & Bacue, A. (1999). Recognition and respect: A content analysis of prime-time television characters across three decades. *Sex Roles, 40*, 527–544.

61. Ganahl, D. J., Prinsen, T. J., & Netzley, S. B. (2003). A content analysis of prime time commercials: A contextual analysis of gender representation. *Sex Roles, 49*, 545–551; Coltrane, S., & Adams, M. (1997). Work-family imagery and gender stereotypes: Television and the reproduction of difference. *Journal of Vocational Behavior, 50*, 323–347; Kaufman, G. (1999). The portrayal of men's family roles in television commercials. *Sex Roles, 41*, 439–458.

62. Bartsch, R. A., Burnett, T., Diller, T. R., & Rankin-Williams, E. (2000). Gender representation in television commercials: Updating an update. *Sex Roles, 43*, 735–743; Hall, C. C. I., & Crum, M. J. (1994). Women and "body-isms" in television beer commercials. *Sex Roles, 31*, 329–337; Strate, L. (1992). Beer commercials: A manual on masculinity. In S. Craig (Ed.), *Men, masculinity, and the media* (pp. 78–92). Newbury Park, CA: Sage; Ogletree, S. M., Williams, S. W., Raffeld, P., Mason, B., & Fricke, K. (1990). Female attractiveness and eating disorders: Do children's television commercials play a role? *Sex Roles, 22*, 791–797.

63. Mastro, D. E., & Stern, S. R. (2003). Representations of race in television commercials: A content analysis of prime-time advertising. *Journal of Broadcasting & Electronic Media, 47*, 638–647; Coltrane, S., & Messineo, M. (2000). The perpetuation of subtle prejudice: Race and gender imagery in 1990s television advertising. *Sex Roles, 42*, 363–389; Seiter, E. (1995). Different children, different dreams: Racial representation in advertising. In G. Dines & J. M. Humez (Eds.), *Gender, race and class in media: A text-free reader* (pp. 99–108). Thousand Oaks, CA: Sage.

64. Morgan, M. (1982). Television and adolescents' sex role stereotypes: A longitudinal study. *Journal of Personality and Social Psychology, 43*, 947–955;

McGhee, P. E., & Frueh, T. (1980). Television viewing and the learning of sex-role stereotypes. *Sex Roles, 6,* 179–188; Signorielli, N., & Lears, M. (1992). Children, television, and conceptions about chores: Attitudes and behaviors. *Sex Roles, 27,* 157–170; Gerbner & Gross.

65. McCauley, C., Thangavelu, K., & Rozin, P. (1988). Sex role stereotyping of occupations in relation to television representations and census facts. *Basic and Applied Social Psychology, 9,* 197–212.

66. Grove, L. (1999, September 16). Captain's Log, Stardate 1999: Mr. Sulu pushes diversity on TV. *Washington Post.* Retrieved September 16, 1999, from http://www.washingtonpost.com; Richards, T. (1997). *The meaning of Star Trek.* New York: Doubleday.

67. Fiske.

68. Beere, C.A. (1979). Bem Sex Role Inventory (BSRI). In *Women and women's issues: A handbook of tests and measures* (pp. 104–113). San Francisco: Jossey-Bass.

69. These two questions were inspired by James Jones, who posed similar questions about race; Jones, J. M. (1991). Psychological models of race: What have they been and what should they be? In J. D. Goodchilds (Ed.), *Psychological perspectives on human diversity in America* (pp. 3–46). Washington, DC: American Psychological Association.

70. Russo, N. F., & Tartaro, J. (2008). Women and mental health. In F. L. Denmark & M. A. Paludi (Eds.), *Psychology of women: A handbook of issues and theories* (2nd ed., pp. 440–483). Westport, CT: Praeger; Doyal, L. (2003). Sex and gender: The challenges for epidemiologists. *International Journal of Health Services, 3,* 569–579.

71. Pleck, J. H. (1981). *The myth of masculinity.* Cambridge, MA: MIT Press; Lippa, R. A., Martin, L. R., & Friedman, H. S. (2000). Gender-related individual differences and mortality in the Terman longitudinal study: Is masculinity hazardous to your health? *Personality and Social Psychology Bulletin, 26,* 1560–1570.

72. U.S. Department of Health and Human Services, Centers for Disease Control and Prevention, National Center for Health Statistics. (2009). *Health, United States, 2008,* tables 25, 26, and 34. Retrieved July 27, 2009, from http://www .cdc.gov/nchs.

73. Doyal; Russo & Tartaro; Verbugge, L. M. (1985). Gender and health: An update of hypotheses and evidence. *Journal of Health and Social Behavior, 26,* 156–182.

CHAPTER 4

Making Employment Decisions

Laura M. Graves & Gary N. Powell

Out of Sight Keeps Women in Mind

Women have better luck auditioning for the major U.S. orchestras if they can be heard and not seen. That is the conclusion of a study by Claudia Goldin of Harvard University and Cecilia Rouse of Princeton University. They found that when musicians auditioned behind a heavy cloth suspended from the ceiling so judges can't see their gender—or race or age—it boosts by 50% the odds that a woman will make it past preliminary rounds and by severalfold the odds that she will get the job. . . .

Blind screens are "the only way to assure a fair audition," says Catherine Pickar, a spokeswoman for the International Alliance for Women in Music in Washington. Sylvia Alimena is certain that performing incognito played at least some role in her hiring 12 years ago to play the French horn—still overwhelmingly a male-dominated instrument—for the National Symphony Orchestra in Washington. She recalls taking off her high heels to walk to her place behind the screen so she wouldn't make the tell-tale clip-clop noises, then slipping them back on her short legs so her five-foot stature would touch the floor.

"The screen assures you that you're going to be taken seriously," says Ms. Allimena, one of two female French horn players at the NSO.[1]

L ike symphony orchestras, many of today's organizations utilize hiring practices designed to prevent sex discrimination, as well as other types of discrimination. Although some organizations have embraced nondiscriminatory practices in order to hire the best talent available, others have been motivated by legal requirements. Because most employers have substantial motivation to avoid sex discrimination in their employment practices, one might assume that sex and gender have little effect on employment decisions. Unfortunately, this assumption is incorrect.

Both job seekers and organizations make employment decisions. Job seekers identify and apply for relevant opportunities, complete job interviews and tests, accept or reject job offers, and negotiate starting salaries. At the same time, organizations promote job openings, evaluate applicants, make job offers, and determine job assignments and starting salaries. As we will see, sex and gender influence the decisions of both job seekers and organizations.

Self-Selection Decisions

The decisions of individual job seekers during the job search process are called **self-selection decisions.** In self-selection decisions, individuals actively choose which opportunities to pursue and which job offers to accept. Of course, job seekers' self-selection decisions affect the nature of the jobs that they obtain. Self-selection decisions, however, also affect organizations. If highly qualified potential applicants do not apply for jobs or accept job offers, organizations may experience shortages of qualified workers.[2]

During the self-selection process, job seekers assess the fit or match between themselves and employment opportunities. Individuals' evaluations of the fit between themselves and specific opportunities are based on the nature of the job and the organization. Women and men may react differently to jobs and organizations, leading to sex differences in fit evaluations and, ultimately, self-selection decisions.[3]

Sex differences in self-selection decisions also result from differences in the techniques that men and women use to find employment. Men and women may obtain different types of employment because their job search methods are dissimilar. We now examine how sex differences in self-selection decisions arise from differences in men's and women's reactions to jobs and organizations and in their job search behavior.

Reactions to Jobs

As women and men seek job opportunities that fit their own characteristics, they may seek different kinds of jobs. Differences in women's and
men's desired jobs could occur if the gender socialization processes
described in Chapter 3 lead women or men to prefer jobs that are consistent with the appropriate gender stereotype and role. Given the increased
labor force participation of women worldwide, do gender stereotypes and
roles continue to dictate individuals' job preferences? In this section, we
consider this question, exploring sex similarities and differences in preferences for job attributes, work activities, and occupations.

Job attribute preferences refer to the extent to which an individual
views different qualities and outcomes of paid work as desirable. Job
attributes represent general characteristics of jobs such as working hours,
geographical location, advancement opportunities, salary, benefits, relationships with coworkers, and opportunities for using skills and abilities.
Preferences for job attributes are most important to job seekers at the
beginning of their job search and play less of a role in actual job choice
decisions, when organizational factors such as reputation and recruiting
practices are more important.[4]

Sex differences in job attribute preferences are prevalent. Most of
these differences align with gender roles and stereotypes, but others do
not. Women are more concerned with job attributes that allow them to
meet demands of the homemaker role (e.g., good hours, easy commute) and the feminine stereotype than are men. The opportunity for
positive interpersonal relations (e.g., working with people, opportunity
to help others, opportunity to make friends) is especially important to
women. However, job attributes normally associated with the male
breadwinner role and the masculine stereotype are not uniformly
endorsed to a greater extent by men than by women. Although men
consider income, autonomy, the opportunity to exercise leadership and
power, challenging work, and promotion opportunities to be more
important than do women, women consider job benefits, the availability of job openings, and feelings of accomplishment as more important. There are no sex differences in the extent to which women and
men seek jobs that provide high status, recognition, meaningful work,
and responsibility.[5]

Job attribute preferences may be influenced by the nature of one's
family structure. For example, women who are mothers value flexibility
more than childless women. Men who are married and fathers value
income and advancement more than single, childless men. The influence

of family structure on individuals' careers and workplace experiences is discussed at greater length in Chapter 8.[6]

Sex differences in job attribute preferences also may be influenced by cultural factors. For example, in Japan, where women typically serve as clerks and leave the workforce after marriage, female employees attach more importance to factors such as working hours, commute, location, salary, benefits, and job security than do male employees. In contrast, male employees are more concerned about their future prospects for advancement with the organization. Lengthy commutes and long working hours are common in Japan. Because Japanese women, unlike Japanese men, do not expect to remain with their employers, they may be more concerned with factors that reduce the everyday stresses of their work schedules than with their long-term prospects with the organization.[7]

Men and women differ in their **preferences for work activities.** Generally, these differences are consistent with gender stereotypes and roles. Young women are more interested in activities that involve people (e.g., taking care of people, performing community service), while young men are more interested in activities that involve things (computers, machines, tools). Individuals may be further classified based on their interests in six activities: realistic (e.g., manipulation of objects, tools, machines, and animals), investigative (e.g., examination of physical, biological, and cultural phenomena), artistic (e.g., creation of art forms and products), social (e.g., informing, training, and developing others), enterprising (e.g., influencing others to attain goals), and conventional (e.g., administrative) activities. Sex differences in preferences for enterprising and conventional activities appear to be small, with young men preferring enterprising and conventional activities somewhat more than do young women. However, sex differences for the other four types of activities are more substantial. Young women are more interested in artistic and social activities than are men, while men are more interested in realistic and investigative activities.[8]

Sex differences in **occupational preferences** are also of interest. As the labor force participation of women has increased, young women have become somewhat less interested in pursuing female-intensive occupations and somewhat more interested in pursuing male-intensive occupations. However, during the same time, the occupational interests of young men have changed very little. As a result, sex differences in occupational preferences have diminished but still remain. Stereotypically masculine occupations such as building contractor, race car driver, stockbroker, and professional athlete are more likely to be preferred by men than by women. In contrast, the occupations of social worker, bank teller, dietician, elementary schoolteacher, and registered nurse are more likely to be preferred by women.[9]

Why do individuals continue to prefer jobs that are regarded as appropriate for members of their sex? Gender socialization processes certainly contribute to sex differences in occupational preferences. The sex segregation of occupations, described in Chapter 2, may also lead job seekers to restrict their occupational choices. People assume generally that individuals possess the characteristics needed for their current work roles. Thus, women are assumed to possess the attributes needed in female-intensive jobs while men are assumed to possess those attributes appropriate for male-intensive jobs. People also believe that success in female-intensive jobs requires feminine personality traits and physical characteristics while success in male-intensive jobs requires masculine personality traits and physical characteristics.[10]

The notion that success in the occupations dominated by one sex requires the personal characteristics associated with that sex is likely to have a chilling effect on job seekers of the other sex. Job seekers may believe that they cannot succeed in occupations that are numerically dominated by the other sex and look elsewhere for employment. Both women and men suffer when they restrict their occupational choices to those that seem suitable for members of their sex. However, women are more likely to suffer financially because female-intensive occupations pay less than male-intensive occupations. In fact, sex differences in occupational choice contribute to the lower pay of women even when we account for differences in the job-related skills and credentials that men and women bring to their jobs.[11]

Job seekers' preferences for work activities and occupations are not a function of their sex only. Gender identity also plays an important role in individuals' interests and occupational preferences. Individuals differ in the extent to which they internalize the lessons of gender socialization and embrace the gender roles prescribed for members of their sex. Masculine individuals are more likely to prefer working with things and to choose male-intensive occupations, whereas feminine individuals are more likely to prefer working with people and to choose female-intensive occupations. College men who endorse antifemininity and toughness norms are more likely to pursue male-intensive occupations such as computer science, engineering, and construction technology, while those who reject these norms are more likely to pursue female-intensive occupations such as nursing, counseling, and elementary education.[12]

In sum, sex differences in preferences for specific job attributes, work activities, and occupations are substantial. As individuals make choices about the kind of work they would like to do, they are influenced by their own socialization experiences and by the distribution of male and female workers across occupations. Individuals tend to seek jobs that are viewed as appropriate for members of their sex, thereby reinforcing the sex segregation of the workforce.

Reactions to Organizations

Sex differences in self-selection decisions may also be due to differences in women's and men's reactions to organizations. Human resource management programs and practices serve as signals for underlying organizational values. Job seekers use these signals to assess the fit between their own values and those of the organization. For women and people of color, initiatives such as diversity and work–family programs may be important signals concerning the value that the organization places on maintaining a diverse workforce and the likelihood of their own fit within the organization. Selection processes, especially the demographic characteristics and behavior of the recruiter and the nature of the procedures used, serve as further signals about working conditions in the organization.[13]

Inclusive diversity policies make it easier for organizations to attract applicants. Organizations that declare their commitment to diversity in recruitment advertisements increase their attractiveness to all job seekers, regardless of the job seeker's sex or race. Nonetheless, women and people of color pay closer attention to a prospective employer's diversity management practices than do men and Whites. Policies concerning affirmative action and the promotion of women and people of color into the managerial and executive ranks are more important to women and people of color, who are more likely to benefit from them.[14]

The presence of **work–family initiatives** such as flextime, reduced hours, and on-site day care also seems to increase organizational attractiveness for all employees. Even individuals who pursue traditional career paths prefer flexible organizations that allow all workers to balance work and family. Flexible organizations may be favored because they are seen as more humane and modern. Also, as individuals devote more time to child rearing and household activities, they seek jobs with organizations that provide more flexibility. Because gender socialization may lead women to emphasize family roles to a greater extent than men, work–family initiatives may be especially attractive to women.[15]

The sex of the recruiter could differentially affect men's and women's evaluations of the organization's attractiveness. For instance, applicants could see job opportunities as less attractive when they are interviewed by female rather than male recruiters because women typically have less power and than men in organizations. In addition, sex similarity between the job seeker and the recruiter could affect the job seeker's attraction to the organization. Sex similarity may lead to perceived similarity in attitudes and values, which in turn leads to interpersonal attraction or liking and more positive evaluations of the other party. Sex similarity may also enhance communication between the applicant and the recruiter. Because individuals are more open to influence from similar others, applicants may be more easily sold on a job by same-sex than by opposite-sex recruiters. The presence of a same-sex recruiter may also serve as a signal that individuals similar to the job seeker are valued at the organization. However, neither recruiter sex nor sex similarity between the recruiter and the applicant have consistent effects on men's or women's evaluations of the attractiveness of job opportunities.[16]

Although recruiter sex and sex similarity do not lead to predictable sex differences in reactions to job opportunities, **recruiting practices** lead to such differences. One study obtained rich evidence on this issue from intensive interviews with undergraduate and graduate students throughout their job searches. In the interviews, the researchers tried to understand why students pursued or rejected various job opportunities. Despite the fact that the researchers asked no questions about sex discrimination, half of the women in their sample mentioned a negative experience that might be a sign of such discrimination. For instance, corporate representatives commented on women's personal appearances or told women that they would not advance as fast as men. In addition, when students described why they became more negative or positive about particular organizations during their job searches, women were much more likely than men to cite their interactions with recruiters and other organizational representatives. Given the negative experiences of women, it is not surprising that their evaluations of job opportunities are more affected by their interactions with organizational representatives. Women may base their assessments of the environment for women and the likelihood of their own success in the organization on their interactions with organizational representatives.[17]

Men and women also differ in their evaluations of the **fairness of selection procedures.** The use of structured selection procedures designed to avoid sex discrimination is more important to women than to men, at least among applicants for entry-level positions. Advertising every open position, using panels of interviewers of both sexes, ensuring equal opportunity regardless of sex, age, or race, and avoiding the use of appearance as a selection criterion are more important in determining the fairness of selection procedures for women than men. In contrast, men are more likely than women to endorse the evaluation of job-related competence as important for fair selection decisions. These sex differences in reactions to selection procedures may arise from differences in men's and women's interview experiences. If women commonly experience sex discrimination, they may feel that formal procedures are needed to address it.[18]

In sum, human resource management programs and practices differentially affect men's and women's attraction to job opportunities. Although both women and men view organizations with diversity and work–family programs in a positive light, these characteristics are especially important to women. In addition, women are more likely to experience offensive behavior in their interactions with organizational representatives. As a result, these interactions are more important in women's than in men's job choice decisions. Women also endorse the use of nondiscriminatory selection procedures to a greater extent than do men. Overall, these findings suggest that organizations that want to attract women need to consider the signals conveyed by their diversity and work–family initiatives and their selection processes.

Job Search Behavior

Sex differences in **job search behavior** also influence the kinds of jobs that men and women obtain. Men devote more time and effort to their searches. According to traditional gender roles, men, who are envisioned as the primary wage earners, should work harder at finding employment than women. Because men have fewer household responsibilities, they have more time available to devote to their job searches and act more independently, whereas women have less time available and are more influenced by the opinions of others in their job searches. If men devote more time and effort to job seeking, they are likely to have better alternatives from which to choose. According to a study of the job search efforts of a broad group of job seekers, women spend less time searching for jobs than do men. However, women in male-intensive occupations spend much more time searching for jobs than women in other occupations. Not surprisingly, individuals who search longer find higher-paying jobs.[19]

Men and women also differ in the methods they use to find jobs. Job search methods may be formal or informal. **Formal job search methods** include obtaining referrals from employment agencies, labor unions, and school placement officers and responding to newspaper ads and help-wanted signs. **Informal job search methods** consist of referrals from networks of friends, family members, and business associates.

Although both methods are useful in the job search process, informal methods are a frequent mechanism for finding employment. In fact, many individuals who find new jobs are not even actively engaged in job searches. Instead, they "fall into" jobs that they hear about through their social networks.[20]

Men's and women's **networks** differ substantially. Women's networks are more kin-centered, and men's networks are more work-centered. Women tend to have networks that are more concentrated in the local community and composed of friends and relatives than are men's, perhaps because of women's greater domestic responsibilities and lower-status positions. In contrast, men have more geographically dispersed, diverse networks containing a greater number of business contacts and high-status individuals. When men and women use their networks to identify desirable jobs, they tend to rely on same-sex contacts. Same-sex contacts restrict the job choices of women compared to those of men, funneling them to female-intensive jobs in their local communities with less status and lower pay than male-intensive jobs. As a result, women benefit less from their social networks during the job search process.[21]

Once they hold jobs, men and women differ in the strategies they use to obtain new jobs and the benefits derived from their chosen strategy. Women often adopt an **internal labor market strategy,** seeking promotions and earnings growth within a single organization. In contrast, men tend to use an **external labor market strategy,** seeking advancement by searching for jobs with new employers while continuing to work for their present employers. Because using an external labor market strategy increases individuals' compensation more than using an internal labor market strategy, sex differences in the strategy used contribute to the pay differential between men and women. Moreover, even when women seek external employment, it yields them little benefit. The primary beneficiaries of an external labor market strategy are White males. Women and people of color who change companies do not increase their pay compared to those who stay with their companies, perhaps because of discrimination in employment systems.[22]

When negotiating with potential employers about job opportunities, sex differences in job seekers' **pay expectations** may lead to sex differences in actual wages. Because women expect and accept less pay than men, they request and receive less pay than men in equivalent positions. For almost all occupations, young women have lower expectations regarding both their entry pay and their pay at the peaks of their careers than do young men. The sex difference in pay expectations is especially striking for male-intensive occupations such as engineering. It occurs even when individuals estimate a fair salary for a particular job. Compared to men, women actually see lower pay as "fair pay."[23]

Several factors account for sex differences in pay expectations. First, women's lower pay expectations may be realistic. As victims of past discrimination in salary decisions, women simply may have lower pay standards. Second, as noted in our discussion of sex differences in job attribute preferences, pay is more important to men than to women. Women appear to be less concerned about pay and more concerned about other aspects of work such as interpersonal relations and convenience. Third, men and women use different reference groups in determining pay expectations. Women typically base their pay expectations on the pay of other women, whereas men base their pay expectations on the pay of other men. Because men are likely to be more highly paid, this tendency to develop pay expectations based on same-sex comparisons may lead to sex differences in pay expectations. Finally, because of their limited business contacts, women's knowledge of pay levels may be less accurate.[24]

Differences in women's and men's job search methods contribute to differences in the jobs available to them and the salaries they receive. Men devote more time to their searches and have more access to beneficial contacts than do women. As a result, men identify more and better job opportunities. Further, even when men and women find equivalent jobs, women's salaries may be lower. Compared to men, women are less likely to obtain wage increases by changing employers. Women appear to have lower pay expectations than men in the same occupation, putting them at a disadvantage when negotiating salaries.

In summary, male and female job seekers make different self-selection decisions regarding employment. They differ in their preferences for job attributes, work activities, and occupations in ways that contribute to the continued sex segregation of the workplace. Women are more influenced than men by the organization's human resource management programs and practices; organizations with policies that emphasize managing diversity and balancing work and family are especially attractive to women. Also, women are more attracted to organizations when they view selection procedures as fair and have positive, nondiscriminatory interactions with recruiters. Finally, sex differences in job search behaviors contribute to the employment of women in jobs that are lower paid than those of men.

Selection Decisions

The decisions of organizations and their representatives during the hiring process are called selection decisions. In selection decisions, organizations choose which applicants will receive further consideration (e.g., by being invited to a formal interview or site visit) and which applicants of those who receive further consideration will actually receive job offers. Although the selection decisions of organizations are based primarily on applicants' qualifications, sex discrimination may occur. We need to consider how and when sex discrimination occurs and who discriminates against whom.[25]

How and When Does Sex Discrimination Occur?

To understand how and when sex discrimination occurs, it is helpful to examine how organizational representatives make selection decisions. Organizational decision makers use a matching process to assess applicants. Decision makers form **mental prototypes** or images of the ideal applicant. These prototypes define the traits and behaviors that are required for success in a particular job. As decision makers evaluate applicants, they favor applicants whose attributes come closest to matching this prototype.[26]

Sex discrimination may arise from decision makers' prototypes of the ideal applicant. These prototypes may include traits that are specifically linked to one sex. When the tasks required for job performance are mostly masculine, the prototype will be masculine and men will be seen as more likely to succeed. For example, the requirements of managerial positions may include stereotypically masculine behaviors such as making tough decisions or competing for scarce organizational resources. As a result, decision makers' prototypes for such positions may emphasize masculine traits and male applicants may be seen as better suited for the job. On the other hand, if the prototype for a job (e.g., day care worker) includes feminine traits, females will be seen as more suitable.[27]

In some cases, decision makers' prototypes explicitly specify the sex of the jobholder. When job incumbents or job applicants are predominantly from one sex, organizational decision makers' prototypes specify the sex of the ideal applicant; applicants whose sex matches the prototype will be seen as more qualified and will be favored in the selection process. Among applicants for female-intensive jobs, female applicants are likely to be rated as more qualified, offered higher starting salaries and more challenging job assignments, and hired more often than males. In contrast, male applicants are likely to be preferred over females for male-intensive jobs. Decision makers do not hire blatantly unqualified applicants of the "correct" sex over qualified applicants of the "wrong" sex. However, they may hire moderately qualified applicants of the correct sex over slightly more qualified applicants of the other sex.[28]

An example from the restaurant industry demonstrates the use of sex as an explicit element of decision makers' ideal applicant prototypes. Imagine going to the most elegant restaurant in a large city to celebrate your birthday. This particular birthday is a significant milestone and you are sparing no expense to enjoy an incredible dining experience. Look around your restaurant. What sex are the servers? They are probably mostly or entirely male. Now, imagine going to a less expensive restaurant such as the nearest sandwich shop that would provide a less elegant dining experience. What sex are the servers? They are probably mostly female. A possible explanation for this phenomenon is that women prefer the limited tips earned in inexpensive restaurants and men prefer the more generous tips in expensive restaurants. Another is that men are more qualified to serve expensive food and women more qualified to serve inexpensive food. A more likely explanation is that managers of expensive restaurants possess ideal applicant prototypes that specify that servers should be male, while managers of inexpensive restaurants have prototypes that specify that servers should be female.

One study suggests that this is indeed the case. In the study, two male and two female students in an undergraduate economics course applied for jobs as servers at selected restaurants in Philadelphia. One male and one female student dropped off equivalent résumés at each restaurant. The students visited 23 high-priced restaurants and received a total of 13 job offers from these restaurants. Eleven of these 13 job offers were made to men. The students visited 21 low-priced restaurants and received a total of 10 offers for jobs from these restaurants. Women received 8 of the 10 offers. Thus, male applicants were preferred at expensive restaurants and female applicants were preferred at inexpensive restaurants. The preference for male servers at high-priced restaurants seems to be due to the managers' beliefs about the preferences of patrons in these restaurants, who are more likely to be male than patrons in low-priced restaurants. Restaurant managers, regardless of their own sex, prefer servers whose sex matches patrons' expectations. Thus, their ideal applicant prototypes specify the sex of the jobholder.[29]

Sex discrimination based on mental prototypes may smolder inside the restaurant kitchen as well. Noted female chefs report that their industry is not comfortable with a woman in charge of overall food preparation. Female chefs are often insulted or ignored by male chefs in the main kitchen. As a result, they often gravitate toward being in charge of pastries, a more traditionally female area of expertise. Sex discrimination even affects who gets to have their own restaurant. Female restaurant owners have a harder time attracting investors and securing funding for their businesses than their male counterparts.[30]

Sex discrimination also arises in the selection process because decision makers have a general tendency to devalue the qualifications of female applicants. In society, individuals are assigned status or esteem based on the demographic groups to which they belong; Whites and men are typically ascribed higher status than women and people of color. Judgments of individuals' task competence are based, in part, on the status assigned to members of their demographic group. Individuals who belong to high-status groups are viewed as more competent than those of low-status groups. Because females are typically ascribed less status or esteem in society, decision makers may believe that women are less qualified than men. As a result, male applicants are valued more than identically qualified female applicants. Moreover, to be seen as qualified, female applicants must provide more evidence of their ability than similarly qualified male applicants.[31]

Thus, sex discrimination in the selection process may lead women to be preferred for jobs that are female-intensive or require feminine traits and men to be preferred for jobs that are male-intensive or require masculine traits. However, if men are generally seen as more qualified than women, men who apply for female-intensive jobs (e.g., male applicant for nursing position) may suffer less discrimination than women who apply for male-intensive jobs (e.g., woman applicant for firefighter position).

Sex discrimination is most likely to occur when jobs are associated with one sex, either because the traits required for the job are stereotypically masculine or feminine or because the job is dominated by members of one sex. However, the presence of sex discrimination is also influenced by other situational factors, especially the amount of information available about applicants and the conspicuousness of the applicant's sex. Recruiters and managers often have insufficient information on which to base their selection decisions. For instance, the initial screening of applicants is typically based on résumés or application forms, which present little information about applicants' personal qualities. When recruiting is conducted on college campuses, decisions about which applicants to consider further are based on interviews of no more than 20 to 30 minutes. These interviews lead to quickly formed impressions that present only a glimpse of the applicant. Follow-up interviews provide more information about applicants, but not so much that employers can be sure that they are making the right choice or offering an appropriate salary.[32]

Insufficient information increases the likelihood that discrimination will occur. In the absence of information, decision makers have no reliable way to evaluate an applicant's potential productivity. They are likely to rely on gender stereotypes and status judgments to form impressions of applicants. Decision makers assume that applicants possess attributes associated with their sex and use these attributes to assess the fit of the applicants with the prototype of the ideal applicant. As a result, when decision makers with limited information evaluate applicants, women are less likely than men to advance into the final applicant pool and to receive job offers. Women also are likely to receive lower starting salaries. On the other hand, when decision makers have extensive information about applicants' abilities, sex discrimination is less likely.[33]

Sex discrimination also occurs when the situation calls attention to the sex of the applicant. When applicant sex is highly conspicuous, decision makers are likely to access their gender stereotypes and status judgments, thereby increasing the chance of sex discrimination. Numerous factors increase the conspicuousness of applicant sex. Applicant sex is likely to be conspicuous when decision makers encounter applicants whose sex is atypical among applicants or job incumbents. Aspects of the applicant's appearance (e.g., a very femininely dressed woman) may also increase attention to the applicant's sex.[34]

A striking demonstration of the importance of the conspicuousness of applicant sex comes from research on the effect of screens on sex discrimination in the selection decisions made by major symphony orchestras. Elite symphonies historically have discriminated against female musicians. In fact, some conductors of major orchestras have been known to make public comments such as "I just don't think women should be in an orchestra," or "The more women in an orchestra, the smaller the sound." Because women musicians are underrepresented in major symphonies, sex is likely to be an explicit aspect of decision makers' prototypes of the ideal applicant and applicant sex is likely to be conspicuous. The use of screens in orchestra auditions reduces the conspicuousness of applicant sex; in fact it makes applicant sex invisible. Thus, by comparing the amount of sex discrimination with and without screens, we can get an idea of how conspicuousness affects the occurrence of discrimination. As we saw in the introductory passage to the chapter, using screens substantially reduces discrimination against women. This finding reinforces the notion that the conspicuousness of applicant sex is an important factor in determining whether sex discrimination occurs.[35]

Sex discrimination, in both symphony orchestras and other employment settings, may also arise when applicant sex is conspicuous in the initial screening phase of the selection process. A study of selection decisions by professional orchestras in Germany illustrates this point. Applicants for orchestra positions first submit a written application, and then selected applicants are invited to audition behind screens. Women composed less than 30% of all musicians in German orchestras; they are more likely to be in the string section and less likely to play woodwinds or brass instruments. Women were discriminated against in decisions about which applicants to invite for auditions, but had an equal chance for men to get a job once they were granted the opportunity to perform in a blind audition. As a result, even though the use of screens accomplished its intended purpose of reducing discrimination at the final hiring stage of the selection process, sex discrimination was still present in decisions at the invitation stage because women's low proportions in German orchestras made applicant sex conspicuous.[36]

In most cases, the processes described above operate at an unconscious level. Most decision makers do not say to themselves, "Women simply aren't qualified for this job" or "I will act on my belief in gender stereotypes in evaluating applicants" or "I must hire a man for this position because this job is usually filled by men." However, some decision makers may consciously use what they believe are other peoples' biases as the basis for their decisions about applicants. If they think, for example, that employees or customers will feel uncomfortable with a female engineer or a male secretary, they may defer to that attitude in their hiring decisions even if they do not share it. Thus, elegant restaurants may hire only male servers because they believe that their patrons prefer to be waited on by male servers. Discrimination on the basis of customer preferences is illegal, as we discuss further in Chapter 9, but it does occur.

Our attention has been on the "how and when" of sex discrimination in selection decisions. Mental prototypes play a large role in selection decisions. These prototypes are most likely to lead to sex discrimination in selection decisions when job applicants or current jobholders are predominantly from one sex, the traits seen as required for the job are either stereotypically masculine or feminine, minimal information is available about applicants, and applicant sex is highly conspicuous. Also, there is a general tendency to devalue the qualifications of female applicants.

Who Discriminates Against Whom?

Whether sex discrimination occurs in selection decisions may be influenced by personal characteristics of decision makers as well as personal characteristics of applicants other than their sex. It is important to examine who discriminates against whom.

As noted earlier, sex similarity between the interviewer and the applicant may enhance their mutual liking and facilitate communication in the interview. As a result, applicants in same-sex interviews may share more information about themselves, thereby providing interviewers a better understanding of what they have to offer. In addition, increased liking may lead interviewers to conduct more positive interviews and focus on positive information when forming their judgments of applicants. These effects of sex similarity may even apply to situations in which organizational representatives are simply evaluating résumés or application forms. However, research findings provide inconsistent support for the idea that sex similarity between the interviewer and the applicant leads to more favorable evaluations of applicants.[37]

Decision-makers' personalities are more useful than their sex in predicting whether they will engage in sex discrimination. The extent to which decision makers endorse traditional gender roles and stereotypes is especially important. Decision makers who adhere to traditional, rather than nontraditional, gender roles and stereotypes are likely to discriminate against women who apply for male-intensive positions. However, even those individuals who reject traditional gender stereotypes may engage in discrimination by favoring women over men.[38]

Applicants' physical attractiveness affects the occurrence of sex discrimination in selection decisions. Even though assessments of attractiveness are highly subjective, people agree on who is attractive and who is not attractive both within and across cultures. They also agree that "what is beautiful is good." Attractive children and adults are judged and treated more positively than unattractive children and adults, even by people who know them. Further, attractive adults, especially men, are judged as being more competent, even when they are not actually more competent, than unattractive adults. In job interviews, physically attractive applicants are seen as more likeable and ultimately as more suitable for hiring. When evaluating job applicants of the opposite sex, people demonstrate a preference for attractive applicants over unattractive applicants. However, although attractive women are more likely than unattractive women to get a job in which job incumbents are predominantly male, attractive men still have an advantage in getting the job. Overall, physical attractiveness is more important in the evaluation of female than of male applicants.[39]

Applicants' weight, a highly visible characteristic that affects judgments of attractiveness, influences whether sex discrimination occurs in selection decisions. Although people have little control over their general level of attractiveness, they are expected to exert control over their body weight. Overweight individuals are stereotyped as being lazier, less conscientious, less attentive to their personal hygiene, and less emotionally stable than their "normal-weight" counterparts, even though there is little supporting evidence. Weight-based discrimination is exhibited in most stages of employment, including decisions about hiring, initial placement, salary, and promotion as well as assessments of career potential. However, biases against hiring overweight applicants have been found to be particularly strong for women. Reflecting differences in physique between the Barbie and G.I. Joe dolls/action figures that are marketed particularly to girls versus boys (see Chapter 3), a "thinness is good" standard is applied more to female applicants than male applicants.[40]

Pregnant applicants also experience discrimination in selection decisions. Intriguing experimental studies have been conducted in which women have played the role of either an applicant who is visibly pregnant, simulated by wearing a prosthesis to make her appear to be 7 or 8 months pregnant, or an applicant who is not visibly pregnant (called "nonpregnant"). Such studies have found that visibly pregnant applicants receive lower hiring recommendations than nonpregnant applicants who are equally qualified. Interestingly, discriminatory treatment appears to be reserved for pregnant job applicants but not pregnant customers. In a study of retail stores, visibly pregnant applicants received more hostile treatment from store employees than nonpregnant applicants, whereas visibly pregnant customers received more benevolent, friendly treatment than nonpregnant customers. Benevolence toward pregnant women in a traditional gender role (customer) and hostility toward pregnant women in a nontraditional gender role (applicant) is, of course, sexist. Biases in selection decisions on the basis of pregnancy violate the U.S. Pregnancy Discrimination Act as well as laws in many other countries. They provide evidence of sex discrimination when women's appearance suggests that they are about to become mothers. Given that men cannot experience anti-pregnancy biases, such biases contribute to the overall level of sex discrimination against women.[41]

In summary, sex discrimination in selection decisions is highly complex and varies as a function of characteristics of the situation (e.g., sex composition, information, desirable traits, conspicuousness of applicant sex), the decision makers (e.g., personality), and the applicants (e.g., physical appearance, weight, pregnancy). We do not fully understand how and when it occurs and who discriminates against whom. However, we certainly know enough to conclude that organizations need to guard against it.

Improving Employment Decisions

We have painted a picture of how job seekers and organizations make employment decisions that heavily emphasizes the influence of sex and gender. In this section, we consider (1) what individual job seekers can do to improve their prospects for attaining a satisfying and rewarding job and (2) what organizations can do to improve their recruitment activities and selection decisions. Tables 4.1 and 4.2 summarize recommended actions for individuals and organizations respectively.

Improving Self-Selection Decisions

Although organizational selection processes have a great impact on the jobs that individuals obtain, individuals can increase the likelihood of obtaining a satisfying and rewarding job by devoting substantial attention to identifying their own interests and to conducting job searches. First, job seekers should engage in self-exploration exercises to identify preferred occupations and job attributes. Career counselors, often available at universities and high schools, may be helpful in this process. Individuals should identify preferred activities and then determine the occupations that will allow them to pursue these activities. Given the influence of the sex segregation of work on occupational preferences, job seekers need to ensure that they do not limit their choices to those that are dominated by their own sex. For instance, females with an interest in medicine might consider becoming surgeons and males with an interest in medicine might explore careers in nursing. Job seekers also should rank their own preferences for specific job attributes. Making such a list clarifies the specific kinds of positions within an occupation that may be suitable for the individual.[42]

Second, job seekers need to devote considerable time and effort to their job searches and to use a broad range of job search methods, both formal and informal. This will allow them to identify more and better alternatives from which to choose. Informal referrals are especially important in the job search process. Women may have fewer business contacts than do men, and may need to make special efforts to establish a broader range of social contacts. For instance, women might want to consider joining local professional or business-related organizations to increase the diversity of their contacts.

Third, applicants should be prepared to make good impressions in their interviews. Applicants who make greater use of **impression management tactics** such as expressed fit with the organization (e.g., stating

Table 4.1 Recommended Actions for Individuals

1. Engage in self-exploration activities to identify your preferred occupations and job attributes.

2. Use a broad range of job search methods.

3. Practice how you will conduct yourself before a job interview.

4. Do research on potential employers before you contact them.

5. Select the job that best matches your preferred job attributes.

6. Be ready to negotiate your starting salary when you take a job.

Table 4.2 Recommended Actions for Organizations

1. Distribute promotional materials to school systems that send a message that both sexes belong in available occupations.

2. Publicize employees who hold jobs that are atypical for their sex.

3. Develop job descriptions that include the full range of activities associated with the job.

4. Seek applicants from multiple sources rather than rely only on referrals.

5. Screen recruiters to determine whether they endorse traditional gender stereotypes.

6. Train recruiters to avoid biased decisions and discriminatory behavior in interviews.

7. Formalize and standardize practices used in selection and promotion decisions.

8. Assess the effectiveness of all selection practices.

9. Reward recruiter effectiveness based on long-term results.

10. Implement diversity and work–family policies to enhance organizational attractiveness.

interest in the position and enthusiasm for working for this organization) and self-promotion (e.g., making positive statements about oneself, one's past accomplishments, or one's future plans) are more likely to receive positive recruiter evaluations in job interviews and invitations for follow-up site visits. To reduce the chances of stereotyping, job seekers should provide as much information as possible to potential employers about their qualifications. Applicants need to make known their positive qualities, both in their paper credentials and in their interactions with employers. Also, job seekers benefit from attending job interview training workshops or holding practice interviews with friends.[43]

Fourth, applicants should carefully assess the merits of each potential employer. During the initial employment interview, applicants should not expect to get much information other than whether there might be a potential match. If job seekers proceed to further discussions with an employer, they need additional information to make a good decision. Such information can be difficult to obtain, but it is available if the right questions are asked at the right time of the right people in a sensitive manner. It may be worthwhile for female applicants to consider the signals provided by recruiter behavior, as well as organizational policies with respect to work and family and managing diversity, in evaluating the extent to which women are valued by the organization.

Finally, applicants should select the job that best matches their preferred job attributes and be ready to negotiate their starting salary. All job seekers should become informed about actual pay levels for the jobs that they are seeking so that they can negotiate fair starting salaries. This is particularly important for women, some of whom may have lower pay expectations than men. Applicants who follow all of these steps will increase their chances of obtaining a satisfying and rewarding job.

Improving Selection Decisions

One key source of sex segregation in today's organizations is the sex difference in occupational preferences. Individuals' occupational preferences are formed at a very young age and typically reflect societal notions about "women's work" and "men's work." If organizations want to lower the level of sex segregation in the workplace, they need to influence the formation of children's occupational expectations.

How can organizations influence the development of occupational preferences? Many organizations distribute materials about careers to high school guidance counselors. These materials portray women and men in a greater variety of occupations than ever before. However, high school is not the place to start. If organizations expect to have an appreciable effect on the development of occupational preferences, they need to provide information about opportunities in their industries to younger children, such as by sending speakers to elementary schools, youth groups, and other places where young children congregate. The best speakers may be members of the sex least represented in the occupations being discussed, or mixed-sex teams that demonstrate that both sexes belong in the occupations. For example, a female engineer or a male nurse who succeeded despite the admonishments of others would be ideal speakers on opportunities in the engineering and nursing professions respectively. Digital media that are distributed to schools and youth groups and posted online can convey similar themes.

Organizations also need to reduce the sex segregation of jobs in their midst and devote more attention to their procedures for attracting and selecting applicants. First, they need to reduce the perception that particular jobs are appropriate for members of one sex. Many jobs require tasks associated with both women's and men's traditional roles. The full range of activities associated with particular jobs should be included in job descriptions. Organizations may also publicize employees who have been successful in positions that are atypical for their sex. The leaders of organizations may be a very powerful force in changing perceptions of jobs. When key leaders select individuals whose sex is "incorrect" for a particular job, employees' perceptions of who belongs in the job may be affected.[44]

Second, organizations need to examine how they solicit applications. Most job seekers obtain jobs through informal contacts of the same sex, and most organizations rely heavily on referrals from employees to make new hires. Organizations must ensure that reliance on referrals does not promote the sex segregation of work. They need to consider alternative sources of applicants (e.g., Internet postings, newspaper advertisements, employment agencies, campus placement centers) if reliance on referrals is limiting the diversity of new hires.

Third, organizations need to screen and train recruiters and other decision makers. Screening of recruiters should include assessments of their beliefs in rigid gender stereotypes and roles and exclude those who are likely to be biased. Training of all those involved in the selection process is critical. A survey of *Fortune* 1000 companies found that less than half offered a standardized training program for recruiters. Given the negative experiences of female applicants in the selection process, employers need to do a better job of training the people who attract and select applicants. Organizations should train individuals to avoid discriminatory behaviors and to be aware of the potential influences of gender stereotypes and the sex segregation of work.[45]

Fourth, organizations can reduce the likelihood of sex discrimination by formalizing and standardizing selection practices. Many organizations rely primarily on employment interviews to make hiring decisions. In the typical interview, interviewers ask vague questions about applicants' opinions and attitudes, goals and aspirations, and self-evaluations.

Interview judgments based on such questions are highly subjective, and, as a result, are susceptible to bias from gender and racial stereotypes. Unlike symphony orchestras, most organizations cannot solve the problem by putting screens between applicants and decision makers. Organizations, however, can implement structured interviews that are less susceptible to bias than traditional interviews. In structured interviews, the content of the interview and the evaluation process are standardized. Specific, job-related interview questions are asked of all applicants. Further, interviewers evaluate each applicant on multiple scales with well-defined descriptions anchoring each level of each scale. These structured procedures force interviewers to obtain and to process information about the applicants' qualifications in a systematic and detailed manner, thereby reducing their reliance on stereotypes. In addition, the use of multiple interviewers with different viewpoints may reduce sex discrimination by offsetting the idiosyncratic biases of a single interviewer. A review of court cases involving employment discrimination should motivate organizations to devote time and money to structuring interviews. The review found that organizations are more likely to win discrimination suits when they use structured interviews.[46]

Fifth, organizations need to monitor selection practices to enhance their effectiveness and ensure that sex discrimination does not occur. Many organizations do poor jobs of assessing the effectiveness of their selection decisions. Recruiter performance is most often evaluated on procedural grounds, such as whether the recruiter kept appointments and filed necessary reports, rather than on actual results. Recruiter performance is seldom tied to rewards, especially for recruiters who are line managers. To assess the effectiveness of selection processes, organizations should track the performance, satisfaction, turnover rate, and subsequent success of new hires. Assessment should also include measurement of the demographic composition of the applicant pool, the demographic composition of new hires, and differences in starting salaries and initial assignments as a function of sex and race. Attention to these measures helps organizations identify potentially discriminatory selection processes. Moreover, organizations should make performance appraisals and rewards contingent on the extent to which selection processes are effective and bias-free.[47]

Finally, organizations that are serious about attracting a diverse workforce should ensure that their policies and procedures are consistent with this goal. They should examine diversity and work–family policies to ensure that these policies enhance organizational attractiveness and do not lead some individuals to self-select out of the selection process.

Policies that signal the organization's commitment to diversity will help attract women and people of color.[48]

In summary, organizations need to take actions to reduce the perception that certain jobs are appropriate for members of only one sex, both among young people and in their own midst. They need to ensure that their hiring process allows them to attract and select the most qualified applicants regardless of sex, race, or any other irrelevant personal characteristics.

The sex segregation of work is a powerful phenomenon and has a great influence on both job seekers and organizations. Their methods of finding and evaluating one another may exacerbate the differential status of men and women in organizations. However, some organizations and job seekers have made substantial changes in how they explore an employment relationship with each other. Otherwise, the National Symphony Orchestra in Washington might never have had a female French horn player.

Notes

1. Duff, C. (1997, March 7). Out of sight keeps women in mind for U.S. orchestra spots, study finds. *Wall Street Journal*, p. B9A. Wall Street Journal Classroom Edition (Only Staff-Produced Materials May Be Used) by C. Duff. Copyright 1997 by DOW JONES & COMPANY, INC. Reproduced with permission of DOW JONES & COMPANY, INC. in the format Textbook via Copyright Clearance Center.

2. Ryan, A. M., Sacco, J. M., McFarland, L. A., & Kriska, S. D. (2000). Applicant self-selection: Correlates of withdrawal from a multiple hurdle process. *Journal of Applied Psychology, 85,* 163–179.

3. Judge, T. A., & Bretz, R. D. (1992). Effects of work values on job choice decisions. *Journal of Applied Psychology, 77,* 261–271.

4. Boswell, W. R., Roehling, M. V., LePine, M. A., & Moynihan, L. M. (2003). Individual job-choice decisions and the impact of job attributes and recruitment practices: A longitudinal field study. *Human Resource Management, 42,* 23–37.

5. Konrad, A. M., Ritchie, J. E., Jr., Lieb, P., & Corrigall, E. (2000). Sex differences and similarities in job attribute preferences: A meta-analysis. *Psychological Bulletin, 126,* 593–641; Tolbert, P. S., & Moen, P. (1998). Men's and women's definitions of "good" jobs: Similarities and differences by age and across time. *Work and Occupations, 25,* 168–194.

6. Corrigall, E. A., & Konrad, A. M. (2006). The relationship of job attribute preferences to employment, hours of paid work, and family responsibilities: An analysis comparing women and men. *Sex Roles, 54,* 95–111.

7. Yamauchi, H. (1995). Factor structure of preferences for job attributes among Japanese workers. *Psychological Reports, 77,* 787–791; Browne, B. A. (1997). Gender and preferences for job attributes: A cross-cultural comparison. *Sex Roles, 37,* 61–71.

8. Lippa, R. (1998). Gender-related individual differences and the structure of vocational interests: The importance of the people-things dimension. *Journal of Personality and Social Psychology, 74,* 996–1009; Holland, J. L. (1985). *Making vocational choices: A theory of vocational personalities and work environments* (2nd ed.). Englewood Cliffs, NJ: Prentice Hall; Aros, J. R., Henly, G. A., & Curtis, N. T. (1998). Occupational sextype and sex differences in vocational preference-measured interest relationships. *Journal of Vocational Behavior, 53,* 227–242.

9. England, P. (2006). Toward gender equality: Progress and bottlenecks. In F. D. Blau, M. C. Brinton, & D. B. Grusky (Eds.), *The declining significance of gender?* (pp. 245–264). New York: Russell Sage Foundation; Jacobs, J. A. (1999). The sex segregation of occupations: Prospects for the 21st century. In G. N. Powell (Ed.), *Handbook of gender and work* (pp. 125–141). Thousand Oaks, CA: Sage.

10. Cejka, M. A., & Eagly, A. H. (1999). Gender-stereotypic images of occupations correspond to the sex-segregation of employment. *Personality and Social Psychology Bulletin, 25,* 413–423; Cleveland, J. N., & Smith, L. A. (1989). The effect of job title and task composition on job and incumbent perceptions. *Journal of Applied Social Psychology, 19,* 744–757.

11. Cejka & Eagly; Lapan, R. T., Shaughnessy, P., & Boggs, K. (1996). Efficacy expectations and vocational interests as mediators between sex and choice of math/science college majors: A longitudinal study. *Journal of Vocational Behavior, 49,* 277–291; Matsui, T. (1994). Mechanisms underlying sex differences in career self-efficacy of university students. *Journal of Vocational Behavior, 45,* 177–184; Subich, L. M., Barrett, G. V., Doverspike, D., & Alexander, R. A. (1989). The effects of sex-role-related factors on occupational choice and salary. In R. T. Michael, H. I. Hartman, & B. O'Farrell (Eds.), *Pay equity: Empirical inquiries* (pp. 91–104). Washington, DC: National Academy Press; Marini, M. M., & Fan, P. (1997). The gender gap in earnings at career entry. *American Sociological Review, 62,* 588–604.

12. Subich, Barrett, Doverspike, & Alexander; Lippa; Jome, L. M., & Tokar, D. M. (1998). Dimensions of masculinity and major choice traditionality. *Journal of Vocational Behavior, 52,* 120–134.

13. Bretz, R. D., & Judge, T. A. (1994). The role of human resource systems in job applicant decision processes. *Journal of Management, 20,* 531–551; Judge & Bretz; Rynes, S. L. (1991). Recruitment, job choice, and post-hire consequences: A call for new directions. In M. D. Dunnette & L. M. Hough (Eds.), *Handbook of industrial and organizational psychology* (2nd ed., Vol. 2, pp. 399–444). Palo Alto, CA: Consulting Psychologists Press; Rynes, S. L., Bretz, R. D., & Gerhart, B. (1991). The importance of recruitment in job choice: A different way of looking. *Personnel Psychology, 44,* 487–521.

14. Avery, D. R., & McKay, P. F. (2006). Target practice: An organizational impression management approach to attracting minority and female applicants. *Personnel Psychology, 59,* 157–187; Williams, M. L., & Bauer, T. N. (1994). The effect of a managing diversity policy on organizational attractiveness. *Group and Organization Management, 19,* 295–308; Saks, A. M., Leck, J. D., & Saunders, D. M. (1995). Effects of application blanks and employment equity on applicant reactions and job pursuit intentions. *Journal of Organizational Behavior, 16,* 415–430; Thomas, K. M., & Wise, P. G. (1999). Organizational attractiveness and individual differences: Are diverse applicants attracted by different factors? *Journal of Business and Psychology, 13,* 375–390.

15. Bretz, R. D., Boudreau, J. W., & Judge, T. A. (1994). Job search behavior of employed managers. *Personnel Psychology, 47,* 275–301; Bretz & Judge; Honeycutt, T. L., & Rosen, B. (1997). Family friendly human resource policies, salary levels, and salient identity as predictors of organizational attraction. *Journal of Vocational Behavior, 50,* 271–290; Corrigall & Konrad; Kulik, L. (2000). Jobless men and women: A comparative analysis of job search intensity, attitudes toward unemployment, and related responses. *Journal of Occupational and Organizational Psychology, 73,* 487–500; Tolbert & Moen.

16. Connerly, M. L., & Rynes, S. L. (1997). The influence of recruiter characteristics and organizational recruitment support on perceived recruiter effectiveness: Views from applicants and recruiters. *Human Relations, 50,* 1563–1587; Taylor, M. S., & Bergmann, T. J. (1987). Organizational recruitment activities and applicants' reactions at different stages of the recruitment process. *Personnel Psychology, 40,* 261–285; Turban, D. B., & Dougherty, T. W. (1992). Influences of campus recruiting on applicant attraction to firms. *Academy of Management Journal, 35,* 739–765; Mauer, S. D., Howe, V., & Lee, T. W. (1992). Organizational recruiting as marketing management: An interdisciplinary study of engineering graduates. *Personnel Psychology, 45,* 807–833.

17. Rynes, Bretz, & Gerhart.

18. Singer, M. (1990). Determinants of perceived fairness in selection practices: An organizational justice perspective. *Genetic, Social, and General Psychology Monographs, 116,* 475–494.

19. Hanson, S., & Pratt, G. (1991). Job search and the occupational segregation of women. *Annals of the Association of American Geographers, 81,* 229–253; Kulik; Leana, C. R., & Feldman, D. C. (1991). Gender differences in responses to unemployment. *Journal of Vocational Behavior, 38,* 65–77; Malen, E. A., & Stroh, L. K. (1998). The influence of gender on job loss coping behavior among unemployed managers. *Journal of Employment Counseling, 35,* 27–39; Wanberg, C. R., Watt, J. D., & Rumsey, D. J. (1996). Individuals without jobs: An empirical study of job-seeking behavior and reemployment. *Journal of Applied Psychology, 81,* 76–87.

20. Drentea, P. (1998). Consequences of women's formal and informal job search methods for employment in female-dominated jobs. *Gender & Society, 12,* 321–338; Hanson & Pratt; Huffman, M. L. & Torres, L. (2001). Job search methods:

Consequences for gender-based earnings inequality. *Journal of Vocational Behavior, 58,* 127–141; Leicht, K. T., & Marx, J. (1997). The consequences of informal job finding for men and women. *Academy of Management Journal, 40,* 967–987; Mencken, F. C. & Winfield, I. (2000). Job search and sex segregation: Does sex of social contact matter? *Sex Roles, 42,* 847–864.

21. Drentea; Hanson & Pratt; Huffman & Torres; Mencken & Winfield; Straits, B. C. (1998). Occupational sex segregation: The role of personal ties. *Journal of Vocational Behavior, 52,* 191–207; Petersen, T., Saporta, I., & Seidel, M. L. (2000). Offering a job: Meritocracy and social networks. *American Journal of Sociology, 106,* 763–816.

22. Keith, K., & McWilliams, A. (1999). The returns to mobility and job search by gender. *Industrial and Labor Relations Review, 52,* 460–477; Lyness, K. S., & Judiesch, M. K. (1999). Are women more likely to be hired or promoted into management positions? *Journal of Vocational Behavior, 54,* 158–173; Brett, J. M., & Stroh, L. K. (1997). Jumping ship: Who benefits from an external labor market career strategy? *Journal of Applied Psychology, 82,* 331–341; Dreher, G. F., & Cox, T. H., Jr. (2000). Labor market mobility and cash compensation: The moderating effects of race and gender. *Academy of Management Journal, 43,* 890–900.

23. Jackson, L. A., Gardner, P. D., & Sullivan, L. A. (1992). Explaining gender differences in self-pay expectations: Social comparison standards and perceptions of fair pay. *Journal of Applied Psychology, 77,* 631–663; Jackson, L. A., & Grabski, S. V. (1988). Perceptions of fair pay and the gender wage gap. *Journal of Applied Social Psychology, 18,* 606–625; Major, B., & Konar, E. (1984). An investigation of sex differences in pay expectations and their possible causes. *Academy of Management Journal, 27,* 777–792; Summers, T. P., Sightler, K. W., & Stahl, M. J. (1992). Gender differences in preference for over-reward and tolerance for over-reward. *Journal of Social Behavior and Personality, 7,* 177–188.

24. Barber, A. E., & Daly, C. L. (1996). Compensation and diversity: New pay for a new workforce? In E. E. Kossek and S. A. Lobel (Eds.), *Managing diversity: Human resource strategies for transforming the workplace* (pp. 194–216). Cambridge, MA: Blackwell; Konrad, Ritchie, Lieb, & Corrigall; Major & Konar; Summers, Sightler, & Stahl; Zanna, M. P., Crosby, F., & Lowenstein, G. (1987). Male reference groups and discontent among female professionals. In B. A. Gutek and L. Larwood (Eds.), *Women's career development* (pp. 28–41). Newbury Park, CA: Sage; McFarlin, D. B., Frone, M. R., Major, B., & Konar, E. (1989). Predicting career-entry pay expectations: The role of gender-based comparisons. *Journal of Business and Psychology, 3,* 331–340; Martin, B. A. (1989). Gender differences in salary expectations when current salary information is provided. *Psychology of Women Quarterly, 13,* 87–96.

25. Graves, L. M., & Powell, G. N. (2008). Sex and race discrimination in personnel decisions. In S. Cartwright & C. L. Cooper (Eds.), *The Oxford handbook of personnel psychology* (pp. 438–463). Oxford, UK: Oxford University Press.

26. Graves, L. M. (1993). Sources of individual differences in interviewer effectiveness: A model and implications for future research. *Journal of Organizational Behavior, 14,* 349–370.

27. Heilman, M. E. (1983). Sex bias in work settings: The lack of fit model. In L. L. Cummings & B. M. Staw (Eds.), *Research in organizational behavior* (Vol. 5, pp. 269–298). Greenwich, CT: JAI; Perry, E. L., Davis-Blake, A., & Kulik, C. T. (1994). Explaining gender-based selection decisions: A synthesis of contextual and cognitive approaches. *Academy of Management Review, 19,* 786–820; Glick, P. (1991). Trait-based and sex-based discrimination in occupational prestige, occupational salary, and hiring. *Sex Roles, 25,* 351–378; Cleveland & Smith; Pratto, F., Stallworth, L. M., Sidanius, J., & Siers, B. (1997). The gender gap in occupational role attainment: A social dominance approach. *Journal of Personality and Social Psychology, 72,* 37–53.

28. Perry, Davis-Blake, & Kulik; Konrad, A. M., & Pfeffer, J. (1991). Understanding the hiring of women and minorities in educational institutions. *Sociology of Education, 64,* 141–157; Heilman, M. E. (1980). The impact of situational factors on personnel decisions concerning women: Varying the sex composition of the applicant pool. *Organizational Behavior and Human Decision Processes, 26,* 386–395; Atwater, L. E., & Van Fleet, D. D. (1997). Another ceiling? Can males compete for traditionally female jobs? *Journal of Management, 23,* 603–626; Davison, H. K, & Burke, M. J. (2000). Sex discrimination in simulated employment contexts: A meta-analytic investigation. *Journal of Vocational Behavior, 56,* 225–248.

29. Neumark, D., Bank, R. J., & Van Nort, K. D. (1996). Sex discrimination in restaurant hiring: An audit study. *Quarterly Journal of Economics, 111,* 915–942.

30. Moroney, R. (2007, October 24). Noted female chefs say bias smolders inside the kitchen. *Wall Street Journal,* p. B13; *New York* (2007, October 29). A woman's place? Retrieved October 25, 2007, from http://nymag.com.

31. Ridgeway, C. L. (2006). Gender as an organizing force in social relations: Implications for the future of inequality. In F. D. Blau, M. C. Brinton, & D. B. Grusky (Eds.), *The declining significance of gender?* (pp. 265–287). New York: Russell Sage Foundation; Jackson, L. M., Esses, V. M., & Burris, C. T. (2001). Contemporary sexism and discrimination: The importance of respect for men and women. *Personality and Social Psychology Bulletin, 27,* 48–61; Biernat, M., & Kobrynowicz, D. (1997). Gender- and race-based standards of competence: Lower minimum standards but higher ability standards for devalued groups. *Journal of Personality and Social Psychology, 72,* 544–557.

32. Seidel, R. P., & Powell, G. N. (1983). On the campus: Matching graduates with jobs. *Personnel, 61*(4), 66–72.

33. Davison & Burke; Tosi, H. L., & Einbender, S. W. (1985). The effects of the type and amount of information in sex discrimination research: A meta-analysis. *Academy of Management Journal, 28,* 712–723; Heilman, M. E., Martell, R. F., & Simon, M. C. (1988). The vagaries of sex bias: Conditions regulating the

undervaluation, equivaluation, and overvaluation of female job applicants. *Organizational Behavior and Human Decision Processes, 41,* 98–110.

34. Perry, Davis-Blake, & Kulik; Davison & Burke.

35. Goldin, C., & Rouse, C. (2000). Orchestrating impartiality: The impact of blind auditions on female musicians. *American Economic Review, 90,* 715–741; Seltzer, G. (1989). *Music matters: The performer and the American Federation of Musicians.* Metuchen, NJ: Scarecrow.

36. Fasang, A. (2006). Recruitment in symphony orchestras: Testing a gender neutral recruitment process. *Work, Employment and Society, 20,* 801–809.

37. Graves, L. M. & Powell, G. N. (1995). The effect of sex similarity on recruiters' evaluations of actual applicants: A test of the similarity-attraction paradigm. *Personnel Psychology, 48,* 85–98; Graves, L. M., & Powell, G. N. (1996). Sex similarity, quality of the employment interview and recruiters' evaluation of actual applicants. *Journal of Occupational and Organizational Psychology, 69,* 243–261; Gorman, E. H. (2005). Gender stereotypes, same-gender preferences, and organizational variation in the hiring of women: Evidence from law firms. *American Sociological Review, 70,* 702–728; Goldberg, C. B. (2004). Relational demography and similarity-attraction in interview assessments and subsequent offer decisions. *Group & Organization Management, 20,* 1–28.   ·

38. Simas, K., & McCarrey, M. (1979). Impact of recruiter authoritarianism and applicant sex on evaluation and selection decisions in a recruitment interview analogue study. *Journal of Applied Psychology, 64,* 483–491; Gallois, C., Callan, V. J., & Palmer, J. M. (1992). The influence of applicant communication style and interviewer characteristics on hiring decisions. *Journal of Applied Social Psychology, 22,* 1041–1060.

39. Langlois, J. H., Kalakanis, L., Rubenstein, A. J., Larson, A., Hallam, M., & Smoot, M. (2000). Maxims or myths of beauty? A meta-analytic and theoretical review. *Psychological Bulletin, 126,* 390–423; Eagly, A. H., Ashmore, R. D., Makhijani, M. G., & Longo, L. C. (1991). What is beautiful is good, but . . . : A meta-analytic review of research on the physical attractiveness stereotype. *Psychological Bulletin, 110,* 109–128; Jackson, L. A., Hunter, J. E., & Hodge, C. N. (1995). Physical attractiveness and intellectual competence: A meta-analytic review. *Social Psychology Quarterly, 58,* 108–122; Luxen, M. F., & Van de Vijver, F. J. R. (2006). Facial attractiveness, sexual selection, and personnel selection: When evolved preferences matter. *Journal of Organizational Behavior, 27,* 241–255; Jawahar, I. M., & Mattsson, J. (2005). Sexism and beautyism effects in selection as a function of self-monitoring level of decision maker. *Journal of Applied Psychology, 90,* 563–573.

40. Roehling, M. V., Roehling, P. V., & Odland, L. M. (2008). Investigating the validity of stereotypes about overweight employees: The relationship between body weight and normal personality traits. *Group & Organization Management, 33,* 392–424; Roehling, M.V. (1999). Weight-based discrimination in employment: Psychological and legal aspects. *Personnel Psychology, 52,* 969–1016;

Pingitore, R., Dugoni, B. L., Tindale, R. S., & Spring, B. (1994). Bias against over-weight job applicants in a simulated employment interview. *Journal of Applied Psychology, 79,* 909–917.

41. Hebl, M. R., King, E. B., Glick, P., Singletary, S. L., & Kazama, S. (2007). Hostile and benevolent reactions toward pregnant women: Complementary interpersonal punishments and rewards that maintain traditional roles. *Journal of Applied Psychology, 92,* 1499–1511; Cunningham, J., & Macan, T. (2007). Effects of applicant pregnancy on hiring decisions and interview ratings. *Sex Roles, 57,* 497–508; Masser, B., Grass, K., & Nesie, M. (2007). "We like you, but we don't want you"—The impact of pregnancy in the workplace. *Sex Roles, 57,* 703–712; Heilman, M. E., & Okimoto, T. G. (2008). Motherhood: A potential source of bias in employment decisions. *Journal of Applied Psychology, 93,* 189–198; Ridgeway, C. L., & Correll, S. J. (2004). Motherhood as a status characteristic. *Journal of Social Issues, 60,* 683–700.

42. Konrad, Ritchie, Lieb, & Corrigall.

43. Stevens, C. K., & Kristof, A. L. (1995). Making the right impression: A field study of applicant impression management during job interviews. *Journal of Applied Psychology, 80,* 587–606.

44. Heilman (1983); Perry, Davis-Blake, & Kulik.

45. Rynes, S. L., & Boudreau, J. W. (1986). College recruiting in large organizations: Practice, evaluation, and research implications, *Personnel Psychology, 39,* 729–757.

46. Campion, M. A., Palmer, D. K., & Campion, J. E. (1997). A review of structure in the selection interview. *Personnel Psychology, 50,* 655–702; Williamson, L. G., Campion, J. E., Malos, S. B., Roehling, M. B., & Campion, M. A. (1997). Employment interview on trial: Linking interview structure with litigation outcomes. *Journal of Applied Psychology, 82,* 900–912.

47. Rynes & Boudreau; Graves, L. M. (1989). College recruitment: Removing personal biases from selection decisions. *Personnel, 66*(3), 48–52; Perry, Davis-Blake, & Kulik; Cox, T. H, Jr., & Blake, S. (1991). Managing cultural diversity: Implications for organizational competitiveness. *Academy of Management Executive, 5*(3), 45–56.

48. Avery & McKay; Williams & Bauer; Martins, L. L., & Parsons, C. K. (2007). Effects of gender diversity management on perceptions of organizational attractiveness: The role of individual differences in attitudes and beliefs. *Journal of Applied Psychology, 92,* 865–875.

CHAPTER 5

Working in Diverse Teams

Laura M. Graves & Gary N. Powell

Lehman Brothers and Sisters

At the recent World Economic Forum in Davos, Switzerland, some of the most interesting discussions revolved around whether we would be in the same mess today if Lehman Brothers [a global financial-services firm that had recently declared bankruptcy] had been Lehman Sisters. The consensus (and this is among the dead White men who parade annually at Davos) is that the optimal bank would have been Lehman Brothers and Sisters.[1]

oday's organizations are increasingly using work teams to achieve their strategic objectives. Teams produce goods and provide services, design new products, solve organizational problems, and even lead entire organizations. Teams are common across industries as diverse as health care, automobile manufacturing, financial services (which once included Lehman Brothers), and electronics. Although the extent to which teams are used is difficult to assess, estimates suggest that about half of the U.S. workforce will soon be working in teams. Moreover, the proliferation of teams is not just a U.S. phenomenon. Multinational corporations such as Heineken, GlaxoSmithKline, and BP use teams to achieve global efficiencies, respond to regional markets, and transfer knowledge throughout the organization.[2]

As a result of women's increased participation in the global labor force, teams are more likely to include both women and men than ever before. Diversity in teams on the basis of member sex may affect the experiences of individual team members and overall team effectiveness in different ways. **Sex effects** arise when men's and women's behavior in teams or experiences as team members differ. **Sex similarity effects** occur when team members' behavior or experiences differ as a function of the extent to which they are similar to their teammates on the basis of sex. **Sex diversity effects** arise when team cohesion and performance vary as a function of the extent to which the team is heterogeneous with respect to sex.[3]

In this chapter, we review the effects of sex, sex similarity, and sex diversity in mixed-sex teams. We then consider how key aspects of the situations in which mixed-sex teams function may determine whether these effects appear. Finally, we consider what actions team members and organizations may take to ensure that mixed-sex teams are effective.

Sex Effects

Although behavior in all-male teams may differ from that in all-female teams, we focus in this section on behavior in mixed-sex teams. When women and men serve on the same team, sex serves as a basis for distinguishing between team members and influences members' interactions. Women's and men's behaviors may differ. Moreover, team members are likely to evaluate the behaviors of males and females differently.

Two dimensions of communication style are important in teams, **self-assertion and dominance** and **deference and warmth.** In general, men display more self-assertion and dominance and women display more deference and warmth. Men talk more, are more powerful and authoritarian in tone, and display more visual dominance by making more eye contact while talking and less eye contact while listening. In contrast, women talk less, smile and lean toward others more, and display less visual dominance. These sex differences are most likely to occur when the team's task is male-intensive (i.e., associated with males) or sex-neutral.[4]

Two types of behavior are important in teams, **task behaviors** and **social behaviors.** Task behaviors contribute directly to the group's task, whereas social behaviors help to maintain morale and interpersonal relations among team members. In groups with assigned tasks, both women and men devote most of their interactions to task-related communications. About two thirds of women's and three quarters of men's communications are task-related; men devote a somewhat higher percentage of their communications to task behavior, and women display a higher percentage of positive social behaviors. These differences may occur because women engage in more in socially oriented behavior than men in general. Women's emphasis on social behaviors in teams is consistent with their desire for positive interpersonal relationships in their jobs (see Chapter 4). Women, more than men, view their teams as like families or communities in which members nurture and support one another.[5]

Consistent with sex differences in societal status and roles, team members tend to evaluate men's **task contributions** more positively than women's contributions. Women may even devalue their own performances. Moreover, team members use a higher standard to judge women. Women thus must provide more evidence of their abilities to be seen as competent.[6]

However, even when women are recognized as better performers, they may receive less **social support** from other team members than men. According to a study of ongoing teams of students in management courses, female members were recognized by their peers as making greater contributions to the completion of group assignments than male members. However, they also participated in fewer social interactions with other team members than their male counterparts. Even when women do more or better work in their teams than men, they still may be excluded from social networks.[7]

Men tend to have more **influence** in mixed-sex teams than women. This is not surprising given men's displays of dominance, greater relative proportion of task behavior, and perceived greater competence. In fact, women's influence attempts are ignored. One study of simulated jury decision making found that unique information (i.e., that possessed by a single group member) influenced the group 72% of the time when it was introduced by a man but only 13% of the time when introduced by a woman! Further, women in mixed-sex teams tend to be more easily influenced than men, perhaps because their lower status and less favorable self-evaluations lessen their confidence in their own views.[8]

Men are also more likely than women to emerge as **informal leaders** in mixed-sex groups that have no assigned leaders. Researchers have measured task leadership, social leadership, and general leadership, in which the exact nature of the leadership behavior is unspecified. Consistent with sex differences in status and social roles, men are more likely to emerge as general leaders and task leaders than are women, and less likely to emerge as social leaders. However, the tendency for men to emerge as general leaders is reduced for tasks that are female-intensive or for tasks that demand longer or more social interaction.[9]

Women cannot increase evaluations of their competence, influence, and leadership in mixed-sex teams simply by behaving like men. Confident, assertive women tend to be less influential than confident, assertive men. In fact, confident, assertive women may be even less influential than nonassertive women, especially among male team members. Men are more likely to be influenced by women who use tentative language (e.g., hedges, disclaimers, tag questions) or who express support for the feminine gender role. In contrast, women are more likely to be influenced by women who use assertive language or reject the feminine gender role. Confident, assertive women are also often viewed by their teammates as less likeable than confident, assertive men. Nonetheless, assertive women can attain influence and acceptance if they combine assertive behaviors with expressions of interpersonal warmth and a desire to cooperate with the group. Women must be "friendly and nice" in their influence attempts and demonstrate that they care for the good of the group. Such behavior is not required of men.[10]

In summary, sex effects in mixed-sex teams are consistent with differences in the status and social roles assigned to women and men. Women tend to be less assertive, engage less in task behavior and more in social behavior, are evaluated more negatively, and exercise less influence and leadership than men in mixed-sex groups. Women who attempt to increase their influence by behaving like men encounter roadblocks.

However, much of the evidence for sex effects comes from laboratory studies in which team members interact briefly and have little information about each other—the very conditions that are most likely to invoke gender-based expectations. There is some evidence that these effects disappear when team members have information about each other's competence or interact extensively over time. When team members know each other better and have worked together for a longer period, status judgments and gender roles play less of a role in dictating behavior.[11]

Sex Similarity Effects

An individual's experience in a team is not simply a function of his or her sex, but is also determined by the sex composition of the team. This section explores how team composition affects women's and men's experiences as team members. Do individuals in teams have more negative experiences when members of their sex are in the minority? Are women who are in the minority (e.g., the only female in a team of engineers) more likely to have negative experiences than men who are in the minority (e.g., the only male in a team of nurses)?[12]

In one of the first major studies of male-female work relationships, Rosabeth Kanter examined the effects of the team's sex composition on individual team members. Based on her observations in a large industrial corporation, she identified four types of work groups. **Uniform groups** of all males or all females represent one extreme. By definition, there are no male–female issues in uniform groups. **Balanced groups** of approximately equal numbers of women and men represent the other extreme. Kanter suggested that attributes other than sex influence how individuals interact in groups that are balanced on the basis of sex.[13]

Between these two extremes are skewed and tilted groups. **Skewed groups** have a ratio of one sex to another ranging from about 85:15 to almost 100:0. Members of the sex in abundance in skewed groups are called "dominants" because they control the group and its culture. Members of the other sex are called "tokens" because they are viewed as representatives of their sex rather than as individuals. **Tilted groups** have less abundance of one sex with the ratio ranging from about 65:35 to about 85:15. In tilted groups, dominants become a majority and tokens become a minority. Minority members may become allies and have more effect on group culture in tilted than in skewed groups. They are distinguishable from each other, as well as from the majority type.

Kanter's primary interest was in the experiences of **tokens in skewed groups.** Because tokens are present only in small numbers, the rest of the group sees them as representing their sex, whether or not they want to represent their sex. A token rarely becomes "just another member of the group." Tokens receive special treatment that is detrimental to their performance in, and attachment to, the group in several ways. First, tokens face performance pressures. Because they are highly visible, they get attention that dominants do not. This does not necessarily lead to recognition of their competence; tokens may have to work harder to get their accomplishments recognized. Second, differences between tokens and dominants tend to be exaggerated. Dominants emphasize what they have in common and exclude tokens from social activities. Third, the characteristics of tokens are often distorted or misperceived because of the dominants' tendency to stereotype them. Tokens are expected to behave in a manner consistent with the stereotype of their sex or risk rejection by the team.

Although Kanter based her conclusions on analysis of an environment in which men vastly outnumbered women in positions of authority, she assumed that her notions would apply equally to women in male-intensive groups and to men in female-intensive groups. Subsequent research has generally failed to support her assumption. Token women experience increased visibility, social isolation, and stereotyping, especially in male-intensive settings such as the military, law enforcement, and medicine. However, token men in female-intensive settings such as nursing, teaching, and social work do not experience the same negative consequences of numerical imbalance as token women. Instead, the visibility that token men receive may work to their advantage. For example, a study of police patrol teams and hospital nursing units found that token female police officers were annoyed at or resigned to their heightened visibility, whereas token male nurses enjoyed the extra attention. Most token male nurses felt that patients attributed a higher status to them than to female nurses, even when they identified themselves as nurses and not physicians. Most also thought that physicians took them more seriously and gave more responsibility to them than to female nurses.[14]

Despite the relatively positive experiences of male tokens in female-dominated groups, men tend to be displeased when the sex composition of a male-dominated group changes in the direction of becoming more balanced. For example, a study of symphony orchestras found that men were highly sensitive to the effects of the sex composition of the orchestra. Men's attitudes toward the orchestra (e.g., integrity of orchestra as an ensemble, player involvement) declined sharply as the proportion of women increased and the orchestra became more balanced in its sex composition. In contrast, women's views changed very little as the sex composition of the orchestra changed.[15]

The effects of sex similarity cannot be predicted solely by looking at the proportions of women and men on a team. To fully understand the effects of team composition on individuals, we need to consider the situation in which the team operates. For example, sex similarity effects are less likely to occur when organizations stress the value of teamwork. In contrast, when organizations stress the importance of acting independently in how they assign tasks, sex similarity effects are more likely to occur.[16]

Sex Diversity Effects

Early research on sex diversity effects focused extensively on the question of whether all-male or all-female teams perform better. All-male teams tend to be better at activities that require a high amount of task behavior, such as brainstorming and generating solutions to a problem (although the mostly all-male teams at the now-defunct Lehman Brothers did not perform well at the task of making financial bets). In contrast, all-female teams are better at activities that call for a high amount of social behavior, such as reaching a consensus on the best solution.[17]

However, these findings are of limited value today. Creating all-female or all-male teams is not feasible given the diversity of today's workforce, and managers who attempt to do so will be vulnerable to charges of sex discrimination. Moreover, assigning all-female and all-male teams to different types of activities is not likely to be effective. The work requirements of teams (e.g., developing global business strategy or a new product) cannot be easily divided into those demanding task-related activity and those demanding interpersonal savvy. In addition, teams are likely to interact over extended periods of time, increasing the importance of interpersonal relationships among members. Poor relationships decrease members' attraction to the team and increase the likelihood that they will choose to leave the team.

Understanding the effects of sex diversity on the effectiveness of mixed-sex teams is of practical importance in today's increasingly diverse organizations. There are two opposing views of the general effect of diversity on team effectiveness.[18] According to the **pessimistic view of sex diversity effects,** the effects of perceived similarity and identification with similar others cause team members to reject those who are different from themselves. This leads to the creation of factions (e.g., men vs. women, Asians vs. Whites vs. Blacks, older members vs. younger members), conflict, and communication problems. Ultimately, poor social relations between subgroups of team members impair the performance of the group as a whole, and members' satisfaction with and commitment to the group are reduced.

According to the **optimistic view of sex diversity effects,** members of diverse teams have different experiences, values, attitudes, and cognitive approaches. They bring varied knowledge and perspectives to the team's task, which enhance its creativity and problem-solving ability. These positive effects of diversity are especially likely to occur on complex tasks such as new-product design and innovation, which require multiple perspectives and varied knowledge. Greater diversity increases the amount of interaction between the two sexes over time and decreases prejudice and discrimination based on sex. This process improves relations among team members and increases member attachment to the team.

Which of these two views better represents the effects of sex diversity in mixed-sex teams? The research evidence regarding the direction and magnitude of sex diversity effects is mixed. Some studies have found that sex diversity has a positive effect on team performance; other studies have found a negative effect; and still other studies have found no effect.[19] These results provide little guidance. Instead, a better answer, which takes into account evidence supporting each view, is that sex diversity in teams has both potential advantages, in the form of increased creativity and enhanced social relations over time that contribute to team performance, and potential disadvantages, in the form of troubled relationships between subgroups and disaffection of team members that detract from team performance.

Thus, the appropriate goal for mixed-sex teams is to maximize the advantages of sex diversity while minimizing the disadvantages. Sex diversity in teams represents a "double-edged sword," offering both an opportunity and a challenge for organizations. The trick is in knowing exactly how to handle the sword.[20]

The Importance of Situational Factors

As we have seen, mixed-sex teams have potential advantages but are susceptible to serious problems. Women's task contributions may be ignored or devalued, and women and men in the numerical minority may suffer. Also, the effectiveness of the team may decline as its diversity increases if subgroups clash and team members drop out. However, these negative consequences are not inevitable. If the conditions under which mixed-sex teams operate de-emphasize the importance of sex as a component of members' identities or promote integration of the sexes, negative outcomes will be averted. Several situational factors appear to be important, including characteristics of the team, the nature of the task, the technologies used in team communications, the demographic composition of the organization and its senior officials, the organizational culture, and the societal culture.

The team's **overall demographic composition** affects interactions among members. The number of subgroups (e.g., young Black males, young White males, young Asian females, middle-aged White females, middle-aged White males, and so on) in a mixed-sex team may vary. When there are many subgroups, effects of sex, sex similarity, and sex diversity on team members' experiences and team effectiveness are minimized. For example, a team comprised of a 40-year-old White male engineer, a 65-year-old Black female engineer, a 45-year-old Asian male sales representative, and a 20-year-old White female sales representative theoretically could form subgroups based on age, race, occupation, or sex. Because forming subgroups based on any one category (e.g., sex) would lead to differences within the subgroup on other categories (e.g., race, occupation, age), subgroup formation is not likely. However, in a team composed of 2 middle-aged White male engineers and 2 young Black female sales representatives, sex is highly related to age, race, and occupation. There are only two possible subgroups in this team, increasing the likelihood of negative effects.[21]

The team's **longevity** is another critical factor. As team members interact over extended periods, they gain additional information about one another and stereotyping is reduced. Relationships between members are formed based on similarity of underlying attitudes, values, and beliefs rather than sex similarity. The greater the team's longevity, the less important its sex composition. However, a great deal of time is needed to eliminate the effects of sex composition. According to a study of teams in hospitals and grocery stores, the negative effects of sex diversity disappear only when the average longevity of team members is 3 or more years.[22]

Tasks that are sex-neutral and require cooperation among team members reduce the negative consequences of diversity in mixed-sex teams. Tasks that are not associated exclusively with women or men and do not create political divisions based on sex minimize attention to sex differences. In contrast, tasks that are typically performed by members of one sex or the other (e.g., nursing, policing) or are likely to create coalitions based on sex (e.g., developing affirmative action plans) increase the likelihood of sex-based categorization. In addition, tasks that require cooperation among team members are beneficial. When team members must work jointly to achieve collective goals and rewards, they are motivated to form accurate, rather than stereotypical, impressions of one another. Moreover, when cooperation leads the team to form a "team identity" (i.e., view themselves as a team), members categorize themselves as a single group rather than as males and females.[23]

The use of **electronic communication technologies** such as e-mail, group decision-making software, and telephone conferences rather than face-to-face meetings reduces the extent to which sex-based categorization occurs. Sex differences in evaluations and influence tend to disappear when group members interact electronically. The benefits of electronic exchanges occur even when individuals are aware of the sex of each group member. The key feature of these types of electronic technologies is they provide visual anonymity, thereby preventing any effects of perceived attractiveness on team members' reactions to each other. Electronic exchanges allow group members to focus more on the content of the arguments than the individuals who make them. Like the screens used in blind auditions for orchestra positions (see Chapter 4), they reduce the attention paid to the sex of the participant. They also benefit women more than men. Women tend to experience stronger feelings of inclusion and support in mixed-sex electronic teams than do men. In addition, women in all-female electronic teams are more satisfied than are men in all-male electronic teams. Women's electronic teams engage in higher levels of self-disclosure and agreement, and men's electronic teams display more conflict and less willingness to change their minds. Perhaps women's relatively greater focus on interpersonal relations enhances their experiences in virtual teams.[24]

The **demographic composition of the larger organization** also affects relationships between men and women in teams. Sex differences are less important in organizations where there is a great deal of sex diversity than in organizations where there is little. In organizations that are balanced on the basis of sex, team members should be accustomed to differences in sex and should not use sex as the basis for categorization. Negative outcomes also may be less likely to occur in female-intensive than male-intensive organizations. In female-intensive organizations, increasing sex diversity means that males are added to female teams. In male-intensive organizations, the reverse is true. Because females are more likely to welcome the addition of males to their teams than males are to welcome the addition of females to their teams, increasing diversity may be less problematic in female-intensive organizations.[25]

Further, the **sex composition of the organization's top management team** affects team members' interactions by influencing the relative status of women and men. When women work in organizations with few women in key roles, they are more likely to invoke gender stereotypes, devalue their own abilities, demonstrate less interest in participating in organizational activities, and compete with their female peers. In contrast, when women and men share power at the top of the organization, status differences between women and men in the team are eliminated or reduced. Although being in the minority still might have a negative effect on women or men, such effects are lessened by the relative equality of the two sexes.[26]

The organization's culture, especially its values regarding cooperation and diversity, has an important influence on what happens in mixed-sex teams. Organizations that foster a **cooperative culture** by encouraging individuals to focus on their common goals rather than on their own self-interests reduce the negative effects of sex diversity. One study assigned diverse teams of MBA students to organizations that had either individualistic (e.g., individual performance valued, individual rewards) or cooperative (e.g., teamwork valued, team-oriented rewards) values. The students who were the most different from their teammates with respect to sex, race, and nationality combined had fewer interactions with others, regardless of the culture of the organization. They did, however, experience more positive conflict (i.e., conflict over ideas) and more creativity in the cooperative organization than the individualistic organization. Thus, an organizational culture that emphasizes cooperation may lessen some of the negative effects of diversity and increase the likelihood that diversity will enhance performance.[27]

Organizations with diversity cultures that foster inclusion also reduce the likelihood of negative consequences in mixed-sex teams. In an **inclusive diversity culture,** organizational members value efforts to increase the representation of women, people of color, and individuals with disabilities, and view members of these groups as qualified. Equality is stressed, and differences in status based on sex and other visible demographic characteristics are reduced. Further, in an inclusive diversity culture, employees acknowledge differences among women and among men, as well as between women and men. Recognition that individual differences are present within each sex allows team members to view each other as distinct persons, not just as representatives of the two sexes. Moreover, organizations that regard the insights, skills, and experiences of individuals from different backgrounds as valuable business resources create a particularly productive environment for diverse teams. In such settings, the input of each individual is valued and respected because of, rather than in spite of, his or her background. We discuss how organizations can create an inclusive diversity culture in Chapter 9.[28]

Finally, the societal culture may affect a mixed-sex team. Although there have been few comparisons of mixed-sex teams across cultures, data collected from members of symphony orchestras in Germany are instructive. As discussed in Chapter 4, women constitute a small proportion of symphony musicians in Germany overall. However, in the former East Germany, musicians believe that male and female orchestra members support one another and work together to achieve common goals. In contrast, in the former West Germany, there is substantial tension over the integration of women into orchestras, and the musicians believe that male and female musicians are treated differently. What might account for this difference? Prior to the unification of Germany, East German women had high rates of labor force participation, and West German women had very low rates. Differences in societal norms concerning women's participation in the labor force may have led to the disparity in the acceptance of female musicians. As a result, a female symphony musician in the minority in the former West Germany may have more negative experiences than her counterpart in the former East Germany.[29]

In conclusion, mixed-sex teams experience fewer disadvantages and greater advantages when the characteristics of the team, task, communication technologies, organization, and society de-emphasize sex differences and promote equality between the sexes. The negative effects of sex diversity are minimized when extremely diverse teams with significant longevity work together. Tasks that require the cooperation of team members or allow electronic interactions reduce the extent to which sex is an important social category in teams. Finally, mixed-sex teams are likely to encounter fewer problems in organizations, and even in societies, with cooperative, egalitarian values and high levels of sex integration in the workplace.

Making Mixed-Sex Teams Work

Mixed-sex teams have both potential advantages and potential disadvantages and are affected by the characteristics of the situation in which they operate. How can organizations ensure that mixed-sex teams are effective, other than by requiring that teams remain intact over a long period (which is not always controllable) or banning face-to-face meetings (which is impractical unless the team is geographically dispersed)? Organizations must create a working environment in which all individuals thrive, regardless of sex, race, and other demographic characteristics. However, team leaders and members also need to take action to ensure that mixed-sex teams are effective, whatever the working environment outside of the team. Tables 5.1 and 5.2 summarize recommended actions for organizations, team leaders, and team members.

Proactive Organizations and Team Leaders

Teamwork is never easy. Some estimates suggest that 7 out of 10 teams fail to achieve the desired results. To ensure team effectiveness, organizations must pay attention to the design and development of teams. Throwing a team together and then ignoring it will sabotage any team, even a homogeneous team. Given the difficulties associated with mixed-sex teams, the need to be proactive in designing and developing such teams is intensified. Team leaders must carefully design mixed-sex teams, train team members, help them get to know one another, and provide ongoing support.[30]

With respect to the design of the team, team leaders should address three questions: (1) Who will be on the team? (2) How will the task be structured? (3) How will performance be measured and rewarded? In choosing team members, they should strive for teams that are diverse on a number of demographic characteristics. It is best if demographic characteristics result in numerous subgroups (e.g., women and men, Latinos and Asians, accountants and engineers) with overlapping memberships. Individuals will belong to and identify with many different subgroups, thereby reducing the likelihood of divisions along sex or any other single dimension. Moreover, differences in the organizational status of team members should be minimized, especially if organizational rank is related to sex or some other demographic characteristic. Women's task contributions are likely to be impaired if they have lower organizational status than men. However, team leaders must achieve a delicate balance between choosing team members for their demographic characteristics and choosing them for their skills. Selecting team members based solely on sex or another visible characteristic may cause more harm than good. When a woman is chosen because of her sex, both the woman and her teammates will question her skills and expertise. Thus, skills and expertise must not be subordinate to demographic characteristics in team formation.[31]

What expertise should leaders look for in choosing team members? They must consider whether potential team members have the necessary technical knowledge, skills, and abilities to accomplish the task. They should also select individuals with values and skills that are conducive to teamwork. Individuals who value collaboration over competition and

Table 5.1 Recommended Actions for Organizations and Team Leaders

1. Strive to have diverse work teams, but do not select team members or managers solely on the basis of sex or other demographic characteristics.

2. Select team members with values and skills conducive to teamwork.

3. Structure work assignments to require cooperation among team members.

4. Make a wide array of electronic communication technologies available to the team.

5. Do not assign tasks to team members on the basis of sex.

6. Encourage rotation of roles and tasks to develop team members to play future roles.

7. Reward team performance in addition to individual performance.

8. Train team members on how to manage team processes and how to deal with the difficulties created by stereotyping and dissimilarity.

9. Publicize qualifications of all individuals assigned to teams as leaders or members.

10. Coach leaders on how to encourage expression of diverse points of view and discourage dysfunctional team processes.

Table 5.2 Recommended Actions for Team Members

1. Understand how your sense of self-identity influences your interactions with other team members.

2. Guard against your own stereotypes and prejudices as you evaluate others' behavior.

3. Build good relationships with other members of your team.

4. If you are a member of the majority group, do not subject minority team members to performance pressures or exaggerate differences between you and them simply because they are in the minority.

5. If you are a member of the minority group, take actions to enhance your own power and guard against stereotypes that limit your behavior.

gain pleasure from others' achievements will be better team players than those who only value competition and personal achievement. Interpersonal skills, such as the ability to communicate and resolve differences, are also critical.[32]

Once the leader has decided who will be on the team, he or she must consider the task structure, task assignments, and the performance measurement and reward system. When possible, tasks should be structured to require high levels of cooperation among team members. When group members are dependent on each other and have to make mutual adjustments, they gain valuable experience working together and are less likely to engage in stereotyping. Giving the team access to a full array of electronic communication technologies may facilitate the participation of all members. Leaders should also ensure that task assignments are not based on the sex of team members. If women and men are assigned tasks consistent with gender stereotypes and roles, sex differences in members' experiences will be accentuated. Rotation of tasks among team members will ensure that tasks are not linked exclusively to one sex and will develop team members for future roles. Finally, performance measurements and rewards should be determined for the entire team. When only individual accomplishment is rewarded, team members have little incentive to cooperate with one another.[33]

Team members should receive training on how to deal with behavioral issues that arise in teams. Because teamwork does not come naturally to many individuals, especially those from individualistic cultures, team members must learn to cooperate with one another. Training in the areas of communication, conflict management, and decision making is valuable. Teams might learn structured decision rules that bring order to team discussions and give all team members a chance to participate. In addition, team members should be trained to observe and evaluate their own processes. This is particularly important in diverse groups because the lack of interpersonal attraction makes interaction more difficult. Being skilled in process observation will help teams correct problems before there are major breakdowns in team functioning.[34]

In addition, diversity training should make team members aware of gender stereotypes and the potential negative effects of these stereotypes and sexist behavior on members' interactions. All team members should receive diversity training, not just women or just men. Women can be coached to increase their task contributions and men to elicit and consider women's contributions. Moreover, all team members should be made aware of the possible negative effects of sex dissimilarity on interpersonal liking and performance. Team members can be taught techniques to reduce the lack of interpersonal attraction created by sex dissimilarity. For example, self-disclosure tends to create openness, trust, and ease of communication. Diversity training will be discussed further in Chapter 9.[35]

Once the team has been designed and members have been trained, the leader should help team members get acquainted so that interactions are based on what individuals bring to the team, not their sex. When the team is formed, the qualifications and achievements of all group members should be publicized. Identifying the expertise of team members in a formal written communication will prevent team members from making erroneous assumptions about each others' qualifications based on sex. Leaders also may provide informal opportunities for team members to interact, such as lunches and other social events.

As the team tackles its task, the leader must provide ongoing support to the team to ensure that it is functioning effectively. The leader should regularly assess the team's performance, including its short-term and long-term accomplishments. The leader should encourage expression of diverse perspectives on problems. The leader should also monitor how well the team is managing its interpersonal processes, including the extent to which it is excluding members on the basis of personal characteristics, failing to take advantage of differences in perspectives, and experiencing miscommunications. Finally, the leader should be ready to identify problems in mixed-sex teams when they occur and then to work with team members to develop and implement solutions to these problems.[36]

Responsible Team Members

Building effective mixed-sex teams is not only an organizational responsibility. Each team member, male and female, must take responsibility for making the team work. Other than by seeking appropriate training, what can team members do? As a first step, each individual must develop an understanding of his or her own social identity. Each team member might ask himself or herself the following questions: (1) What social categories do I use to describe myself and others? (2) How important is each of these categories to my identity? (3) How do I behave toward individuals who are of the opposite sex (or a different race, profession, etc.)? (4) How do I feel about myself when I am in the presence of members of the opposite sex (or a different race, profession, etc.)? (5) How are others' behaviors toward me influenced by my sex (race, profession, etc.)? Answering such questions will give individuals some idea of which social categories are most important to them and how these social categories affect their interactions with other team members.[37]

Second, team members must hone their ability to evaluate the behaviors of their teammates. Most people are not good at understanding the causes of others' behaviors and are even worse when they evaluate those who are different from them. To address this problem, team members' evaluations of other members' behaviors should be based on careful, repeated observations. Quick judgments, which are likely to be based on gender stereotypes, are to be avoided. Team members also may check the accuracy of their evaluations by comparing them with those of others.[38]

Third, team members should establish and maintain good working relationships with other team members. People sometimes feel awkward and uncomfortable working with people whom they view as unlike themselves. To overcome this discomfort, team members should identify common interests that provide a basis for relating. Such interests can be identified through informal conversation about nonwork topics. Observing a teammate's office area (e.g., pictures, plaques, coffee mug) can offer useful clues about his or her interests (e.g., alma mater, travel destinations, family, hobbies) and provide a good starting point for conversation. Identifying common interests eases interactions, contributes to the development of relationships, and, ultimately, reduces stereotyping. Team members also may benefit by sharing appropriate personal information with other team members. As noted earlier, self-disclosure by one team member is likely to lead to self-disclosure by other team members and create an environment of openness and trust.

Fourth, members of skewed or tilted teams need to ensure that both male and female members are fully integrated into the team. Members of the numerical majority should be especially careful to avoid the exclusion of those in the minority. A team member can be assigned to monitor member participation and ensure that all team members have an equal opportunity to contribute. Moreover, members of the majority should include those in the minority in social activities and make them feel welcome.

Those who are in the minority need to take responsibility for their own roles in the team. There are several strategies that tokens or others in the numerical minority can adopt to build their power and influence in a team. Tokens can make themselves indispensable to the team by developing special areas of expertise. Other team members then will pay attention to them because of their expertise, not their sex. Tokens should also learn to diagnose power dynamics in teams so that they can maximize their own influence. In a particular situation, they might determine whether they should attempt to influence the assumptions on which decisions are based, the alternatives to be considered, or the information available about alternatives. Tokens also need to ensure that their own gender stereotypes do not dictate the nature of their participation in the team. Individuals sometimes limit their own behaviors to reflect gender stereotypes, even if these stereotypes do not reflect their true selves. Tokens may be especially likely to engage in stereotypical behavior because their numerical status makes gender stereotypes so prominent. Thus, tokens may find it valuable to consider whether their behaviors reflect their true selves or gender stereotypes.[39]

In conclusion, mixed-sex teams face challenges in reaching their full potential. Women's task contributions are often ignored or devalued by other team members. Individuals who are members of teams composed primarily of the opposite sex have more negative experiences than do individuals who are members of teams comprised primarily of the same sex. Although the effects of being in the minority are not identical for women and men, both men and women are vulnerable to negative experiences when their sex is underrepresented. Moreover, as the level of sex diversity in a team increases, the effectiveness of the team may decline. These effects are not inevitable, but depend on a host of factors, such as the team's characteristics and task, the organization's demographic composition and values, and even the values of the society in which the organization operates. Mixed-sex teams are likely to experience problems in poorly integrated organizations that do not value collaboration and diversity.

Although organizations, team leaders, and team members cannot address all of these problems, there is much that they can do to improve the functioning of a mixed-sex team. Team leaders must carefully design the team, provide proper training, help team members to get acquainted, and provide continual support to the team. Team members need to understand their own social identities, improve the accuracy of their perceptions, develop relationships with one another, and avoid the dynamics created by a disproportionate representation of one sex.

Above all, team leaders and their members must be patient. Mixed-sex teams require more time to come together than same-sex teams, and there may be frustrating moments for everyone. However, with appropriate nurturing, mixed-sex teams can be more effective than either all-male or all-female teams.[40]

As for Lehman Brothers, how would the financial services organization have fared if it had looked more like Lehman Brothers and Sisters, with an abundance of mixed-sex teams rather than all-male teams? We will never know, but it might have survived to the present day so we could have found out.[41]

Notes

1. Kristof, Nicholas D. (2009, February 8). Mistresses of the universe. *New York Times.* Retrieved February 9, 2009, from http://www.nytimes.com.

2. Lawler, E. E., III, Mohrman, S. A., & Ledford, G. E., Jr. (1995). *Creating high performance organizations: Practices and results of employee involvement and total quality management in Fortune 1000 companies.* San Francisco: Jossey-Bass; Cohen, S. G., & Bailey, D. E. (1997). What makes teams work: Group effectiveness research from the shop floor to the executive suite. *Journal of Management, 23,* 239–290; Snow, C. C., Snell, S. A., Davison, S. C., & Hambrick, D. C. (1996). Use transnational teams to globalize your company. *Organizational Dynamics, 24*(4), 50–67.

3. Graves, L. M., & Powell, G. N. (2007). Sex, sex similarity and sex diversity effects in teams: The importance of situational factors. In D. Bilimoria & S. K. Piderit (Eds.), *Handbook of women in business and management* (pp. 217–231). Cheltenham, UK: Edward Elgar.

4. Carli, L. L., & Eagly, A. H. (1999). Gender effects on social influence and emergent leadership. In G. N. Powell (Ed.), *Handbook of gender and work* (pp. 203–222). Thousand Oaks, CA: Sage; Carli, L. L., & Bukatko, D. (2000). Gender, communication, and social influence: A developmental perspective. In T. Eckes & H. M. Trautner (Eds.), *The developmental social psychology of gender* (pp. 295–331). Mahwah, NJ: Erlbaum; Dovidio, J. F., Ellyson, S. L., Keating, C. F., Heltman, K., & Brown, C. E. (1988). The relationship of social power to visual displays of dominance between men and women. *Journal of Personality and Social Psychology, 54,* 233–242; Balkwell, J. W., & Berger, J. (1996). Gender, status and behavior in task situations. *Social Psychology Quarterly, 59,* 273–283.

5. Carli & Eagly; Anderson, L. R., & Blanchard, P. N. (1982). Sex differences in task and social-emotional behavior. *Basic and Applied Social Psychology, 3*(2), 109–139; Wood, W., & Karten, S. J. (1986). Sex differences in interaction style as a product of perceived sex differences in competence. *Journal of Personality and Social Psychology, 50,* 341–347; Carli & Bukatko; Ridgeway, C. L., & Smith-Lovin, L. (1999). Gender and interaction. In J. S. Chafetz (Ed.), *Handbook of the sociology of gender* (pp. 247–274). New York: Kluwer Academic/Plenum; Gibson, C. B., &

Zellmer-Bruhn, M. E. (2001). Metaphors and meaning: An intercultural analysis of teamwork. *Administrative Science Quarterly, 46,* 274–303.

6. Carli & Eagly; Wood & Karten; Carli, L. L. (1991). Gender, status, and influence. In E. J. Lawler, B. Markovvsky, C. Ridgeway, & H. A. Walker (Eds.), *Advances in group processes* (Vol. 8, pp. 89–113). Greenwich, CT: JAI; Cohen, B. P., & Zhou, X. (1991). Status processes in enduring work groups. *American Sociological Review, 56,* 179–188; Foschi, M. (1996). Double standards in the evaluation of men and women. *Social Psychology Quarterly, 59,* 237–254.

7. Graves, L. M., & Elsass, P. M. (2005). Sex and sex dissimilarity effects in ongoing teams: Some surprising findings. *Human Relations, 58,* 191–221.

8. Carli & Eagly; Carli & Bukatko; Lockheed, M. E. (1985). Sex and social influence: A meta-analysis guided by theory. In J. Berger & M. Zelditch (Eds.), *Status, rewards, and influence: How expectations organize behavior* (pp. 406–429). San Francisco: Jossey-Bass; Propp, K. M. (1995). An experimental examination of biological sex as a status cue in decision making groups and its influence on information use. *Small Group Research, 26,* 451–457; Eagly, A. H., & Carli, L. L. (1981). Sex of researchers and sex-typed communications as determinants of sex differences in influenceability: A meta-analysis of social influence studies. *Psychological Bulletin, 90,* 1–20.

9. Eagly, A. H., & Karau, S. J. (1991). Gender and emergence of leaders: A meta-analysis. *Journal of Personality and Social Psychology, 60,* 685–710; Hall, R. J., Workman, J. W., & Marchioro, C. A. (1998). Sex, task, and behavioral flexibility effects on leadership perceptions. *Organizational Behavior and Human Decision Processes, 74,* 1–32; Dobbins, G. H., Long, W. S., Dedrick, E. J., & Clemons, T. C. (1990). The role of self-monitoring and gender on leader emergence: A laboratory and field study. *Journal of Management, 16,* 609–618.

10. Carli & Bukatko; Ridgeway & Smith-Lovin; Carli, L. L., LaFleur, S. J., & Loeber, C. C. (1995). Nonverbal behavior, gender, and influence. *Journal of Personality and Social Psychology, 68,* 1030–1041; Rudman, L. A. (1998). Self-promotion as a risk factor for women: The costs and benefits of counterstereotypical impression management. *Journal of Personality and Social Psychology, 74,* 629–645; Butler, D., & Geis, F. L. (1990). Nonverbal affect responses to male and female leaders: Implications for leadership evaluations. *Journal of Personality and Social Psychology, 58,* 48–59.

11. Carli & Bukatko; Carli & Eagly; Eagly & Karau; Wood & Karten; Dovidio, Ellyson, Keating, Heltman, & Brown.

12. Riordan, C. M. (2000). Relational demography within groups: Past developments, contradictions, and new directions. In G. Ferris (Ed.), *Research in personnel and human resource management* (Vol. 19, pp. 131–173). New York: Elsevier; Konrad, A. M., Winter, S. & Gutek, B. A. (1992). Diversity in work group sex composition: Implications for majority and minority members. In P. S. Tolbert & S. B. Bacharach (Eds.), *Research in the sociology of organizations,* (Vol. 10, pp. 115–140). Greenwich, CT: JAI; Tolbert, P.S., Graham, M. E., &

Andrews, A. O. (1999). Group gender composition and work group relations: Theories, evidence, and issues. In G. N. Powell (Ed.), *Handbook of gender and work* (pp. 179–202). Thousand Oaks, CA: Sage.

13. Kanter, R. M. (1977a). *Men and women of the corporation.* New York: Basic; Kanter, R. M. (1977b). Some effects of group proportions on group life: Skewed sex ratios and responses to token women. *American Journal of Sociology, 82,* 965–990.

14. Yoder, J. D. (1991). Rethinking tokenism: Looking beyond numbers. *Gender & Society, 5,* 178–192; Floge, L., & Merrill, D. M. (1986). Tokenism reconsidered: Male nurses and female physicians in a hospital setting. *Social Forces, 64,* 925–947; Ott, E. M. (1989). Effects of the male-female ratio at work: Policewomen and male nurses. *Psychology of Women Quarterly, 13,* 41–57; Fairhurst, G. T., & Snavely, B. K. (1983). Majority and token minority group relationships: Power acquisition and communication. *Academy of Management Review, 8,* 292–300.

15. Allmendinger, J., & Hackman, J. R. (1995). The more the better? A four-nation study of the inclusion of women in symphony orchestras. *Social Forces, 74,* 423–460.

16. Chatman, J. A., Polzer, J. T., Barsade, S. G., & Neale, M. A. (1998). Being different yet feeling similar: The influence of demographic composition and organizational culture on work processes and outcomes. *Administrative Science Quarterly, 43,* 749–780; Graves & Elsass; Riordan, C. M., & Shore, L. M. (1997). Demographic diversity and employee attitudes: An empirical examination of relational demography within work units. *Journal of Applied Psychology, 82,* 342–358.

17. Wood, W. (1987). Meta-analytic review of sex differences in group performance. *Psychological Bulletin, 102,* 53–71.

18. Tsui, A. S., & Gutek, B. A. (1999). *Demographic differences in organizations: Current research and future directions.* Lanham, MD: Lexington Books; Williams, K. Y., & O'Reilly, C. A., III. (1998). Demography and diversity in organizations: A review of 40 years of research. In B. M. Staw & L. L. Cummings (Eds.), *Research in organizational behavior* (Vol. 20, pp. 77–140). Stamford, CT: JAI; Milliken, F. J., & Martins, L. L. (1996). Searching for common threads: Understanding the multiple effects of diversity on occupational groups. *Academy of Management Review, 21,* 402–433; Elsass, P. M., & Graves, L. M. (1997). Demographic diversity in decision-making groups: The experiences of women and people of color. *Academy of Management Review, 22,* 946–973.

19. Jackson, S. J., Joshi, A., & Erhardt, N. L. (2003). Recent research on team and organizational diversity: SWOT analysis and implications. *Journal of Management, 29,* 801–830; van Knippenberg, D., & Schippers, M. C. (2007). Work group diversity. *Annual Review of Psychology, 58,* 515–541.

20. Milliken & Martins, p. 400.

21. Lau, D. C., & Murnighan, J. K. (1998). Demographic diversity and faultlines: The compositional dynamics of organizational groups. *Academy of*

Management Review, 23, 325–340; Lau, D. C., & Murnighan, J. K. (2005). Interactions within groups and subgroups: The effects of demographic faultlines. *Academy of Management Journal, 48,* 645–659; Brewer, M. B. (2000). Reducing prejudice through cross-categorization: Effects of multiple social identities. In S. Oskamp (Ed.), *Reducing prejudice and discrimination* (pp. 165–183). Mahwah, NJ: Erlbaum.

22. Harrison, D. A., Price, K. H., & Bell, M. P. (1998). Beyond relational demography: Time and the effects of surface- and deep-level diversity on work group cohesion. *Academy of Management Journal, 41,* 96–107; Chatman, J. A., & Flynn, F. J. (2001). The influence of demographic heterogeneity on the emergence and consequences of cooperative norms in work teams. *Academy of Management Journal, 44,* 956–974; Schippers, M. C., Den Hartog, D. N., Koopman, P. L., & Wienk, J. A. (2003). Diversity and team outcomes: The moderating effects of outcome interdependence and group longevity and the mediating effect of reflexivity. *Journal of Organizational Behavior, 24,* 779–802.

23. Hall, Workman, & Marchioro; Karakowsky, L. & Siegel, J. P. (1999). The effects of proportional representation and gender orientation of the task on emergent leadership behavior in mixed-sex groups. *Journal of Applied Psychology, 84,* 620–631; Chatman, Polzer, Barsade, & Neale; Schippers, Den Hartog, Koopman, & Wienk.

24. Staples, D. S., & Zhao, L. (2006). The effects of cultural diversity in virtual teams versus face-to-face teams. *Group Decision and Negotiation, 15,* 389–406; Bhappu, A. D., Griffith, T. L., & Northcraft, G. B. (1997). Media effects and communication bias in diverse groups. *Organizational Behavior and Human Decision Processes, 70,* 199–205; Lind, M. (1999). The gender impact of temporary virtual work groups. *IEEE Transactions on Professional Communication, 42,* 276–285; Savicki, V., Kelley, M., & Oesterreich, E. (1998). Effects of instructions on computer-mediated communication in single- or mixed-gender small task groups. *Computers in Human Behavior, 14,* 163–180.

25. Joshi, A., & Roh, H. (2009). The role of context in work team diversity research: A meta-analytic review. *Academy of Management Journal, 52,* 599–627; Milliken & Martins; Williams & O'Reilly.

26. Ely, R. J. (1995). The power in demography: Women's social constructions of gender identity at work. *Academy of Management Journal, 38,* 589–634; Elvira, M. M., & Cohen, L. E. (2001). Location matters: A cross-level analysis of the effects of organizational sex composition on turnover. *Academy of Management Journal, 44,* 591–605; Burke, R. J., & McKeen, C. A. (1996). Do women at the top make a difference? Gender proportions and the experiences of managerial and professional women. *Human Relations, 49,* 1093–1104.

27. Chatman & Flynn.

28. Ely, R. J., & Thomas, D. A. (2001). Cultural diversity at work: The effects of diversity perspectives on work group processes and outcomes. *Administrative Science Quarterly, 46,* 229–273; Kossek, E. E., & Zonia, S. C. (1993). Assessing

diversity climate: A field study of reactions to employer efforts to promote diversity. *Journal of Organizational Behavior, 14,* 61–81; Cox, T., Jr. (1993). *Cultural diversity in organizations: Theory, research, and practice.* San Francisco: Berrett-Koehler.

29. Allmendinger & Hackman.

30. Thompson, D. E., & Gooler, L. E. (1996). Capitalizing on the benefits of diversity through work teams. In E. E. Kossek & S. A. Lobel (Eds.), *Managing diversity: Human resource strategies for transforming the workplace.* (pp. 392–437). Cambridge, MA: Blackwell.

31. Heilman, M. E. (1994). Affirmative action: Some unintended consequences for working women. In B. M. Staw & L. L. Cummings (Eds.), *Research in organizational behavior* (Vol. 16, pp. 125–169). Greenwich, CT: JAI.

32. Northcraft, G. B., Polzer, J. T., Neale, M. A., & Kramer, R. M. (1995). Diversity, social identity, and performance: Emergent social dynamics in cross-functional teams. In S. E. Jackson & M. N. Ruderman (Eds.), *Diversity in work teams: Research paradigms for a changing workplace* (pp. 69–96). Washington, DC: American Psychological Association; Tsui & Gutek.

33. Sessa, V. I., & Jackson, S. E. (1995). Diversity in decision-making teams: All differences are not created equal. In M. M. Chemers, S. Oskamp, & M. A. Costanzo (Eds.), *Diversity in organizations: New perspectives for a changing workplace* (pp. 133–156). Thousand Oaks, CA: Sage; Thompson & Gooler; Tsui & Gutek.

34. Tsui & Gutek; Thompson & Gooler.

35. Sessa & Jackson; Tsui & Gutek.

36. Thompson & Gooler; Northcraft, Polzer, Neale, & Kramer.

37. Cox, T., Jr., & Beale, R. L. (1997). *Developing competency to manage diversity: Readings, cases, & activities.* San Francisco: Berrett-Koehler.

38. Tsui & Gutek.

39. Fairhurst & Snavely; Tsui & Gutek.

40. Northcraft, Polzer, Neale, & Kramer.

41. Kristof.

CHAPTER 6

Leading People

The Gender and Leadership Wars

The *New York Times* recently published an interview with Carol Smith, a top executive at the Elle Group, a media company, about her views on leadership. In the interview, Ms. Smith said, "In my experience, female bosses tend to be better managers, better advisors, mentors, rational thinkers. Men love to hear themselves talk." She added that she intentionally arrives late for meetings with men to miss their inevitable, boring conversations about golf and football before the meeting actually starts.[1]

After the interview triggered an outpouring of comments posted to its web site, the *Times* invited six people to participate in an online debate one week later on what research says about the question, "Do women make better bosses?" I was one of the participants in this debate; the other five participants, all women, included researchers, consultants, and executives. As before, readers were invited to respond to the debate. Over 500 responses were received, some of which are excerpted below. Some of the responses were more fascinating than the debate itself.[2]

Several themes emerged in the responses. One theme was criticism of the composition of the debate panel. The panel was alternatively disparaged as "five females and one guy who wants to make his wife happy" (*NC*, response #85, not knowing that my wife, Laura Graves, is also my coauthor on two chapters in this book as well as other publications), "five women and one man who was formerly the Chair of the Women in Management Division of the Academy of Management" (*Disillusioned*, #289, implying that this credential provided a good basis to dismiss anything I had to say), and "five women and one boomer man" (*Becky*, #66, presumably after seeing my Web page photo).

Many respondents took strong positions on the question that was posed, writing passionately about their own experiences pro and con with female bosses, male bosses, or both. They tended to draw conclusions about what all male and female bosses are like. Some argued that female bosses are inferior to male bosses:

I can't understand them, (so) how can I work for them? —*katman*, #4

No! As a female, I'll take the male egos any day. At least you know what to expect from a guy. Men are more level tempered. They lay it on the line. Women are egotistical BIT…es. —*smitel*, #344

From my humble experience and that of virtually all of my business associates, women managers are more ruthless, more arbitrary, less compassionate, more sociopathic, and tend to be less knowledgeable and less involved in whatever they are doing. It seems to be all about climbing the ladder. —*BJ*, #426

Other respondents argued that female bosses are superior to male bosses:

In my experience, women make better bosses. Generally, they do not have that asinine alpha male schoolyard crap baggage. —*Paulie*, #84

Women make better leaders when given the chance, and not only lately. —*John*, #439

As far as I can tell, women are better than men at just about anything. —*daldoc*, #444

A few respondents argued that neither male nor female bosses are superior:

Women are no better or worse than men, in general. There are only good managers and bad managers. —*Nancy*, #3

I have had good and bad experiences with both sexes. It completely depends upon the individual and not the sex. —*Joel*, #223

Still other respondents argued that both male and female bosses leave a lot to be desired:

I have had two female bosses. Both were dishonest and manipulative. . . . The male bosses I had were merely incompetent. —*hb*, #125

All bosses suck. This is a trick question. —*Jonathan*, #346

As the online debate continued, it turned on itself as some women criticized what they perceived as a sexist or clueless tone exhibited in many of the previous comments from men:

Response to *katman*, #4: This is one of the challenges women have faced in working for/with men. We deal with it. I suggest you do the same. —*Brenda*, #179

The vitriol with which so many male commentators have greeted this (debate) demonstrates well the obstacles that women still face in the workplace. —*Rachel*, #244

The outpouring of "women make the most inferior, back-stabbing, emotional, menopausal, passive-aggressive, ineffectual, lazy bosses" or "have a family" sentiment in these comments is a pretty stark picture of how overt sexism is still alive and acceptable today. —*Caroline*, #302

Questions about sex differences and leadership have always been a topic of keen public interest and often a source of debate. This topic is not simply "hot" in the sense of being fashionable; it is also inflammatory. Some people tend to exaggerate sex differences (alpha bias), whereas other people tend to minimize or ignore sex differences (beta bias). Many people have strong beliefs about male and female similarities and differences in basic interests, abilities, attitudes, and behaviors.

As the number and vehemence of the responses to the *New York Times* debate suggest, questions about sex differences among managers or leaders (terms I will use interchangeably) stimulate especially heated debate. This is because corporate leaders are given an enormous amount of attention, especially in societies that place a high value on individualism rather than collectivism such as the United States, the United Kingdom, Australia, Canada, and the Netherlands.[3] In such societies, the success of organizations is attributed to the wisdom, values, and practices of their founders or current leaders. When organizations fail to achieve expected results, their leaders are the first to be blamed. Consider the issues of sex differences and leadership together, and it is clear why so many people from all walks of life have strong opinions about what constitutes effective leadership as well as which sex, if either, is more likely to exhibit it.

The purpose of this chapter is to offer a live update from what may be called the "gender and leadership wars." It examines preferences, stereotypes, attitudes, and behaviors associated with the leader role in relation to traditional gender stereotypes and roles. First, it considers preferences for male versus female leaders in general. Second, it compares stereotypes of leaders with gender stereotypes and examines whether leader stereotypes have changed over time. Third, it reviews attitudes toward female leaders. Fourth, it investigates whether (and, if so, how) female and male managers differ in their behavior and overall effectiveness as leaders. Finally, it considers what can be done to promote effective leadership by managers of both sexes.[4]

Leader Preferences

Due to the increased representation of women in management, more employees than ever before have had a female boss. In fact, many employees have become accustomed to working for a woman, having had two or more female bosses in their careers. Nonetheless, when people state a preference, they still tend to prefer a male manager over a female manager. Over time, the Gallup Organization has asked people in 22 countries, "If you were taking a new job and had your choice of a boss, would you prefer to work for a man or a woman?" Respondents could also state that the sex of their new boss would make no difference to them. All over the globe, respondents have consistently expressed a preference for a male boss.[5]

According to the most recent poll results, obtained in 2006, twice as many Americans said that, if they were taking a new job, they would prefer a male boss (37%) than those who said they would prefer a female boss (19%); however, "It makes no difference to me" was the slight favorite (44%). Among men who stated a preference, 34% favored a male boss and 10% a female boss. Among women who stated a preference, 40% favored a male boss and 26% a female boss. Note that a greater proportion of women than men said they would prefer a male boss. In contrast, according to 1975 poll results, 63% of men and 60% of women preferred a male boss, whereas 4% of men and 10% of women preferred a female boss. Overall, while preferences for a male boss have declined over time, a male boss is still preferred over a female boss by a 2–1 margin.[6]

Why do people who state a preference tend to prefer a male boss? There are several possible explanations. First, stereotypes suggesting that leaders are more effective if they display personal characteristics associated with men rather than those associated with women may account for the preference for men as leaders. Second, prejudice directed toward female leaders may make it difficult for women to be as effective in the leader role as men and reduce their desirability as leaders. Third, women and men may differ in their actual behaviors in the leader role, with the behaviors exhibited by male leaders yielding better financial results for the organization and more satisfied subordinates, contributing to a preference for male leaders. We will consider the merits of these possible explanations for leader preferences as we proceed.

However, it is important to note that leader preferences differ according to the age of the person being asked. In the 2006 poll results, 18- to 34-year-olds were equally likely to say they preferred a male (31%) or female (29%) boss if they were taking a new job. Twice as many 35- to 54-year-olds preferred a male boss (38%) than a female boss (19%). Four times as many Americans who were 55 years old or older preferred a male boss (40%) than a female boss (11%). Thus, Generation Yers, who have had greater experience in working with women as peers in educational programs and professional jobs, are less likely to prefer a male boss and more likely to prefer a female boss than Generation Xers or baby boomers. These results suggest that, assuming that individuals' leader preferences do not change over their life spans, the overall sex bias in leader preferences favoring male leaders may diminish over time as new entrants to the labor force progress in their careers.

Leader Stereotypes

Studies of the relationships among sex, gender stereotypes, and leader stereotypes were first conducted in the 1970s. Virginia Schein compiled a list of 92 characteristics that people commonly believe distinguish between men and women, the basis for gender stereotypes. She then asked a sample of U.S. middle managers to describe how well each of the characteristics fit women in general, men in general, or successful middle managers in general. Schein hypothesized that because the vast majority of managers were men, the managerial job would be regarded as requiring personal attributes thought to be more characteristic of men than women. In support of her hypothesis, she found that both male and female middle managers believed that a successful middle manager possessed personal characteristics that more closely matched beliefs about the characteristics of men in general than those of women in general.[7]

In more recent studies, U.S. women have less inclination to view management as the domain of men. They now associate the characteristics of successful managers more equally with those of women in general and men in general. A similar pattern of results is exhibited in countries with very different national cultures such as the United Kingdom, Germany, Japan, China, Turkey, and Sweden: Both men and women believe that men are more similar to successful managers than women are, but men endorse such beliefs to a greater extent than women do. These results suggest that international beliefs about managers may be best expressed as **think manager—think male,** especially among men.[8]

Tony Butterfield (my mentor) and I have taken a different approach to the analysis of leader stereotypes in a research program that also began in the 1970s. For three decades, we have periodically asked part-time MBA students in the United States, nearly all of whom work full-time, and undergraduate business students to describe both themselves and a "good manager" on the Bem Sex-Role Inventory (BSRI).[9] We assess individuals' self-descriptions and good-manager descriptions on both masculinity and femininity.

When we first collected data, the proportion of women in management positions in the United States was just beginning to rise. Based on this trend, we hypothesized that a good manager would be seen as possessing similarly high levels of masculine and feminine traits, what may be called an "androgynous" personal profile. However, contrary to our hypothesis, a good manager was seen as possessing predominantly masculine characteristics by a majority of respondents in all groups, including undergraduate and part-time graduate males and females. I obtained similar results in a separate study of actual managers' stereotypes of a good manager. Thus, the idea of **think manager—think masculine** prevailed in these studies.[10]

Since then, as we have continued to assess individuals' good-manager descriptions, the new results have been essentially the same as the earlier results. Although the proportion of respondents from different groups that describe a manager as possessing predominantly masculine characteristics has declined somewhat over time, men and women still describe a good manager in predominantly masculine terms.[11]

Overall, in studies conducted over three decades, men and women at different career stages, including undergraduate business students preparing to enter the workplace, part-time MBA students preparing for managerial careers, and practicing managers, have described a good manager as higher in stereotypically masculine traits than stereotypically feminine traits. Further, additional evidence suggests that support for these stereotypes is strong within specific occupations such as the military ("think military leader, think male") and athletic administration ("think athletic director, think masculine").[12] Thus, managerial stereotypes continue to reflect the dual notions of think manager—think masculine and think manager—think male.

Are these leader stereotypes important? The answer to this question is a resounding yes. Leader and gender stereotypes put aspiring female leaders at a distinct disadvantage by forcing them to deal with the perceived incongruity between the leader role and their gender role. If women conform to the female gender role by displaying predominantly feminine characteristics, they fail to meet the requirements of the leader stereotype. However, if women compete with men for leadership positions and conform to the leader role by displaying predominantly masculine characteristics, they fail to meet the requirements of the female gender role, which calls for feminine niceness and deference to the authority of men.[13]

This incongruity between the leader role and the female gender role may affect women's aspirations to seek management positions. For example, undergraduate business students' self-descriptions on the BSRI exhibited stereotypical sex differences, with male students seeing themselves as more masculine and less feminine than female students. However, female and male undergraduates agreed on a description of the good manager as highly masculine. As a result, undergraduate women tended to describe a good manager as less like themselves than undergraduate men did. Undergraduate women who do not see themselves as fitting the stereotype of a good manager may not develop management competencies and may be diverted from pursuing managerial careers. Those who see themselves as fitting the stereotype may be the ones who go on to graduate business programs and eventually attain managerial positions.[14]

When women decide to pursue management positions, they may encounter barriers in the selection process. Given leader stereotypes that focus on masculine characteristics and males, women may be less likely than men to be hired for management positions. Moreover, once women assume leader roles, leader stereotypes act as constraints on their behavior. Many organizations exert strong pressures on their members to conform to standards of behavior dictated by those in power. As long as men remain in the majority in the top management ranks, the masculine leader stereotype is likely to prevail, and women throughout the organization will be expected to behave as men. Thus, a masculine stereotype of the good manager is self-reinforcing and inhibits the expression of femininity by women in management positions.

In addition, the mismatch between the leader role and the female gender role constrains the advancement of female managers. When performance evaluations are conducted, women may receive lower ratings than men for similar levels of performance. Women may also be subjected to discrimination when decisions are made about promotions into higher leadership positions, resulting in a "glass ceiling" that makes it difficult for them to rise in managerial hierarchies. Thus, being competent does not ensure that a female manager will have the same amount of organizational success as her male equivalent.[15]

Do leader stereotypes depend on sex ratios in management ranks? If the proportion of female managers rises more, will there be some point at which stereotypes of managers no longer agree with the masculine gender stereotype? Probably not. As reported in Chapter 3, support for gender stereotypes has not diminished over the past three decades, despite considerable changes in women's and men's roles in the workplace and in society. Similarly, stereotypes of leaders have remained essentially the same despite the substantial increase in female managers during the same time period. There is little reason to believe that these stereotypes will change if even more women become managers. The upper levels of management remain a male bastion, despite the overall increase in the proportion of female managers. If stereotypes of leaders are influenced at all by sex ratios, they may be influenced most by the sex ratio of top executives.[16]

Are stereotypes of leaders dependent on the racial and ethnic composition of the management ranks? The vast majority of both female and male managers are non-Hispanic Whites. Stereotypes of male and female leaders in general may largely reflect beliefs about the characteristics of leaders from the dominant racial and ethnic group in the managerial ranks and ignore the characteristics of leaders from other groups.[17]

How well do leader stereotypes apply to the practice of management? Stereotypes are resistant to change and do not necessarily reflect current realities. Widely held stereotypes that men are better managers and that better managers are masculine may not reflect what makes good managers. Instead, these stereotypes could reflect only that most managers have been men and that most men have been expected to live up to the masculine stereotype.

Attitudes Toward Women as Leaders

In 1965, *Harvard Business Review* (which then used the subtitle *The Magazine of Thoughtful Businessmen,* a choice that reflected the times) published results from a survey of executives' attitudes toward women in managerial roles. Most female executives (82%) had a favorable attitude toward women in management; they believed that women should be treated as individuals rather than as a uniform group. In contrast, a large proportion of male executives (41%) had an unfavorable attitude toward women in management. They believed not only that women were special but also that they had a special place, which was outside the ranks of management; this is what benevolent sexists would think. Older men tended to be more accepting of women in managerial roles than were younger men. Also, men who had been superiors or peers of women managers thought more favorably of them than did men who had worked only for men. Overall, few men (27%) thought that they would feel comfortable working for a woman boss.[18]

Respondents to the 1965 survey gave several reasons for their negative attitudes toward female executives. According to a large proportion of both male and female executives, women themselves were part responsible for the negative attitudes because they had accepted their exclusion from managerial ranks without major protest. Societal prejudices against women working outside the home were also cited. Many men did not want to contend with women as well as with other men for the keenly competitive managerial jobs; younger men particularly may have felt in competition with women for managerial jobs.

Over the next four decades, the composition of the managerial ranks changed considerably. According to replications of the original *Harvard Business Review* survey conducted 20 and 40 years later, male executives' attitudes about whether women belong in leader roles also changed considerably. The proportion of male executives who expressed a favorable attitude toward women in management increased from 35% in 1965 to 88% in 2005. Similarly, the proportion who would feel comfortable working for a woman boss increased from 27% in 1965 to 71% in 2005. These are *huge* shifts in male executives' attitudes. In comparison, the proportion of female executives who expressed a favorable attitude toward women in management remained generally high, ranging from 82% in 1965 to 88% in 2005.[19]

Moreover, male executives in 2005 were more positive about how female executives were being accepted in business than the women themselves. The proportion of men who thought that a woman must be exceptional to succeed in business dropped from 90% in 1965 to 32% in 2005, whereas this proportion dropped by a lesser amount, from 88% to 69%, for women. Similarly, the proportion of men who thought that the business community would never fully accept women executives fell from 61% in 1965 to 16% in 2005, whereas this proportion fell from 47% to 34% for women, a smaller drop-off. Thus, female executives viewed the business community's general attitude toward women as executives in a less favorable light than male executives did.

Another way of examining attitudes toward male versus female leaders is to conduct laboratory or field studies in which participants evaluate the behaviors of leaders. In laboratory studies, leader behavior is held constant; only the sex of the leader is varied. In field studies, real subordinates evaluate the behaviors of real managers. A meta-analysis of laboratory studies of sex differences in evaluations of leaders found a tendency for female leaders to be evaluated less favorably than male leaders. This tendency, however, was more pronounced under certain specific circumstances. Female leaders were particularly devalued relative to male leaders when they (a) used a stereotypically masculine leadership style, (b) occupied a traditionally male-intensive leader role, and (c) were evaluated by males. These findings suggest that attitudes toward women as leaders are most negative when the leadership style or situation invokes traditional male norms. Women who exhibit the same leader behavior as men may be evaluated less favorably because of their sex.[20]

In studies of actual managers and their subordinates, subordinates typically express similar satisfaction with male and female managers. Subordinates do not appear to respond differently to male and female leaders for whom they have actually worked. The experience of having been supervised by a woman contributes to more positive attitudes toward women as leaders. Being in direct contact with or proximity to women as leaders may serve to dispel stereotypes about whether women belong in leader roles. However, individuals' attitudes toward women as leaders do not become more positive with experience unless that experience itself is positive. When individuals are more *satisfied* with their interactions with women leaders, they are more positive about women in leader roles.[21]

As noted earlier, many people still see an incongruity between the female gender role and the leader role, which often puts female leaders in a glaring spotlight solely because they are women. For example, after PepsiCo announced that Indra Nooyi would become its new CEO in 2006, the headline of the *New York Times* story was "A Woman to Be Chief at PepsiCo." Nooyi's ascent to the position increased the number of female CEOs of *Fortune* 500 companies at the time from 10 to 11, a 10% increase, which may seem noteworthy. However, it decreased the number of male CEOs of such companies from 490 to 489, hardly a significant decline (.2%). No headline has ever announced "A Man to Be Chief at Acme Corp."[22]

The focus of this section has been on attitudes toward women, not men, as leaders. Male leaders essentially are taken for granted. Having a woman as a manager has only recently become a common experience for workers. As more people have more experience with women in leader roles, female leaders may elicit less negative reactions. However, prejudices against women as leaders resulting from sexist attitudes are unlikely to disappear completely. Hostility toward women as leaders may be less openly expressed than in the past, but this does not mean that it does not exist. Women continue to face prejudices in the leader role that men do not face. These prejudices make it more difficult for women to be effective as leaders.[23]

Leader Behavior and Effectiveness

To what extent do perceptions of leadership match current realities? Are men and masculine behaviors really best in leadership positions as leader stereotypes suggest? To consider these questions, let's review how the major theories of leadership regard the merits of stereotypically feminine or masculine behaviors. Finally, we will examine research evidence on sex differences in leader behavior and effectiveness.

Theories of Leadership

Early theories of what leaders do and what does and does not work well were based almost entirely on studies of male managers. A classic

1974 compendium of research results, Ralph Stogdill's *Handbook of Leadership*, discovered few studies that examined female leaders exclusively or even included female leaders in their samples.[24] When female managers were present in organizations being studied, they were usually excluded from the analysis because their few numbers might distort the results! It was as if female managers were less legitimate or less worthy of observation than were male managers. Although management researchers no longer exclude female managers from their samples, many of the existing theories of leadership were developed with male managers in mind. However, most theories refer to feminine and sex-neutral as well as masculine characteristics.

There are two distinct types of behavior that managers may use to influence the actions of their subordinates. The first type, **task style** or task accomplishment, refers to the extent to which the manager initiates and organizes work activity and defines the way work is to be done. For example, a manager who reorganizes a department, develops a description of the function of each department member, formulates department and individual goals, assigns projects, and gives details on how projects should be conducted may be considered high in task style. The second type, **interpersonal style** or maintenance of interpersonal relationships, refers to the extent to which the manager engages in activities that tend to the morale and welfare of people. For example, a manager who expresses appreciation to subordinates for work performed well, demonstrates concern about their job and work satisfaction, and tries to build their self-esteem may be considered high in interpersonal style. A manager may be high in both task and interpersonal style, low in both, or high in one but not the other.[25]

Managers may also exhibit different decision-making styles. A leader who exhibits a **democratic style of decision making** allows subordinates to participate in decision making, whereas a leader who exhibits an **autocratic style of decision making** discourages such participation. These are generally considered to be opposite decision-making styles.[26]

Some leadership theories regard different types of leader behavior as appropriate for different situations. For example, **situational leadership theory,** originated by Paul Hersey and Ken Blanchard, recommends that managers adopt high task–low interpersonal, high task–high interpersonal, low task–high interpersonal, and low task–low interpersonal styles in that order as their subordinates' maturity increases. More mature subordinates are more willing and able to take responsibility and have greater education and experience relevant to the task at hand. Also,

Tannenbaum and Schmidt's leadership theory recommends that managers become more democratic and less autocratic in decision making as subordinates display a greater need for independence, readiness to assume responsibility, and ability to solve problems as a team.[27]

In recent years, transformational and transactional leadership have become the primary focus of leadership theories.[28] **Transformational leaders** motivate subordinates to transcend their own self-interests for the good of the group or organization by setting exceptionally high standards for performance and then developing subordinates to achieve these standards. In this way, they turn followers into leaders. Transformational leaders exhibit four types of behavior: (1) *charisma,* by displaying attributes that induce followers to view them as role models and behaviors that communicate a sense of values, purpose, and the importance of the mission; (2) *inspirational motivation,* by exuding optimism and excitement about the mission and its attainability; (3) *intellectual stimulation,* by encouraging followers to question basic assumptions and consider problems and tasks from new perspectives; and (4) *individualized consideration,* by focusing on the development and mentoring of followers as individuals and attending to their specific needs.[29]

In contrast, **transactional leaders** focus on clarifying the responsibilities of subordinates and then responding to how well subordinates execute their responsibilities. They exhibit two kinds of behavior: (1) *contingent reward,* by promising and providing suitable rewards if followers achieve their assigned objectives, and (2) *management by exception,* by intervening to correct follower performance either in anticipation of a problem or after a problem has occurred. Transactional leaders who engage in active management by exception systematically monitor subordinate performance for mistakes, whereas those who engage in passive management by exception wait for subordinate difficulties to be brought to their attention before intervening. Transformational leaders may be transactional when it is necessary to achieve their goals. However, transactional leaders are seldom transformational.

Distinct from both transformational and transactional leadership is **laissez-faire leadership.** Laissez-faire leaders avoid taking responsibility for leadership altogether. Such leaders refrain from giving direction or making decisions and do not involve themselves in the development of their followers.

The call for transformational leadership has occurred partly in recognition of the changing economic environment in which organizations operate. As global environments become more turbulent, highly competitive, and reliant on new technologies, they call for "high-involvement" organizations with decentralized authority, flexible structures, and fewer managerial levels. Individuals who are able to articulate and rally followers behind a unified vision, stimulate creativity in achieving the vision, and develop rewards, recognition, and career opportunities for high-performing specialists are best suited for leader roles in such organizations. Management approaches that emphasize open communications and delegation are most conducive to the rapid innovation and response to customers that organizations need to survive in such environments. As a result, successful organizations are shifting away from an authoritarian model of leadership and toward a more transformational and democratic model.[30]

Gender Stereotypes and Leadership Theories

Several linkages may be made between gender stereotypes and leadership theories. A high propensity to exhibit task-oriented behaviors such as setting goals and initiating work activity is associated with the masculine stereotype. The feminine stereotype is associated with a high propensity to exhibit interpersonally oriented behaviors such as showing consideration toward subordinates and demonstrating concern for their satisfaction. When individuals are high in the propensity to exhibit both task-oriented and interpersonally oriented behavior, they adopt the profile of an androgynous leader. However, when individuals are low in the propensity to exhibit either type of behavior, they may be regarded as undifferentiated. In contrast, situational leadership theory suggests that leaders should be masculine, androgynous, feminine, and finally undifferentiated (low in both masculine and feminine traits) in turn as followers increase in maturity and the leader's need to demonstrate task behavior abates.[31]

Further, the autocratic style of decision making is more associated with the masculine stereotype, reflecting a greater emphasis on dominance and control over others. In contrast, the democratic style of decision making is more associated with the feminine stereotype, reflecting a greater emphasis on the involvement of others. Tannenbaum and Schmidt's leadership theory recommends that leaders behave in an increasingly feminine manner as their followers gain independence, responsibility, and the ability to work well as a team.[32]

Overall, the transformational leadership style appears to be more congruent with the feminine than the masculine gender role, whereas the transactional leadership style appears to be more congruent with the masculine than the feminine gender role. Transformational leadership is positively associated with nurturance and agreeableness, feminine traits, and negatively associated with aggression, a masculine trait. Individualized consideration is congruent with the feminine gender role because its developmental focus reflects a high concern with relationships and the needs of others. However, both active and passive management by exception seem congruent with the masculine gender role in their focus on correcting followers' mistakes because they stress immediate task accomplishment over long-term building of relationships and favor use of the leadership position to control others. In addition, contingent reward appears to be congruent with the masculine gender role because it is primarily task-oriented.[33]

Recall that leader stereotypes place a high value on masculine characteristics. Even though early leadership theories were developed at a time when there were far fewer women in leader roles, review of major theories does not support these stereotypes. Leadership theories also do not endorse feminine characteristics exclusively. The recent calls for transformational leadership over transactional leadership and for democratic decision making over autocratic decision making place somewhat more emphasis on feminine characteristics than masculine characteristics. Other theories, such as situational leadership theory and Tannenbaum and Schmidt's leadership theory, recommend that leaders vary the amount of masculine and feminine characteristics they display according to the situation. Thus, leadership theories do not suggest that either feminine or masculine behaviors are the key to leader effectiveness.

Sex Differences

Although leadership theories do not exclusively promote either masculinity or femininity, researchers have devoted a great deal of attention to sex differences in leader behavior and effectiveness. Over time, three distinct perspectives have emerged regarding these differences:

1. **Stereotypical differences favoring men.** Female and male managers differ in ways predicted by gender stereotypes, with men's preponderance of masculine traits making them better suited as managers.

2. **Stereotypical differences favoring women.** Female and male managers differ in accordance with gender stereotypes, but femininity is particularly needed by managers to be effective in today's workplace.

3. **No differences.** Women who pursue the nontraditional career of manager do not adhere to the feminine stereotype and behave similarly to men who pursue managerial careers.

Sex differences have been examined in several types of leader behaviors. A meta-analysis of sex differences in task style, interpersonal style, and democratic versus autocratic decision-making style divided studies into three types: (1) laboratory experiments, which compare the behavior of male and female leaders in group simulations; (2) assessment studies, which compare the behavioral inclinations of men and women who do not currently hold leadership roles, such as business students; and (3) organizational studies, which compare the actual behavior of men and women in equivalent leadership roles. As gender stereotypes would predict, women tended to be higher in interpersonal style than men, but only in laboratory experiments and assessment studies. That is, this sex difference was present only for individuals who participated in laboratory experiments and for nonleaders who were assessed on how they would behave if they actually were leaders; there was no sex difference in the interpersonal style of actual managers. Contrary to gender stereotypes, men and women did not differ in task style in any type of study. However, a consistent sex difference emerges in individuals' tendencies to adopt a democratic versus autocratic style of decision making. In support of gender stereotypes, women tended to be more democratic, less autocratic leaders than men in all settings and circumstances—for actual leaders, nonleaders, and participants in laboratory experiments.[34]

A meta-analysis of sex differences in transformational and transactional leadership found that female leaders are more transformational than their male counterparts. Women rated higher than men on all dimensions of transformational leadership: charisma (especially attributes that motivate pride and respect), inspirational motivation, intellectual stimulation, and individualized consideration. Women also rated higher than did men on the contingent reward dimension of transactional leadership. In contrast, men rated higher than women did on two dimensions of transactional leadership: active management by exception and passive management by exception. Men also rated higher than did women in laissez-faire leadership.[35]

Evidence from meta-analysis also suggests that all of the dimensions of transformational leadership and the contingent reward dimension of transactional leadership are positively associated with leader effectiveness as reflected in individual, group, and organizational performance. In contrast, passive management by exception and laissez-faire leadership are negatively associated with leader effectiveness.[36] Thus, the above results suggest that women rate higher than men do in behavior that contributes to their effectiveness as leaders and lower than do men in behavior that would detract from their effectiveness.

A separate meta-analysis on sex differences in leader effectiveness found that women and men overall did not differ in their effectiveness as leaders. Most of the studies included in this meta-analysis were conducted in organizational settings. Men were more effective than women in military settings, which are extremely male-intensive, whereas women were more effective than men in education, government, and social service settings, which are less male-intensive. Neither men nor women were more effective in business settings. Men were more effective than women when the particular leader role examined was more congruent with the male gender role and when there was a larger proportion of men as both leaders and subordinates. Further, men were more effective than women in lower-level management positions, whereas women were more effective than men in middle-level management positions. The position of middle manager is often regarded as requiring heavy use of interpersonal skills to wield influence, which would favor women according to gender stereotypes. There have not been sufficient studies of men and women in top management positions to allow a comparison of the sexes using meta-analysis.[37]

In summary, the bulk of evidence regarding sex differences in leader behavior suggests the existence of stereotypical differences. As gender stereotypes would predict, women are higher in interpersonal style than men in laboratory experiments and assessment studies (but not organizational studies), and they are higher in democratic decision making than men in all types of studies. Women are also higher than men in dimensions of transformational leadership, which are associated with the feminine stereotype, and lower than men in active and passive management by exception, which are associated with the masculine stereotype. Contrary to gender stereotypes, women are higher than men in the contingent reward dimension of transactional leadership. Offering some support for the "no differences" perspective, women and men do not differ in task style in any type of study.

However, the stereotypical differences that were found favor women, not men. Women are higher than men in dimensions of behavior that contribute to leader effectiveness (charisma, inspirational motivation, intellectual stimulation, individualized consideration, contingent reward) and lower than men in dimensions of behavior that detract from leader effectiveness (passive management by exception, laissez-faire leadership). Women also make greater use of a democratic decision-making style than men. Moreover, trends in the economic environment seem to call for a transformational and democratic leadership style that is associated more with women than men.

Studies that directly measure leader effectiveness, however, rate women as no more or less effective than men. Additional evidence suggests that situational factors influence whether men or women are more effective as leaders. These factors include the nature of the organizational setting and leader role, the proportions of male leaders and followers, and the managerial level of the position. As a result, some leader roles are more congenial to male leaders, whereas other leader roles are more congenial to female leaders.

Thus, the evidence clearly refutes the stereotypes that men are better leaders and that better leaders are masculine. Effective leadership today requires a combination of behaviors that are masculine (e.g., contingent reward) and feminine (e.g., individualized consideration) and the absence of other behaviors that are sex-neutral (e.g., laissez-faire leadership). Women exhibit more of behaviors that contribute to leader effectiveness than do men. However, situations differ in whether they favor women or men as leaders.

Promoting Effective Leadership

In Chapter 3, Sandra Bem was quoted as saying that "behavior should have no gender."[38] Ideally, to amend Bem's statement, leader behavior should have no gender. As Nancy and Joel said in their comments on the *New York Times* online debate quoted earlier, the sex of individuals who hold leader roles should be of little concern. What should matter is how well individuals, male and female, respond to the demands of the particular leader role that they occupy. However, the sex of leaders often makes a difference to others in different cultures. Many individuals, especially men, describe leaders in stereotypical terms that favor males over females. Individuals who state a preference tend to prefer male over female leaders. They also tend to hold attitudes that make it difficult for female leaders to be effective in their roles.

What is required to create a working environment in which members of both sexes with equal leadership abilities have an equal chance to be effective in the leader role? Table 6.1 summarizes recommended actions. To achieve this objective, prejudices against women as leaders must be confronted. Such prejudices are most likely to be exhibited in masculinized work settings in which the majority of leaders and followers are men and the leader role is associated with the male gender role. In such settings, the playing field is tipped in favor of men.[39]

To give women a greater chance of being effective in highly masculinized settings, organizations need to consider the ways in which leaders are evaluated. When leaders in masculinized settings are evaluated on the basis of whether they promote group cohesiveness and develop subordinates for future roles as well as accomplish tasks, female leaders, who rank higher in individualized consideration than male leaders, have more of an opportunity to be seen as effective. To take advantage of this opportunity, they need to have resources to promote subordinate development.

Organizations also need to take steps to increase the legitimacy of female leaders. As for the selection of team members (see Chapter 5), the appointment of individuals to leadership roles should be accompanied by publicity about their special skills, expertise, and accomplishments. This information should be provided for all individuals who assume

Table 6.1   Recommended Actions

1. Confront prejudices against leaders on the basis of their sex.

2. Evaluate leaders on the basis of task accomplishment, group cohesiveness, and development of subordinates for future roles.

3. Publicize qualifications of individuals assigned to leader positions.

4. Develop the capabilities of all individuals to play leader roles.

5. Create conditions that give leaders of both sexes equal chances to succeed.

6. Confront beliefs that you do not have what it takes to be a great leader and prove them wrong.

7. If you are the first woman to hold a particular leader position, take advantage of being seen as a symbol of change.

leader roles, not just women, to avoid drawing attention to female leaders as a group. Such an action will reduce the potential for stereotyping of leaders according to their sex because of insufficient or inaccurate information.[40]

Male leaders in settings that are more congenial to women face somewhat different issues. Because men have more societal status than women, they are likely to be granted higher status in a feminized work setting than female leaders are granted in a masculinized work setting. However, male leaders may still be subjected to sexist attitudes. As discussed in Chapter 3, attitudes toward men range from hostility to benevolence, with women scoring higher in hostility toward men and lower in benevolence toward men.[41] Male leaders do not deserve to be the target of sexist attitudes any more than female leaders do. When sexist attitudes are directed toward male as well as female leaders, they have to be addressed.

No matter what the setting, organizations need to be ready to act when their members embrace stereotypical views or display prejudices toward members of one sex as leaders. Although beliefs (e.g., leader stereotypes) and attitudes (e.g., prejudice against women as leaders) are difficult to change, organizations must take steps to counteract problematic beliefs and attitudes. Diversity training programs should make individuals aware of the ways in which biases related to sex (as well as race, ethnicity, age, sexual orientation, and so on) can affect their decisions, and to teach them how to move beyond their own biases. Organizations should also encourage employees to engage in the most effective kinds of behavior, whatever their beliefs or attitudes may be.

When stereotyping of leaders does occur in an organizational setting, the risk is that potential or actual leaders will fall for the stereotypes and see themselves as others see them, whether or not their personal traits actually fit the stereotypes. No matter how they may be stereotyped, leaders of both sexes need to be ready to demonstrate their capabilities as leaders and to disprove anyone who thinks otherwise. Asking their superiors to back them up when others second-guess them may also be helpful in establishing their leadership credentials.[42]

Women who beat the odds and enter leadership levels previously controlled by men are often seen as powerful symbols of changing organizational realities. The appointment of women to top management positions may mean that the organization now values the attributes associated with women and may give newly appointed female executives a surprising degree of influence. They should be ready to take advantage of their status as symbols of change.[43]

In conclusion, evidence increasingly suggests that women tend to be better suited than men to serve as leaders in the ways required in the global economy. However, this is *not* to say that organizations should choose women for leader roles on the basis of their sex. The challenge for organizations is to take advantage of and develop the capabilities of all individuals in leader roles and then to create conditions that give leaders of both sexes an equal chance to succeed. The proper goal for leadership training programs is not to teach men how to behave more like women, nor is it to teach women how to behave more like men. No matter what the linkage between gender and leadership may be, the goal should be to enhance the likelihood that all people, women and men, will be effective in leader roles.

The last word in this live update from the gender and leadership wars appropriately comes from a response to the *New York Times* online debate:[44]

Rather than looking backward, I hope that we will look toward the potential of men and women to be great managers and remove obstacles in their way. —*Julie*, #387

Notes

1. Bryant, A. (2009, July 26). No doubt: Women are better managers. *New York Times*. Retrieved July 26, 2009, from http://www.nytimes.com.

2. Room for debate: Do women make better bosses? (2009, August 2). *New York Times*. Retrieved August 2, 2009, from http://roomfordebate.blogs .nytimes.com.

3. Hofstede, G. (2001). *Culture's consequences: Comparing values, behaviors, institutions, and organizations across nations* (2nd ed.). Thousand Oaks, CA: Sage, p. 215.

4. Portions of this chapter are based on Powell, G. N., & Graves, L. M. (2006). Gender and leadership: Perceptions and realities. In K. Dindia & D. J. Canary (Ed.), *Sex differences and similarities in communication* (2nd ed., pp. 83–97). Mahwah, NJ: Erlbaum; Powell, G. N., Butterfield, D. A., & Bartol, K. M. (2008). Leader evaluations: A new female advantage? *Gender in Management, 23*, 156–174.

5. Simmons, W. W. (2001, January 11). When it comes to choosing a boss, Americans still prefer men. *Gallup News Service*. Retrieved September 10, 2001, from http://www.gallup.com.

6. Carroll, J. (2006, September 1). Americans prefer male boss to a female boss. *Gallup News Service.* Retrieved May 6, 2009, from http://www.gallup.com.

7. Schein, V. E. (1973). The relationship between sex role stereotypes and requisite management characteristics. *Journal of Applied Psychology, 57,* 95–100; Schein, V. E. (1975). Relationships between sex role stereotypes and requisite management characteristics among female managers. *Journal of Applied Psychology, 60,* 340–344.

8. Heilman, M. E., Block, C. J., Martell, R. F., & Simon, M. C. (1989). Has anything changed? Current characterizations of men, women, and managers. *Journal of Applied Psychology, 74,* 935–942; Brenner, O. C., Tomkiewicz, J., & Schein, V. E. (1989). The relationship between sex role stereotypes and requisite management characteristics revisited. *Academy of Management Journal, 32,* 662–669; Schein, V. E. (2001). A global look at psychological barriers to women's progress in management. *Journal of Social Issues, 57,* 675–688; Schein, V. E., Mueller, R., Lituchy, T., & Liu, J. (1996). Think manager—think male: A global phenomenon? *Journal of Organizational Behavior, 17,* 33-41; Fullagar, C. J., Sumer, H. C., Sverke, M., & Slick, R. (2003). Managerial sex-role stereotyping: A cross cultural analysis. *International Journal of Cross Cultural Management, 3,* 93–107.

9. Bem, S. L. (1974). The measurement of psychological androgyny. *Journal of Consulting and Clinical Psychology, 42,* 155–162; Bem, S. L. (1981). *Bem Sex-Role Inventory: Professional manual.* Palo Alto, CA: Consulting Psychologists Press.

10. Powell, G. N., & Butterfield, D. A. (1979). The "good manager": Masculine or androgynous? *Academy of Management Journal, 22,* 395–403; Powell, G. N. (1978). *Management styles.* Address to Allstate Insurance Company, Farmington, CT.

11. Powell, G. N., Butterfield, D. A., & Parent, J. D. (2002). Gender and managerial stereotypes: Have the times changed? *Journal of Management, 28,* 177–193; Powell, G. N., & Butterfield, D. A. (1989). The "good manager": Did androgyny fare better in the 1980s? *Group & Organization Studies, 14,* 216–233.

12. Boyce, L. A., & Herd, A. M. (2003). The relationship between gender role stereotypes and requisite military leadership characteristics. *Sex Roles, 49,* 365–378; Burton, L. J., Barr, C. A., Fink, J. S., & Bruening, J. E. (2009). "Think athletic director, think masculine?": Examination of the gender typing of managerial subroles within athletic administration positions. *Sex Roles, 61,* 416–426.

13. Eagly, A. H., & Karau, S. J. (2002). Role congruity theory of prejudice toward female leaders. *Psychological Review, 109,* 573–598; Eagly, A. H. & Carli, L. L. (2007). *Through the labyrinth: The truth about how women become leaders.* Boston: Harvard Business School Press; Rudman, L. A., & Glick, P. (2001). Prescriptive gender stereotypes and backlash toward agentic women. *Journal of Social Issues, 57,* 743–762; Catalyst (2007). *The double-bind dilemma for women in leadership: Damned if you do, doomed if you don't.* New York: Author. Retrieved

October 20, 2009, from http://www.catalyst.org; Johnson, S. K., Murphy, S. E., Zewdie, S., & Reichard, R. J. (2008). The strong, sensitive type: Effects of gender stereotypes and leadership prototypes on the evaluation of male and female leaders. *Organizational Behavior and Human Decision Processes, 106,* 39–60.

14. Powell, Butterfield, & Parent.

15. Eagly & Karau; Heilman, M. E. (2001). Description and prescription: How gender stereotypes prevent women's ascent up the organizational ladder. *Journal of Social Issues, 57,* 657–674; Powell, G. N. (1999). Reflections on the glass ceiling: Recent trends and future prospects. In G. N. Powell (Ed.), *Handbook of gender and work* (pp. 325–345). Thousand Oaks, CA: Sage.

16. Martell, R. F., Parker, C., Emrich, C. G., & Crawford, M. S. (1998). Sex stereotyping in the executive suite: "Much ado about something." *Journal of Social Behavior and Personality, 13,* 127–138.

17. Parker, P. S., & ogilvie, d. t. (1996). Gender, culture, and leadership: Toward a culturally distinct model of African-American women executives' leadership strategies. *Leadership Quarterly, 7,* 189–214.

18. Bowman, G. W., Worthy, N. B., & Greyser, S. A. (1965). Are women executives people? *Harvard Business Review, 4*(4), 14-28, 164–178.

19. Carlson, D. S., Kacmar, K. M., & Whitten, D. (2006). What men think they know about executive women. *Harvard Business Review, 84*(9), 28; Sutton, C. D., & Moore, K. K. (1985). Executive women—20 years later. *Harvard Business Review, 63*(5), 42–66.

20. Eagly, A. H., Makhijani, M. G., & Klonsky, B. G. (1992). Gender and the evaluation of leaders: A meta-analysis. *Psychological Bulletin, 111,* 3–22.

21. Ezell, H. F., Odewahn, C. A., & Sherman, J. D. (1981). The effects of having been supervised by a woman on perceptions of female managerial competence. *Personnel Psychology, 34,* 291–299; Bhatnagar, D., & Swamy, R. (1995). Attitudes toward women as managers: Does interaction make a difference? *Human Relations, 48,* 1285–1307.

22. Deutsch, C. H. (2006, August 15). A woman to be chief at PepsiCo. New York Times. Retrieved on February 25, 2008, from http://www.nytimes.com; Eagly & Karau.

23. Glick, P., Fiske, S. T., Mladinic, A., Saiz, J. L., Abrams, D., Masser, B., et al. (2000). Beyond prejudice as simple antipathy: Hostile and benevolent sexism across cultures. *Journal of Personality and Social Psychology, 79,* 763–775; Glick, P., Diebold, J., Bailey-Werner, B., & Zhu, L. (1997). The two faces of Adam: Ambivalent sexism and polarized attitudes toward women. *Personality and Social Psychology Bulletin, 23,* 1323–1334; Rudman, L. A., & Kilianski, S. E. (2000). Implicit and explicit attitudes toward female authority. *Personality and Social Psychology Bulletin, 26,* 1315–1328; Masser, B. M., & Abrams, D. (2004). Reinforcing the glass ceiling: The consequences of hostile sexism for female managerial candidates. *Sex Roles, 51,* 609–615.

24. Stogdill, R. M. (1974). *Handbook of leadership.* New York: Free Press.

25. Eagly, A. H., & Johnson, B. T. (1990). Gender and leadership style: A meta-analysis. *Psychological Bulletin, 108,* 233–256.

26. Eagly & Johnson.

27. Hersey, P., Blanchard, K. H., & Johnson, D. E. (2008). *Management of organizational behavior: Utilizing human resources* (9th ed.). Upper Saddle River, NJ: Pearson Education; Tannenbaum, R., & Schmidt, W. H. (1973). How to choose a leadership pattern. *Harvard Business Review, 51*(3), 162–180.

28. Judge, T. A., & Piccolo, R. F. (2004). Transformational and transactional leadership: A meta-analytic test of their relative validity. *Journal of Applied Psychology, 89,* 755–768; Judge, T. A., & Bono, J. E. (2000). Five-factor model of personality and transformational leadership. *Journal of Applied Psychology, 85,* 751–765.

29. Bass, B. M. (1998). *Transformational leadership: Industry, military, and educational impact.* Mahwah, NJ: Erlbaum; Bass, B. M., Avolio, B. J., & Atwater, L. (1996). The transformational and transactional leadership of men and women. *Applied Psychology: An International Review, 45*(1), 5–34; Rafferty, A. E., & Griffin, M. A. (2004). Dimensions of transformational leadership: Conceptual and empirical extensions. *Leadership Quarterly, 15,* 329–354.

30. Drucker, P. F. (1988). The coming of the new organization. *Harvard Business Review, 88*(1), 45–53; Hitt, M. A., Keats, B. W., & DeMarie, S. M. (1998). Navigating in the new competitive landscape: Building strategic flexibility and competitive advantage in the 21st century. *Academy of Management Executive, 12*(4), 22–42; Lawler, E. E., III, Mohrman, S. A., & Ledford, G. E., Jr. (1995). *Creating high performance organizations: Practices and results of employee involvement and total quality management in* Fortune *1000 companies.* San Francisco: Jossey-Bass.

31. Cann, A., & Siegfried, W. D. (1990). Gender stereotypes and dimensions of effective leader behavior. *Sex Roles, 23,* 413–419; Hersey, Blanchard, & Johnson.

32. Eagly & Johnson; Tannenbaum & Schmidt.

33. Ross, S. M., & Offermann, L. R. (1997). Transformational leaders: Measurement of personality attributes and work group performance. *Personality and Social Psychology Bulletin, 23,* 1078–1086; Bono, J. E., & Judge, T. A. (2004). Personality and transformational and transactional leadership: A meta-analysis. *Journal of Applied Psychology, 89,* 901–910; Bass, Avolio, & Atwater; Eagly, A. H., & Johannesen-Schmidt, M. C. (2001). The leadership styles of women and men. *Journal of Social Issues, 57,* 781–797; Kark, R. (2004). The transformational leader: Who is (s)he? A feminist perspective. *Journal of Organizational Change Management, 17,* 160–176.

34. Eagly & Johnson.

35. Eagly, A. H., Johannesen-Schmidt, M. C., & van Engen, M. L. (2003). Transformational, transactional, and laissez-faire leadership styles: A meta-analysis comparing women and men. *Psychological Bulletin, 129,* 569–591.

36. Lowe, K. B., Kroeck, K. G., & Sivasubramaniam, N. (1996). Effectiveness correlates of transformational and transactional leadership: A meta-analytic review of the MLQ literature. *Leadership Quarterly, 7,* 385–425.

37. Eagly, A. H., Karau, S. J., & Makhijani, M. G. (1995). Gender and the effectiveness of leaders: A meta-analysis. *Psychological Bulletin, 117,* 125–145; Eagly & Karau.

38. Bem, S. L. (1978). Beyond androgyny: Some presumptuous prescriptions for a liberated sexual identity. In J. A. Sherman & F. L. Denmark (Ed.), *The psychology of women: Future direction in research* (pp. 1–23). New York: Psychological Dimensions, p. 19.

39. Yoder, J. D. (2001). Making leadership work more effectively for women. *Journal of Social Issues, 57,* 815–828; Eagly & Karau.

40. Hogue, M. B., Yoder, J. D., & Ludwig, J. (2002). Increasing initial leadership effectiveness: Assisting both women and men. *Sex Roles, 46,* 377–384; Falkenberg, L. (1990). Improving the accuracy of stereotypes within the workplace. *Journal of Management, 16,* 107–118.

41. Glick, P., & Fiske, S. T. (1999). The Ambivalence toward Men Inventory: Differentiating hostile and benevolent beliefs about men. *Psychology of Women Quarterly, 23,* 519–536.

42. Hymowitz, C. (2005, October 24). Too many women fall for stereotypes of selves, study says. *Wall Street Journal,* p. B1; White, E. (2007, August 28). Advice for women on developing a leadership style. *Wall Street Journal.* Retrieved September 5, 2007, from http://online.wsj.com.

43. Adler, N. J. (1999). Global leaders: Women of influence. In G. N. Powell (Ed.), *Handbook of gender and work* (pp. 239–261). Thousand Oaks, CA: Sage.

44. Room for debate.

CHAPTER 7

Dealing With Sexuality in the Workplace

Touching Me, Touching You—at Work

Every workplace seems to have at least one "toucher"—someone constantly doling out hugs, shoulder rubs or high fives. Some people hate this attention and quickly put an end to it. For better or worse, that leaves a lot more love for the rest of us.

But is it ever really OK to put your hand on someone else in the office, even in friendship and support? It depends on whom you ask. Corporate lawyers and human-resource types say we should always keep our hands to ourselves in the workplace. After all, touch is subjective. One person's friendly pat can quickly turn into another's threatened lawsuit.

"There aren't standards about what touching is nonsexual other than handshakes," says Larry Stybel, a Boston management consultant. "If we are sitting alongside each other and I put my hand on your knee, is that a friendly sign of affection or a sexual come-on? I don't know, and I don't know how you will perceive it. So let's not even go there."[1]

Issues pertaining to the expression of sexuality in the workplace arise in all cultures. In this chapter, we discuss **sexual harassment,** the directing of unwelcome sexual attention by one member of an organization toward another, and **workplace romance,** the sharing of welcome sexual attention by two members of an organization. Sexual harassment is a matter of public concern with potential legal ramifications. Workplace romances are a frequent subject of public debate: How should participants and their organizations handle them? Even when men and women in organizations do not participate in romances, they frequently have to deal with the intermingling of work roles and sexual roles by other employees.

Sexual harassment is a pervasive phenomenon. Although the proportion of women who report having experienced sexually harassing behavior at work has depended somewhat on the research method used to assess the prevalence of sexual harassment, it is 54% across all types of studies. The proportion of men who have been sexually harassed at work is not as high but still worthy of note; in a survey of U.S. government employees, 19% of men (as well as 44% of women) reported having experienced sexually harassing behavior during the previous 2 years. In 2008, over 13,000 sexual harassment complaints were filed with the U.S. Equal Employment Opportunity Commission (EEOC), 16% of which were filed by men. Companies such as Dial, Mitsubishi, and Astra USA have paid millions of dollars to settle sexual harassment charges filed by the EEOC on behalf of employees. The CEO of W. R. Grace was asked to resign by the board of directors because its members believed that he sexually harassed female employees.[2]

Further, sexual harassment is a cross-cultural phenomenon. Studies have confirmed the prevalence of sexual harassment in many nations, and public consciousness of the issue has spread worldwide. For example, in Japan, public consciousness of sexual harassment, or *sekuhara,* emerged after the nation's first hostile environment court case received considerable media attention in 1989. However, norms regarding the acceptability of sexually oriented behavior at work vary across national cultures, with American laws and customs stricter in many cases than those elsewhere. When employees from a country with more relaxed norms are assigned to work in a country with stricter norms, they often need training on how to work within the norms of the unfamiliar culture.[3]

Workplace romance is also pervasive, with about 40% of workers having dated a coworker at some point in their careers. When a public figure is involved, workplace romances receive extensive media coverage, as was most prominently the case with U.S. President Bill Clinton. Although Clinton kept his job, CEOs at Boeing and the Red Cross were forced to resign their jobs after affairs they had with female employees became public knowledge. Suzy Wetlaufer, the editor of *Harvard Business Review (HBR),* was forced to resign from her post after admitting to an affair with then-married Jack Welch, the former General Electric CEO, while she was interviewing him for the magazine. Two lower-ranking *HBR* editors conducted a second interview of Welch that was published instead of that written by Wetlaufer (who eventually married Welch after his divorce).[4]

Sexual harassment is illegal, but there are no laws against workplace romance. Also, sexual harassment typically victimizes and offends the target person. There is not necessarily a "victim" of a workplace romance, although one or both parties may pay a price in their emotional health, task assignments, or career advancement if others are offended by the romance. In such cases, the participants are seen as having brought on their own troubles rather than having been victimized by others.

In this chapter, we examine explanations for and experiences with both sexual harassment and workplace romance. In addition, we discuss what organizations and individuals can do in response to sexual harassment and workplace romance. As we will see, sexual behavior in the workplace poses a challenge for managers. Managers cannot ban sexuality at work, but they also cannot ignore it.

Sexual Harassment

In this section, we address the following questions: (1) How may sexual harassment be defined? (2) How may sexual harassment be explained? (3) What are peoples' experiences with sexual harassment?[5]

Definitions

The U.S. EEOC defines sexual harassment as an unlawful employment practice under Title VII of the 1964 Civil Rights Act. Its guidelines on sexual harassment state, "Unwelcome sexual advances, requests for sexual favors, and other verbal or physical conduct of a sexual nature constitute sexual harassment when (1) submission to such conduct is made either explicitly or implicitly a term or condition of an individual's employment, (2) submission to or rejection of such conduct by an individual is used as the basis for employment decisions affecting such individual, or (3) such conduct has the purpose or effect of unreasonably interfering with an individual's work performance or creating an intimidating, hostile, or offensive working environment." An employer is held responsible for acts of sexual harassment by its employees when it knew or should have known of the conduct, unless it can show that it took immediate and appropriate corrective action. According to the EEOC guidelines, an employer should take all steps necessary to prevent sexual harassment from occurring, including raising the subject, expressing strong disapproval, developing appropriate sanctions, informing employees of their right to raise the issue of sexual harassment and how to raise it, and developing methods to sensitize all concerned.[6]

Definitions of sexual harassment have been incorporated into laws around the world. For example, the European Union (EU) has established standards for what constitutes illegal sexual harassment. An EU resolution stated that "conduct of a sexual nature, or other conduct based on sex affecting the dignity of women and men at work, constitutes an intolerable violation of the dignity of workers or trainees and is unacceptable." The resolution called for member states to inform employers that they have a responsibility to ensure that employees' work environment is free from sexual harassment and to develop campaigns to promote public awareness of the issue. The EU later issued a legally enforceable Code of Practice on sexual harassment. Most EU countries as well as many other countries have passed their own sexual harassment laws.[7]

The U.S. Supreme Court generally upheld the EEOC guidelines in *Meritor Savings Bank vs. Vinson,* the first case of sexual harassment it considered. It concluded that two types of harassment are actionable under Title VII, quid pro quo harassment and hostile environment harassment. In **quid pro quo sexual harassment,** the harasser asks the victim to participate in sexual activity in return for gaining a job, promotion, raise, or other reward. In **hostile environment sexual harassment,** one employee makes sexual requests, comments, looks, and so on toward another employee and thereby creates a hostile work environment. The Supreme Court later affirmed in *Oncale vs. Sundowner Offshore Services* that the EEOC guidelines apply to same-sex as well as opposite-sex harassment. In federal court cases involving sexual harassment below the Supreme Court level, plaintiffs have been more likely to win their cases when (1) the harassment was more severe, (2) supporting witnesses were present, (3) supporting documents were available, (4) they had complained to superiors or management prior to filing charges, and (5) management took no action upon being notified of the alleged harassment. If plaintiffs have none of these factors in their favor, their odds of winning the case are less than 1%. If all five factors are in their favor, their odds of winning are almost 100%. In addition, plaintiffs are less likely to win their case if they were involved in a prior workplace romance with the alleged harasser.[8]

Court decisions may be influenced by the instructions that judges give to juries. Judges have historically instructed juries, when making judgments about the guilt or innocence of a party accused of illegal behavior, to consider what a "reasonable person" would do in the same or similar circumstances. However, given that men have higher status in most societies than do women, a juror, when asked to adopt the point of view of a "reasonable person," may adopt that of a "reasonable man." Such a tendency could affect the outcome of court decisions regarding sexual harassment because men are less likely than women to perceive behavior as sexual harassment. In some court cases, juries have been instructed to decide the case based on a "reasonable woman" rather than a "reasonable person" standard: Would a reasonable women consider the alleged conduct to be sufficiently severe or pervasive to alter conditions of employment and thus constitute sexual harassment? When a reasonable woman standard is used, jurors may be more likely to find alleged conduct as harassing than if a reasonable person standard is used.[9]

Although the legal definition of sexual harassment is complex and subject to interpretation by the courts, most people agree that some line needs to be drawn between acceptable and unacceptable sexually oriented behavior in the workplace. However, the question remains as to exactly what constitutes sexual harassment: **Where should the line be drawn?**

As the opening passage suggests, even behavior that some consider harmless and nonsexual may be seen by others as a violation of their personal space and sexual harassment. In addition, some types of sexually oriented behavior at work are welcome to some people and unwelcome to others. To answer this question, we need to consider which types of sexually oriented behavior individuals find most offensive. Some types of sexually oriented behavior are universally regarded as more offensive than other types. However, judgments of which behaviors constitute sexual harassment may vary from person to person.[10]

Behaviors that may be considered sexual harassment include verbal requests, verbal comments, and nonverbal displays. Specific behaviors of each type may be classified from more severe (presented first) to less severe. **Verbal requests** include sexual bribery (pressure for sexual favors with threat or promise of reward), sexual advances (pressure for sexual favors with no threat or promise), relationship advances (repeated requests for date or relationship), and more subtle advances (questions about one's sex life). **Verbal comments** include personally directed remarks (insulting jokes or remarks made directly to you), other-directed remarks (insulting jokes or remarks about you to others), and general sexual remarks (insulting sexual references about men or women in general). **Nonverbal displays** include sexual assault, sexual touching (however "sexual" is defined), sexual posturing (looks or gestures), and sexual materials (display of pornography or other materials). In addition, sexually oriented behavior is considered more severe when (1) the harasser is at a higher hierarchical level than the victim, (2) the harasser has behaved similarly toward the victim and others over time, and (3) there are job consequences for the victim.[11]

Individuals' definitions of sexual harassment differ according to their personal and job characteristics. The sex difference in definitions is strongest: Men perceive a narrower range of behaviors as constituting sexual harassment than women do. In addition, men are more likely than women to perceive victims as contributing to their own harassment, either by provoking it or by not properly handling "normal" sexual attention. There is also an age difference: Younger individuals have a broader, more lenient view of whether sexually oriented behavior constitutes sexual harassment than older individuals. Individuals who rate higher in hostile sexism are less likely to perceive sexual harassment. Finally, perceptions of sexual harassment differ across managerial levels, with lower-level managers more likely to see sexual harassment as a problem than higher-level managers. Top executives are least likely to acknowledge the existence of sexual harassment.[12]

In conclusion, laws and court decisions define sexual harassment and dictate legally acceptable standards of behavior in the workplace. Individuals' own definitions of sexual harassment, however, influence the kinds of sexually oriented behaviors they feel entitled to initiate and their responses to behaviors initiated by others, whether they are jurors, victims, or simply bystanders. Individuals' definitions are in turn influenced by their personal and job characteristics, especially their sex. Thus, drawing a line between acceptable and unacceptable sexually oriented behavior in the workplace is not simple. Opinions differs over where the line should be drawn, making it difficult for organizations to fulfill their obligation to take corrective action against sexual harassment and to prevent it.

Explanations

Several models have been offered as explanations for why sexual harassment occurs.[13] According to the **evolutionary model** of sexual harassment, it represents a type of behavior to be accepted rather than a problem to be solved. Individuals with strong sex drives are sexually aggressive toward others due to their biological needs. Therefore, it is not surprising or of particular concern that individuals exhibit sexual aggressiveness in work settings. Men and women are naturally attracted to each other and enjoy interacting sexually in the workplace.[14]

According to the **sociocultural model,** sexual harassment has little to do with sexuality. Instead, it is an expression of power and dominance. In this view, individuals with the least amount of power in society are the most likely to be harassed. In patriarchal societies that expect men to be dominant and women to be compliant, sexual harassment may be regarded almost as a male prerogative. Its purpose is to keep women economically dependent and subordinate.[15]

The **organizational model** suggests that certain organizational characteristics set the stage for sexual harassment. For example, the hierarchical structure of organizations grants higher-level employees legitimate power over lower-level employees. Also, employees who have critical expertise or information valued by other employees may have personal power over others independent of their position in the organizational hierarchy. Power differentials allow some employees to use the promise of rewards or the threat of punishments to obtain sexual gratification from others. Therefore, the higher the power differential in organizations, the greater the level of sexual harassment. In addition, some workplace cultures are more tolerant of sexual harassment than others.[16]

In the **gender role spillover model,** the effects of gender role expectations are emphasized. The term gender role spillover refers to the carryover into the workplace of gender role expectations that are irrelevant to the conduct of work (e.g., expectations regarding sexual behaviors). Gender role spillover is most likely to occur when the sex ratio of a group is skewed, making members of the minority sex more noticeable and subject to special attention (see Chapter 5). Women in male-intensive groups and men in female-intensive groups experience gender role spillover because they are assumed to be basically different from members of the dominant sex and therefore are treated differently. They will experience more harassment than individuals who stand out less in their work environments.[17]

According to this model, incidents of sexual harassment vary according to the sex ratio of the pertinent group, which may consist of employees in the occupation, job, or immediate work group. The sex ratio of an occupation is determined by the proportions of men and women who hold jobs in it. The sex ratio of a job within a particular organization does not necessarily mirror the sex ratio of the occupation. Even if the sex ratio of an occupation is skewed in one direction, the sex ratio of the job may be skewed in the other direction. For example, more expensive restaurants tend to employ waiters rather than waitresses (see Chapter 4), even though waitresses comprise over two thirds of all food servers overall. Finally, the sex ratio of the individual's work group, consisting of the people with whom he or she interacts on a daily basis, may differ from the other two sex ratios.[18]

The three types of sex ratios vary in the immediacy of their impact on work experiences. The sex ratio of the occupation has the least impact on daily behavior at work, but it is part of the context in which this behavior occurs. The sex ratio of the job has some impact, but the sex ratio of the work group, those people with whom one most interacts, has the most immediate effect. In a work group with a skewed sex ratio, the greater visibility of members of the minority sex, especially if they are newcomers, may lead to their being scapegoats for the frustration of members of the majority sex. If they have peers who resent their presence, token members of work groups may be subjected to sexual harassment to make them feel so isolated and uncomfortable that they resign.

The **individual differences model** of sexual harassment recognizes that some people engage in sexual harassment and others do not, even when they live and work under the same conditions. Although most harassers are men, most men are not harassers. Most women are not harassers either. Individuals' tendencies to embrace benevolent or hostile sexism predict whether they will engage in sexual harassment. For example, male employees who are higher in benevolent sexism direct milder forms of sexual attention toward female employees in the belief that they are flattering the targets. However, male employees who are higher in hostile sexism direct more hostile types of sexual attention toward female employees, thereby creating a hostile work environment for all employees.[19]

In summary, although the evolutionary model views sexual harassment as arising from individuals' basically sexual nature, other models suggest that power differences in society and organizations and the sex ratio of the occupation, job, and work group contribute to the occurrence of sexual harassment. However, individuals vary widely in their likelihood to harass others and their reactions to harassment by others. Each of these explanatory models may provide a partial explanation of why sexual harassment occurs. In addition, many of the factors described may operate simultaneously. To understand the relative merits of these models, we need to examine experiences with sexual harassment in a variety of work situations.

Experiences

An extensive survey of U.S. federal employees sheds light on the underlying causes and effects of sexual harassment.[20] In the survey, 44% of female and 19% of male federal employees said that they had been harassed at some time during the previous 2 years. Most male and female victims had experienced milder forms of unwanted behaviors rather the more serious forms.

The vast majority of female victims (93%) had been harassed by men, whereas most male victims (65%) had been harassed by women. About 1% of female victims had been harassed by women, and 21% of male victims had been harassed by men. Other sources of harassment were mixed groups of men and women or unknown sources, as in the case of anonymous letters.

Female victims were harassed more by their immediate or higher-level supervisors (28%) than by their subordinates (3%). This difference supports the organizational model of sexual harassment. The power differential resulting from the relative positions in the organizational hierarchy of the harasser and victim appeared to contribute to the experiences of female victims. In contrast, male victims were harassed by their superiors (14%) and subordinates (11%) in similar proportions. However, coworkers and other employees without supervisory authority over victims were the most common harassers for both sexes (77% for female victims, 79% for male victims). (Percentages add to more than 100% because some victims had been harassed by more than one type of individual.)

In the federal survey, male and female victims of sexual harassment were more likely than nonvictims to work exclusively or mostly with members of the opposite sex, supporting the gender role spillover model. Victims of both sexes were more likely than nonvictims to be under the age of 35 and unmarried, which supports the evolutionary model if younger and unmarried employees are assumed to be the more sexually attractive and available. Victims also were more likely than nonvictims to have gone to college.

In response to unwanted sexual attention, approximately equal proportions of female (45%) and male (44%) federal employees ignored the behavior or did nothing. Very few of the female (6%) and male (7%) victims went along with the sexual attention directed toward them, refuting the evolutionary model from the victim's perspective. Contrary to the sociocultural and organizational models, both of which assume a power differential favoring men, female victims (41%) were more likely to ask harassers to stop than male victims (23%). However, female victims (33%) were also more likely to avoid the harassers than male victims (20%). Few female (13%) or male (8%) victims reported the behavior to a supervisor or other official.

The costs of sexual harassment to individual federal employees and the federal government overall were high. Twenty-one percent of victims reported that they suffered a decline in productivity as a result having been harassed, which would also affect the productivity of their work groups. About 8% used sick leave and 1% used leave without pay. Three percent received medical assistance and/or emotional counseling as a result of the unwanted attention, and 7% would have found such assistance or counseling helpful. Another 4% were transferred or fired, or quit without a new job. The cost of sexual harassment to the federal government over the 2-year period of the study was estimated to be $327 million.

Meta-analyses of studies across a variety of work settings confirm that the costs of sexual harassment are substantial. Sexual harassment has negative effects on both physical health (e.g., headaches, sleep disturbance, fatigue) and mental health (e.g., loss of self-esteem and self-confidence, anxiety, depression). In addition, even at low frequencies, it exerts a significant negative impact on employees' job-related attitudes such as their sense of job satisfaction, organizational commitment, and feeling of involvement in their work. Further, it interferes with the functioning and performance of work teams and the organization as a whole.[21]

We have focused on the effects of sexual harassment on the immediate victim. However, sexual harassment may create a hostile work environment for employees not personally targeted by offensive behavior. The perspective of witnesses of sexual harassment is important. Witnesses' responses to unwanted sexual attention directed toward others range from ignoring the behavior, to intervening personally in an incident, to reporting it to authorities. Witnesses generally are more likely to take action when the behavior has more serious consequences for the victim, when they believe that most people would consider the behavior sexual harassment, and when they believe that the behavior poses a moral issue.[22]

We have also focused on sexual harassment within organizations directed by some employees toward other employees. However, individual employees may be sexually harassed by customers and clients as well; the customer should not always be "king." Such harassment is increasing as service industries that bring employees into close contact with customers and clients represent an increasingly large component of the global economy.[23]

In conclusion, women's and men's experiences with sexual harassment are considerably different. Although both sexes may be the targets of unwanted sexual attention, women are more likely to be harassed. It is not surprising that women see more sexual harassment in the workplace than men do: They are more conscious of sexual harassment than are men because they experience it more. The personal costs of being harassed for both male and female victims are high. Their employers also face the prospect of diminished individual productivity, increased employee health care expenses, and costly litigation. The evolutionary model suggests that sexual harassment will never be completely eliminated in the workplace. However, all parties benefit when its occurrence is minimized. In the last section of this chapter, we discuss steps that organizations and individuals can take to prevent sexual harassment and to deal with it when it occurs.

Workplace Romance

Sexual interest in a coworker is not always unwelcome.[24] In some cases, it is reciprocated and serves as the basis for a relationship between two employees that goes beyond their work roles. Workplace romances, or mutually desired relationships between two people at work in which some element of sexuality or physical intimacy exists, have become more prevalent in recent years due to fundamental changes in the workplace. Individuals have greater opportunity to become romantically involved with an organizational member of the opposite sex due to the increased proportion of women in the labor force, especially in managerial and professional jobs. Also, employees are expected to work longer hours, leading to their spending more time with coworkers and less time with family members. As a result, the work environment has become increasingly conducive to the formation of romantic relationships. In this section, we examine the causes, dynamics, and consequences of workplace romances.

Causes

Robert Sternberg's triangular theory of love provides a perspective on loving relationships in general that may be applied to the formation of romantic relationships in the workplace. Love may be explained in terms of three components: intimacy, feelings of closeness and connectedness in a relationship; passion, feelings of romance and sexual attraction and the desire for sexual consummation; and decision/commitment, the decision that one loves someone else and the commitment to maintain that love. Intimacy is at the core of many kinds of loving relationships, such as love of parent, sibling, child, or close friend. Passion is linked to certain kinds of loving relationships, especially romantic ones involving sexual activity. Decision/commitment is highly variable over different kinds of loving relationships. The importance of these components depends in part on whether the relationship is short term or long term, with passion being prominent in a short-term romance.[25]

Sternberg's theory may be used to distinguish between factors that contribute to interpersonal attraction (i.e., feelings of intimacy) and factors that contribute to romantic attraction (i.e., feelings of passion and, in some cases, decision/commitment as well as feelings of intimacy). Workplace romance takes place in three stages. First, feelings of interpersonal attraction arise toward another organizational member. Second, feelings of romantic attraction toward the same person follow. Third, the decision is made to engage in a workplace romance.[26]

Interpersonal attraction is influenced by physical and functional proximity. Physical proximity refers to closeness that results from the location of employees' areas of work. Functional proximity refers to closeness that results from the actual conduct of work. Employees who are closer in rank and status are likely to be higher in functional proximity. Employees who interact with each other more frequently or more intensely because of ongoing work relationships are higher in both physical and functional proximity. Generally, employees with higher physical and functional proximity are more likely to be attracted to each other. Interpersonal attraction is also influenced by attitude similarity; individuals who are more similar in attitudes like each other more.[27]

Whether interpersonal attraction leads to romantic attraction is determined by the perceived physical attractiveness of the other person. Whether romantic attraction in turn leads to a workplace romance is influenced by several factors. Individuals' general attitudes toward workplace romance influence whether they act on feelings of romantic attraction. In addition, individuals may engage in a workplace romance if they believe that doing so will fulfill job motives (e.g., desire for advancement, job security, financial rewards), ego motives (e.g., desire for excitement, adventure, ego satisfaction), or love motives (e.g., desire for intimacy, passion, and decision/commitment).[28]

As for sexual harassment, there is a sex difference in attitudes toward workplace romance: Women have more negative reactions than men do. Women are more likely to worry that a workplace romance would hurt them on the job, more reluctant to get involved in one, and more discreet about it when they do. In general, women are more likely than men to believe that their private life and work life should not mix.[29]

The nature of individuals' jobs influences whether they get involved in a workplace romance. Individuals whose jobs are more autonomous, allowing them to make more decisions about their own work and to move more freely inside and outside the organization, are less subject to the constraining presence of others and more likely to participate in workplace romances. Business trips, which entail high levels of both physical and functional proximity away from coworkers and supervisors, are particularly conducive to romance.[30]

The prevailing culture of the organization, work group, or profession regarding the acceptability of workplace romance influences whether coworkers act on their feelings of mutual attraction. Younger and growing organizations that emphasize creativity and innovation are more likely to have an open culture regarding workplace romance. In contrast, older and more staid organizations that emphasize traditional values and ways of doing things are less conducive to workplace romance. Also, as for sexual harassment, the culture regarding workplace romance may be influenced by the sex ratio in an organization, department, or group. Recall that gender role spillover, or the carryover into the workplace of individuals' expectations based on gender roles, is more likely to occur when the sex ratio is skewed in favor of either sex. Employees may be more inclined to become romantically involved when the work setting is numerically dominated by one sex. In this kind of environment, employees may be more likely to see each other as sex objects and thereby search for romantic partners.[31]

In summary, interpersonal attraction created by high functional or physical proximity at work sets the stage for workplace romance. As employees interact, interpersonal attraction may evolve into romantic attraction, and, ultimately, a workplace romance. Romantic attraction is most likely to lead to an actual romance when employees have positive attitudes toward workplace romance and work autonomously in work environments that are more accepting of it.

Dynamics

Once two people enter into a workplace romance, what kinds of dynamics occur, and how do they evolve over time? Workplace romances differ according to the match between the motives (job, ego, love) of the two participants. Nine different combinations of these three motives are possible. However, four combinations of partners' motives tend to be more prevalent than other combinations: (1) ego for both partners, a **fling**; (2) love for both partners, **true love**; (3) job for both partners, a **mutual user relationship**; and (4) ego for one partner and job for the other partner, a **utilitarian relationship**. Flings are characterized by high excitement for both participants and tend to be short-lived. True love relationships are characterized by the sincerity of both participants and tend to result in marriage. Mutual user relationships are primarily job motivated. Utilitarian relationships involve a trade-off between different motives of the two participants, with the less powerful partner seeking to further job-related goals through involvement with a more powerful partner in pursuit of ego gratification.[32]

Power and dependency are key variables in understanding the dynamics of workplace romances. Three types of dependency may be present in a work relationship. **Task dependency** occurs when a worker depends on another in order to perform his or her function effectively. **Career dependency** occurs when individuals desire advancement that is dependent on the consent of others. In normal manager-subordinate relationships, managers depend on subordinates to perform tasks while subordinates rely on managers for career advancement. In a workplace romance, a **personal/sexual dependency** is introduced. The addition of this third dependency threatens the normal exchange of task and career dependencies.[33]

Whenever there is an imbalance of power in a romantic relationship, there is a high potential for exploitation of the participant with the higher level of dependency. The potential for exploitation is especially high in a **hierarchical romance** in which participants are at different organizational levels with high task and career dependency. For example, the higher-level participant in a hierarchical relationship can use the lower-level participant's personal/sexual dependency to force an increase in task performance. In addition, the lower-level participant can use the higher-level participant's personal/sexual dependency to argue for favorable task assignments or work conditions. When either of these instances occur, the relationship becomes utilitarian. Exploitation, however, is not only limited to hierarchical romance, but also may appear in a **lateral romance** in which participants are at the same organizational level with less task and career dependency. A power imbalance may occur in a lateral romance simply because one participant is more dependent on the personal/sexual exchange than the other.

Most couples try to keep their workplace romance hidden from coworkers but fail in the attempt. In less open cultures, workplace romances are likely to go underground with participants making a greater effort to keep the relationship secret because the consequences of exposure are more severe. Because coworkers disapprove of hierarchical romances more than lateral romances, participants in hierarchical romances are more likely to try to hide the relationship. Workplace romances in which one or both partners are married also create greater incentives for secrecy.[34]

The components of love, dependencies, and motives in workplace romances are seldom static and evolve over time. The levels of intimacy, passion, and decision/commitment felt by participants in a loving relationship seldom remain constant. Changes in task and career dependencies may alter the dynamics of their work relationship and romance. In addition, participants' motives for engaging in the romance may change. Growing satisfaction with the relationship may lead to increasing mutual commitment, or declining satisfaction may lead to terminating the relationship. Each participant has to deal with the other's changing feelings about the relationship, even if his or her own feelings remain the same.[35]

There are great difficulties associated with the end of a romance and the return to being only coworkers, including the rejected lover's lower self-image and self-esteem. In addition, what was once workplace romance may become sexual harassment if one participant desires to continue the relationship. Dissolved hierarchical romances between a supervisor and an immediate subordinate are the relationships most likely to become sexual harassment.[36]

We purposely have not distinguished between the dynamics of opposite-sex and same-sex workplace romance. We would expect the dynamics of both types of relationships to be similar. However, same-sex romance is particularly hazardous for participants due to homophobia in some pockets of the workplace. Because of this, individuals interested in a same-sex romance face greater risks when they look for a partner at work than do straight individuals. Participants in a same-sex workplace romance, whether or not their sexual orientation is known to coworkers, have more reasons for secrecy: They face more serious repercussions.[37]

Consequences

There may be both positive and negative consequences of workplace romances for participants, their partners outside of work, coworkers, and the organization as a whole. Participants in workplace romances face a variety of outcomes. For example, their productivity, motivation, and involvement may decrease during the early stages of the romance (when they are more distracted) and increase in later stages of the romance (when it has become a normal part of their lives). As for Jack Welch, the former General Electric CEO, and Suzy Wetlaufer, the former *Harvard Business Review* editor (now Suzy Welch) who interviewed him for the magazine, the romance may lead to their marrying each other, but it may also lead to their divorcing or breaking up with their current partner.[38]

Participants who are more satisfied with the romance tend to be more satisfied with other aspects of their jobs. In particular, workplace romance has a positive impact on the performance, motivation, and involvement of participants who enter the romance with a love motive. Love-motivated individuals may feel the need to impress their partners through higher productivity and to alleviate their supervisors' fears that the romance will negatively affect their work. In addition, they may simply be happier because they have filled their need for companionship and now have more time and energy for work.

Romance within mentoring relationships, however, may lead to negative consequences for the protégé. Successful mentoring relationships, judged by the development of the protégé, are characterized by a productive level of intimacy between the mentor and protégé that does not result in workplace romance. Less successful mentoring relationships are characterized by either unproductive intimacy, leading to a romantic relationship and poor development of the protégé, or unproductive distance, which also leads to insufficient development of the protégé.[39]

Depending on the circumstances, coworkers' reactions to workplace romances range from approval to tolerance to outright objection. At a minimum, workplace romance stimulates gossip among coworkers. Whether the gossip is positive or negative depends on the type of romance. A true love relationship stimulates the most positive gossip. Most people root for lovers in principle because they want to believe that romances can have happy endings. However, a utilitarian relationship stimulates more negative gossip, especially if it represents a hierarchical romance between a superior and subordinate. When coworkers strongly disapprove of a workplace romance, they may adopt extreme strategies such as ostracism of participants in informal interactions, quitting the organization to remove themselves from what they see as an intolerable situation, or informing the spouse of one or both participants with whom they may have socialized at corporate functions. If a coworker adopts the latter strategy, the romance may lead to divorce.[40]

In general, people do not care what their fellow employees do as long as it does not affect the conduct of work. When coworkers perceive the lower-level participant in a hierarchical romance to be motivated by job concerns such as advancement or job security, however, they have strong negative reactions. These perceptions differ according to the sex of the lower-level participant. Women who are involved in a hierarchical romance with a senior-level executive are seen as more motivated by job concerns than men in a similar relationship, leading coworkers to direct the most negative reactions to lower-level women.[41]

Why are lower-level women in hierarchical romances subjected to negative evaluations to a greater extent than are lower-level men? When a lower-level woman becomes involved with a higher-level man, coworkers tend to see the woman as motivated more by job concerns and the man by ego concerns. That is, coworkers perceive a utilitarian relationship, even if the relationship is better characterized as true love or a fling. In contrast, a workplace romance between a lower-level man and a higher-level woman is less likely to trouble coworkers. Although he may be seen as her "boy toy" if he is significantly younger than she, he is still seen as satisfying his ego needs. These perceptions work to the disadvantage of women.

The managerial response to a workplace romance also influences coworkers' reactions. Possible managerial actions, to be discussed at greater length in the last section of the chapter, range from ignoring the romance, to positive action (e.g., counseling), to punitive action (e.g., warning, reprimand, transfer, or termination). Coworkers prefer that punitive action be taken when the romance is hierarchical rather than lateral, one or both participants is motivated by job concerns, and there is a greater conflict of interest and disruption of the conduct of work. When managerial action is to be taken at all, coworkers prefer that equivalent actions be directed toward both participants. Thus, coworkers' reactions are influenced by the ramifications of a workplace romance, not just the existence of the romance itself.[42]

In conclusion, as with sexual harassment, women's and men's experiences with workplace romance differ greatly. Women are more likely to be judged negatively, and suffer the consequences, if they engage in a hierarchical romance. Thus, it is not surprising that women have more negative attitudes toward workplace romance than men do. The overall effects of workplace romance on organizations vary widely. These effects may be positive (e.g., increased individual productivity, motivation, involvement; improved work climate), neutral (e.g., increased levels of gossip with no other impact), or negative (e.g., decreased productivity, work motivation, involvement; worsened work climate). When a workplace romance has negative effects on the conduct of work, organizations need to be ready to act.

Addressing the Intersection of Sexuality and Work

Table 7.1 summarizes recommended actions for organizations and individuals in dealing with both sexual harassment and workplace romance to make the work environment a comfortable place for all.

Table 7.1 Recommended Actions

> 1. Adopt a zero-tolerance policy against sexual harassment.
>
> 2. Train managers to recognize and deal with sexual harassment.
>
> 3. Designate a party to whom employees may bring complaints of sexual harassment and other offensive behavior without fear of reprisal.
>
> 4. Investigate employee allegations of sexual harassment and take appropriate action.
>
> 5. Offer counseling to employees who need help in handling sexual, or other types of harassment, and workplace romances.
>
> 6. Do not ignore sexual harassment or other offensive behavior directed toward you or others thinking that it will eventually cease; either confront the offending party directly or use your organization's procedure to file a complaint.
>
> 7. Take organizational action when workplace romance affects the conduct of work, especially when it is a hierarchical or utilitarian romance, but ignore it otherwise.
>
> 8. Weigh the potential costs of a workplace romance against the potential benefits before getting involved.

Sexual Harassment

Unless organizations address sexual harassment, they may be held in violation of the law and risk loss of productivity and alienation of a large portion of their work force. Many cases of sexual harassment, though not all, require managerial action. In addition, organizations and their employees benefit from managerial actions that discourage harassment from ever occurring.

Organizations must create cultures that prevent sexual harassment in the first place. They may do so by adopting a zero-tolerance policy against it, educating employees about the issue, and establishing formal grievance procedures to deal with allegations of harassment. The organization's policy on sexual harassment should clearly specify the types of behaviors that are forbidden and their penalties. New employees should be informed of the policy on sexual harassment during their initial orientation. A training program for managers should detail the reasons for the policy, the variety of forms of sexual harassment, and proper responses to allegations of harassment. Managers and nonsupervisory employees should be made aware that sexual harassment could cost them their careers.[43]

In dealing with cases of alleged harassment, organizations should follow this general principle: *The severity of the action taken should be based on the severity of the alleged offense and the certainty that an offense was committed.*

After a complaint of sexual harassment has been directed to a designated party, organizational policy can be effectively implemented by a formal grievance procedure:[44]

1. Interview the complainant, the accused, and possible witnesses.

2. Check personnel files for evidence that documents prior animosities between the parties, previous complaints against the accused or by the complainant, and recent discrepancies in the work record of the complainant or the accused.

3. Assess the severity of the alleged offense, considering the type of behavior, intent, power position of the accused relative to the complainant, and frequency of occurrence. Actions by complainants' supervisors should be considered more serious offenses than the same actions by coworkers. Repeated incidents should be considered more serious offenses than isolated cases. The severity of both quid pro quo and hostile environment sexual harassment should be considered.

4. Assess the certainty that an offense was committed. Solid evidence, in the form of either witnesses or documents, to support the complaint provides assurance that there actually was an offense.

Matters are less certain when there is less than overwhelming evidence to support the complaint. Whether an offense was committed is in greatest doubt when the only evidence to support the complaint is the complainant's word.

5. Determine appropriate actions to be taken. Severe actions (e.g., dismissal, demotion, suspension, transfer of accused) are to be taken when the alleged offense is severe and the certainty that it was committed is high. In such cases, the work record of the complainant should be restored if unjustly blemished. Mild actions (e.g., no record of complaint in file of accused, or record with annotation that accusation not proved; letter to the accused stressing organizational policy against sexual harassment; announcement reminding employees of organizational policy) are to be taken when the alleged offense is mild and the certainty that it was committed is low. Moderate actions (e.g., warning or disciplinary notice in file of accused with removal of the notice if no subsequent offense within a specified period; required counseling for accused) are to be considered in cases that fall between these two extremes. A combination of actions of different levels of severity may be appropriate.

Such a procedure demonstrates that an organization is willing to take action to minimize the incidence of sexual harassment. It also acknowledges individual differences in definitions of sexual harassment by matching the action taken with the severity of the offense and the certainty of its occurrence. Clear and objective administration of such procedures protects organizations from liability and increases the probability that their work environment is free of harassment.

Formal grievance procedures, however, have little effect if the organization exhibits **deaf ear syndrome** when it receives complaints of sexual harassment. Many organizations have poorly written policies and cumbersome reporting procedures. For example, one U.S. company stated its sexual harassment policy in a single paragraph in the middle of a 50-page handbook that no one was expected to read. Other organizations couch their policies in language that only a lawyer could understand. In another company, an employee reported a manager who would not stop making sexual comments to her after she repeatedly asked him to stop. She was told to keep notes on his actions. When the comments escalated to physical harassment, she left the company and reported the incident to headquarters. She finally filed a charge with the EEOC after headquarters failed to take any action. The company denied liability for its inaction, stating that the employee did not follow proper procedure and had reported the incidents to the wrong person. This is how *not* to administer a sexual harassment reporting procedure. Organizations exhibit deaf ear syndrome by minimizing the seriousness of the offense, blaming the victim, protecting valued employees, ignoring habitual harassers, and retaliating against employees who "blow the whistle" on inappropriate behavior and on inadequate corporate responses to it.[45]

No matter how well intentioned a formal grievance procedure is, it will have little effect unless individuals who feel that they have been harassed are willing to make formal complaints against their harassers. Many victims are reluctant to use formal procedures. In the federal study described earlier, only 6% of victims used formal complaint channels. If they take any action at all, most victims choose to deal with the situation themselves. In fact, this may be their only recourse if they do not have solid evidence that harassment has taken place or if the organization turns a deaf ear to such complaints. Oral requests may alleviate sexual harassment, especially if they are assertively delivered and consistent across time and all types of offensive behavior. In the federal study described earlier, this "knock-it-off" approach improved conditions for 60% of female victims and 61% of male victims. Telling colleagues, or threatening to tell, is also an effective response. On the other hand, going along with the offensive behavior, making a joke of it, or pretending to ignore it usually does not resolve the issue.[46]

If oral requests do not stop offensive behavior, victims may be more successful if they write a letter to the harasser. The letter should contain (1) a detailed description of the offending behavior, when it occurred, and the circumstances under which it occurred; (2) the feelings of the victim about the behavior and the damage that has been done (e.g., "Your behavior has made me feel uncomfortable about working in this unit"; "You have caused me to ask for a change in job"); and (3) what the victim wants in addition to an end to the harassment, such as rewriting of an unjust evaluation that was prepared after the victim rejected sexual advances. The letter should be delivered in person with a witness present. The harasser will usually accept the letter and say nothing. There is rarely a response in writing, and, nearly always, the harassment stops.[47]

Victims' reluctance to make formal complaints does not relieve organizations of their obligations to create an environment free of sexual harassment and to provide support for employees who have been harassed. Even if no formal complaint has been filed, the organization should be prepared to initiate action if it uncovers significant evidence of wrongdoing. In investigating and redressing the wrongdoing, it should respect the wishes of those victims who wish to remain anonymous. The organization should also provide support for employees who have been harassed. Support should include off-the-record counseling to help victims identify and understand the available options for resolving the problem and to assist them in coping with the emotional consequences of harassment.[48]

In summary, we have detailed actions that organizations and individuals may take to deal with sexual harassment. Organizations should (1) establish a firm policy against sexual harassment; (2) provide training to employees about sexual harassment, including workplace norms and regulations in cultures with which they have contact; (3) set up and administer a formal grievance procedure; (4) ensure that employees are aware of both policies and procedures; and (5) provide counseling to help employees cope psychologically with harassment and decide what to do about it. Victims, however, should not bear the burden of solving the problems. Organizations have a responsibility to monitor the work environment and make it as harassment-free as possible.

Workplace Romance

There are sharp differences of opinion over whether workplace romance can and should be banned. Catharine MacKinnon, one of the first scholars of sexual harassment, argued that most of what passes for workplace romance is actually sexual harassment in disguise, resulting from a patriarchal system in which women are powerless to avoid being exploited sexually, and should be treated accordingly. Margaret Mead, a famed anthropologist, argued that, much like taboos against sexual expression in the family that are necessary for children to grow up safely, taboos against sexual involvement at work are necessary for men and women to work together effectively. However, others claim that it is foolish to try to regulate welcome sexual attention. As one manager put it, "Trying to outlaw romance is like trying to outlaw the weather."[49]

In practice, most organizations are realistic and do not try to outlaw workplace romance. According to a survey of human resource management professionals, only 25% of companies have written or unwritten policies about workplace romance. When policies exist, the two most frequent restrictions are on relationships between supervisors and subordinates (80%) and on public displays of affection (35%). The reasons most frequently cited for restrictions on workplace romance include the fear of sexual harassment claims (77%), the perception that it represents unprofessional behavior (58%), the potential for retaliation between employees involved in the romance if it ends (50%), and concerns about the lowered productivity of participants (52%) and lowered morale of coworkers (44%). The most frequent managerial responses to violations of the policy on workplace romance, if one exists, include transfer within the organization (42%), formal reprimand (36%), counseling (34%), and termination (27%).[50]

How should organizations respond when two employees become romantically involved? The general principle to follow in dealing with workplace romance is the same as that for dealing with sexual harassment: The severity of the action taken should be based on the severity of the alleged offense and the certainty that an offense was committed. However, unlike sexual harassment, the existence of a workplace romance does not necessarily represent an offense. *The primary concern of management ought not to be who is involved with whom, but whether the necessary work is getting done, and done well.*

If there is no disruption to the accomplishment of work goals, then there is little need to take any action. However, a relationship in which there is the potential for task-related or career-related decisions to be influenced by romantic considerations presents some threat. Coworkers may fear that the relationship will influence the conduct of work or suspect that it is already having an effect, causing their morale and productivity to suffer. When the romantic partners have committed no actual offense but there is the potential for offense, management should step in. The couple should be told that if they continue the relationship, work assignments and/or reporting responsibilities will be changed to reduce the potential for disruption of the conduct of work. In this case, punitive action is not in order, but the situation does need to be addressed by management.

When it is certain that task-related or career-related decisions have been influenced by romantic considerations, there is greater cause for concern. This situation calls for punitive action against *both* participants. The hierarchical level of the participants should not be allowed to affect the actions taken. This recommendation runs counter to the common practice that the lower-status person bears the brunt of punitive action. However, when both individuals are punished, rather than only the person at the lower level, the appearance of an equitable decision will have the most positive effect on morale and productivity.[51]

Management can also contribute to a satisfactory resolution of romance-related issues by offering counseling to all individuals involved—the couple, the managers of work areas that are disrupted by the relationship, and the coworkers in those areas. Coworkers need to have a designated neutral party with whom they can consult about a troublesome romantic relationship. As their manager may be one of the participants, they need freedom to report their concerns without fear of reprisal.

Individuals need to weigh the potential costs against the potential benefits when deciding whether to begin a workplace romance. The potential costs include negative effects of a workplace romance on their careers (e.g., loss of coworkers' respect, lack of advancement due to violations of workplace norms), self-esteem (e.g., questioning of basis for their work-related rewards), and family (e.g., marital strife, divorce). The potential benefits include meeting their personal needs at work and being happier as a result. When caught up in the passion of the moment, individuals may not be thinking clearly of the consequences. Nonetheless, they may gain from considering these consequences before they act on their feelings.[52]

In conclusion, although workplace romance seldom poses a legal threat unless a dissolved romance leads to sexual harassment, it poses potential problems for organizations. Two types of romances have the most damaging effects on individual, group, and organizational effectiveness: (1) a hierarchical romance in which one participant directly reports to the other and (2) a utilitarian romance in which one participant satisfies personal/sexual needs in exchange for satisfying the other participant's task-related or career-related needs. Negative effects of workplace romance on the conduct of work need to be addressed by organizations in some manner. However, workplace romance often has only positive effects, such as when both participants are single and committed to each other. In such cases, coworkers will be happy for the couple, and organizations need not respond.

Although sexuality in the workplace cannot be fully "managed," we have outlined steps that organizations can take to respond to the negative effects of both sexual harassment and workplace romance. In taking such steps, organizations help create a more comfortable work environment for their employees, even if it is not an asexual or "touch-free" zone. We also have suggested actions that individuals may take to influence their own destinies. As a convenient site for people to meet their personal needs, the workplace may be more exotic than ever before. However, it need not be a battlefield over issues of sexuality and work.

Notes

1. Bernstein, E. (2009, July 2). Touching me, touching you—at work. *Wall Street Journal*, WALL STREET JOURNAL ONLINE EDITION (ONLY STAFF-PRODUCED MATERIALS MAY BE USED) by C. BERNSTEIN. Copyright 2009 by DOW JONES & COMPANY, INC. Reproduced with permission of DOW JONES & COMPANY, INC. in the format Textbook via Copyright Clearance Center.

2. Ilies, R., Hauserman, N., Schwochau, S., & Stibal, J. (2003). Reported incidence rates of work-related sexual harassment in the United States: Using meta-analysis to explain reported rate disparities. *Personnel Psychology, 56,* 607–631; U.S. Merit Systems Protection Board. (1995). *Sexual harassment in the federal workplace: Trends, progress, and continuing challenges.* Washington, DC: Government Printing Office; U.S. Equal Employment Opportunity Commission. (2009). *Sexual harassment charges, EEOC and FEPAs combined: FY 1997—FY 2008.* Retrieved October 26, 2009, from http://www.eeoc.gov; Ellison, S., & Lublin, J. S. (2003, April 30). Dial to pay $10 million to settle a sexual-harassment lawsuit. *Wall Street Journal*, p. B4; Miller, J. P. (1998, June 12). Mitsubishi will pay $34 million in sexual-harassment settlement. *Wall Street Journal,* p. B4; Maremont, M. (1998, February 6). Astra USA settles harassment suit, to pay $9.9 million. *Wall Street Journal*, p. B6; Lublin, J. S., & Simmons, J. (1995, April 5). A second CEO falls on charges of harassment. *Wall Street Journal,* p. B2.

3. Webb, S. L. (1994). *Shockwaves: The global impact of sexual harassment.* New York: MasterMedia Limited; Uggen, C., & Shinohara, C. (2009). Sexual harassment comes of age: A comparative analysis of the United States and Japan. *Sociological Quarterly, 50,* 201–234; Lublin, J. S. (2006, May 15). Harassment law in U.S. is strict, foreigners find. *Wall Street Journal.* Retrieved May 17, 2006, from http://www.online.wsj.com; Reitman, V. (1996, July 9). Cramming for the exotic U.S. workplace. *Wall Street Journal,* p. A15.

4. Parks, M. (2006). *2006 workplace romance: Poll findings.* Alexandria, VA: Society for Human Resource Management. Retrieved October 26, 2009, from http://www.shrm.org; Holmes, S. (2005, March 8). The affair that grounded Stonecipher. *Business Week.* Retrieved October 26, 2009, from http://www.businessweek.com; Beatty, S., & Lublin, J. S. (2007, November 28). Red Cross ousts CEO Everson. *Wall Street Journal.* Retrieved November 28, 2007, from http://www.online.wsj.com; Bandler, J. (2002, March 4). Harvard editor faces revolt over Welch story. *Wall Street Journal,* pp. B1, B4; Hymowitz, C. (2002, May 14). An *HBR* case study: How magazine failed to respond to a crisis. *Wall Street Journal,* p. B1.

5. O'Leary-Kelly, A. M., Bowes-Sperry, L., Bates, C. A., & Lean, E. R. (2009). Sexual harassment at work: A decade (plus) of progress. *Journal of Management, 35,* 503–536; Bowes-Sperry, L., & Tata, J. (1999). A multiperspective framework of sexual harassment: Reviewing two decades of research. In G. N. Powell (Ed.), *Handbook of gender and work* (pp. 263–280). Thousand Oaks, CA: Sage.

6. U.S. Equal Employment Opportunity Commission. (2009). *Code of Federal Regulations, Title 29—Labor, Part 1604—Guidelines on discrimination because of sex, Section 1604.11—Sexual harassment.* Retrieved October 27, 2009, from http://www.eeoc.gov.

7. Collier, R. (1995). *Combating sexual harassment in the workplace.* Buckingham, UK: Open University Press; Webb.

8. Conte, A. (1997). Legal theories of sexual harassment. In W. O'Donohue (Ed.), *Sexual harassment: Theory, research, and treatment* (pp. 50–83). Boston: Allyn & Bacon; Meritor Savings Bank, FSB v. Vinson, 477 U.S. 57, 40 FEP Cases 1822 (1986); Oncale v. Sundowner Offshore Services, Inc., 118 S. Ct. 998 (1998); Terpstra, D. E., & Baker, D. D. (1992). Outcomes of federal court decisions on sexual harassment. *Academy of Management Journal, 35,* 181–190; Pierce, C. A., Muslin, I. S., Dudley, C. M., & Aguinis, H. (2008). From charm to harm: A content-analytic review of sexual harassment court cases involving workplace romance. *Management Research, 6,* 27–45.

9. Wiener, R. L., Hackney, A., Kadela, K., Rauch, S., Seib, H., Warren, L., & Hurt, L. E. (2002). The fit and implementation of sexual harassment law to workplace evaluations. *Journal of Applied Psychology, 87,* 747–764; Wiener, R. L., & Hurt, L. E. (2000). How do people evaluate social sexual conduct at work? A psycholegal model. *Journal of Applied Psychology, 85,* 75–85; Blumenthal, J. A. (1998). The reasonable woman standard: A meta-analytic review of gender differences in perceptions of sexual harassment. *Law and Human Behavior, 22,* 33–57; Gutek, B. A., & O'Connor, M. (1995). The empirical basis for the reasonable woman standard. *Journal of Social Issues, 5*(1), 151–166.

10. Berdahl, J. L., & Aquino, K. (2009). Sexual behavior at work: Fun or folly? *Journal of Applied Psychology, 94,* 34–47; Bernstein.

11. Gruber, J. E., Smith, M., & Kauppinen-Toropainen, K. (1996). Sexual harassment types and severity: Linking research and policy. In M. S. Stockdale (Ed.), *Sexual harassment in the workplace: Perspectives, frontiers, and response strategies* (pp. 151–173). Thousand Oaks, CA: Sage.

12. O'Connor, M., Gutek, B. A., Stockdale, M., Geer, T. M., & Melançon, R. (2004). Explaining sexual harassment judgments: Looking beyond gender of the rater. *Law and Human Behavior, 28,* 69–95.; Rotundo, M., Nguyen, D-H., & Sackett, P. R. (2001). A meta-analytic review of gender differences in perceptions of sexual harassment. *Journal of Applied Psychology, 86,* 914–922; Collins, E. G. C., & Blodgett, T. B. (1981). Sexual harassment: Some see it . . . some won't. *Harvard Business Review, 59*(2), 76–95.

13. O'Leary-Kelly, Bowes-Sperry, Bates, & Lean.

14. Browne, K. R. (2006). Sex, power, and dominance: The evolutionary psychology of sexual harassment. *Managerial and Decision Economics, 27,* 145–158.

15. Berdahl, J. L. (2007). Harassment based on sex: Protecting social status in the context of gender hierarchy. *Academy of Management Review, 32,* 641–658; Bourgeois, M. J., & Perkins, J. (2003). A test of evolutionary and sociocultural explanations of reactions to sexual harassment. *Sex Roles, 49,* 343–351.

16. Chamberlain, L. J., Crowley, M., Tope, D., & Hodson, R. (2008). Sexual harassment in organizational context. *Work and Occupations, 35,* 262–295; Ilies, Hauserman, Schwochau, & Stibal.

17. Gutek, B. A., & Done, R. S. (2001). Sexual harassment. In R. K. Unger (Ed.), *Handbook of the psychology of women and gender* (pp. 367–387). New York: Wiley; Chamberlain, Crowley, Tope, & Hodson; Berdahl, J. L. (2007). The sexual harassment of uppity women. *Journal of Applied Psychology, 92,* 425–437.

18. Gutek, B. A. (1985). *Sex and the workplace: The impact of sexual behavior and harassment on women, men, and organizations.* San Francisco: Jossey-Bass.

19. Pryor, J. B. (1987). Sexual harassment proclivities in men. *Sex Roles, 17,* 269–290; Perry, E. L., Schmidtke, J. M., & Kulik, C. T. (1998). Propensity to sexually harass: An exploration of gender differences. *Sex Roles, 38,* 443–460; Fiske, S. T., & Glick, P. (1995). Ambivalence and stereotypes cause sexual harassment: A theory with implications for organizational change. *Journal of Social Issues, 51*(1), 97–115.

20. U.S. Merit Systems Protection Board.

21. Willness, C. R., Steel, P., & Lee, K. (2007). A meta-analysis of the antecedents and consequences of workplace sexual harassment. *Personnel Psychology, 60,* 127–162; Bowling, N. A., & Beehr, T. A. (2006). Workplace harassment from the victim's perspective: A theoretical model and meta-analysis. *Journal of Applied Psychology, 91,* 998–1012; Raver, J. A., & Gelfand, M. J. (2005). Beyond the individual victim: Linking sexual harassment, team processes, and team performance. *Academy of Management Journal, 48,* 387–400.

22. Bowes-Sperry, L., & O'Leary-Kelly, A. M. (2005). To act or not to act: The dilemma faced by observers of sexual harassment. *Academy of Management Review, 30,* 288–306; Bowes-Sperry, L., & Powell, G. N. (1999). Observers' reactions to social-sexual behavior at work: An ethical decision making perspective. *Journal of Management, 25,* 779–802; Bowes-Sperry, L., & Powell, G. N. (1996). Sexual harassment as a moral issue: An ethical decision-making perspective. In M. S. Stockdale (Ed.), *Sexual harassment in the workplace: Perspectives, frontiers, and response strategies* (pp. 105–124). Thousand Oaks, CA: Sage.

23. Gettman, H. J., & Gelfand, M. J. (2007). When the customer shouldn't be king: Antecedents and consequences of sexual harassment by clients and customers. *Journal of Applied Psychology, 92,* 757–770.

24. This section is primarily based on Powell, G. N., & Foley, S. (1999). Romantic relationships in organizational settings: Something to talk about. In G. N. Powell (Ed.), *Handbook of gender and work* (pp. 281–304). Thousand Oaks,

CA: Sage; Powell, G. N., & Foley, S. (1998). Something to talk about: Romantic relationships in organizational settings. *Journal of Management, 24,* 421–448.

25. Sternberg, R. J. (1998). *Cupid's arrow: The course of love through time.* Cambridge, UK: Cambridge University Press; Sternberg, R. J. (1986). A triangular theory of love. *Psychological Review, 93,* 119–135.

26. Pierce, C. A., Byrne, D., & Aguinis, H. (1996). Attraction in organizations: A model of workplace romance. *Journal of Organizational Behavior, 17,* 5–32.

27. Dillard, J. P., & Miller, K. I. (1988). Intimate relationships in task environments. In S. Duck (Ed.), *Handbook of personal relationships* (pp. 449–465). Chichester, UK: Wiley; Quinn, R. (1977). Coping with cupid: The formation, impact, and management of romantic relationships in organizations. *Administrative Science Quarterly, 22,* 30–45; Pierce, Byrne, & Aguinis.

28. Quinn; Pierce, Byrne, & Aguinis.

29. Gurchiek, K. (2007, February 13). Women more leery than men about workplace romances. *HR News.* Retrieved October 26, 2009, from http://www .shrm.org/Publications/HRNews; Powell, G. N. (1986). What do tomorrow's managers think about sexual intimacy in the workplace? *Business Horizons, 29*(4), 30–35.

30. Pierce, C. A., & Aguinis, H. (2003). Romantic relationships in organizations: A test of a model of formation and impact factors. *Management Research, 1,* 161–169; Pierce, Byrne, & Aguinis.

31. Mainiero, L. A. (1989). *Office romance: Love, power, and sex in the workplace.* New York: Rawson Associates; Gutek (1985); Riach, K., & Wilson, F. (2007). Don't screw the crew: Exploring the rules of engagement in organizational romance. *British Journal of Management, 18,* 79–92.

32. Dillard, J. P. (1987). Close relationships at work: Perceptions of the motives and performance of relational participants. *Journal of Social and Personal Relationships, 4,* 179–193.

33. Mainiero, L. A. (1986). A review and analysis of power dynamics in organizational romances. *Academy of Management Review, 11,* 750–762.

34. Mainiero (1989).

35. Berscheid, E. (2010). Love in the fourth dimension. *Annual Review of Psychology, 61,* 1–25.

36. Pierce, C. A., & Aguinis, H. (1997). Bridging the gap between romantic relationships and sexual harassment in organizations. *Journal of Organizational Behavior, 18,* 197–200.

37. Friskopp, A., & Silverstein, S. (1995). *Straight jobs, gay lives: Gay and lesbian professionals, the Harvard Business School, and the American workplace.* New York: Scribner; Mainiero (1989).

38. Pierce, Byrne, & Aguinis; Dillard & Miller; Parks; Bandler; Hymowitz.

39. Clawson, J. G., & Kram, K. E. (1984). Managing cross-gender mentoring. *Business Horizons, 2* (3), 22–32.

40. Shellenbarger, S. (2003, November 13). Co-workers can wreck a marriage: At the office, divorce is contagious. *Wall Street Journal,* p. D1; Åberg, Y.

(2003). *Social interactions: Studies of contextual effects and endogenous processes.* Doctoral dissertation, Stockholm University; Dillard & Miller; Quinn; Pierce, Byrne, & Aguinis.

41. Powell, G. N. (2001). Workplace romances between senior-level executives and lower-level employees: An issue of work disruption and gender. *Human Relations, 54,* 1519–1544.

42. Foley, S., & Powell, G. N. (1999). Not all is fair in love and work: Coworkers' preferences for and responses to managerial interventions regarding workplace romances. *Journal of Organizational Behavior, 20,* 1043–1056; Powell (2001).

43. Bell, M. P., Quick, J. C., & Cycyota, C. S. (2002). Assessment and prevention of sexual harassment of employees: An applied guide to creating healthy organizations. *International Journal of Selection and Assessment, 10,* 160–167; Gutek, B. A. (1997). Sexual harassment policy initiatives. In W. O'Donohue (Ed.), *Sexual harassment: Theory, research, and treatment* (pp. 185–198). Boston: Allyn & Bacon.

44. Powell, G. N. (1983). Sexual harassment: Confronting the issue of definition. *Business Horizons, 26*(4), 24-28.

45. Peirce, E., Smolinski, C. A., & Rosen, B. (1998). Why sexual harassment complaints fall on deaf ears. *Academy of Management Executive, 12*(3), 41–54.

46. U.S. Merit Systems Protection Board; Yagil, D., Karnieli-Miller, O., Eisikovits, Z., & Enosh, G. (2006). Is that a "no"? The interpretation of responses to unwanted sexual attention. *Sex Roles, 54,* 251–260; Malamut, A. B., & Offermann, L. R. (2001). Coping with sexual harassment: Personal, environmental, and cognitive determinants. *Journal of Applied Psychology, 86,* 1152–1166; Knapp, D. E., Faley, R. H., Ekeberg, S. E., & Dubois, C. L. Z. (1997). Determinants of target responses to sexual harassment: A conceptual framework. *Academy of Management Review, 22,* 687–729; Rowe, M. P. (1996). Dealing with harassment: A systems approach. In M. S. Stockdale (Ed.), *Sexual harassment in the workplace: Perspectives, frontiers, and coping strategies* (pp. 241–271). Thousand Oaks, CA: Sage.

47. Rowe, M. P. (1981). Dealing with sexual harassment. *Harvard Business Review, 59*(3), 42–46.

48. Rowe (1981); Rowe (1996).

49. MacKinnon, C. A. (1979). *Sexual harassment of working women: A case of sex discrimination.* New Haven, CT: Yale University Press; Mead, M. (1980). A proposal: We need taboos on sex at work. In D. A. Neugarten and J. M. Shafritz (Eds.), *Sexuality in organizations: Romantic and coercive behaviors at work* (pp. 53–56). Oak Park, IL: Moore; Hymowitz, C., & Pollock, E. J. (1998, February 4). Corporate affairs: The one clear line in interoffice romance has become blurred. *Wall Street Journal,* pp. A1, A8.

50. Parks.

51. Quinn.

52. Mainiero (1986); Quinn.

CHAPTER 8

Managing the Work–Family Interface

Jennifer's Story

> *[One] Saturday, Jennifer (not her real name) held a fiftieth birthday party for her mother. She worked for several months in arranging the party and in getting her family to agree to the arrangements. She lined up the restaurant at which the party would be held. She arranged the group gifts, prepared for the follow-up party to be held at her house afterwards, the whole works. It was going to be a special day for Jennifer, her mother, and everyone else involved. Early on that Saturday morning, Jennifer received a call from her boss and was told that she had to come to work that day. When she began to describe her plans for the day, she was cut off and told, "The board doesn't want excuses. The board wants work." The fiftieth birthday party was held, but without Jennifer present. She spent the whole Saturday at work. According to Jennifer, it wasn't even an emergency that led her to be called in.*[1]

Stories like Jennifer's are increasingly common in today's workplace. Many organizations expect their employees, especially managers and professionals who are not bound by labor contracts, to put work first at all times. They do not display even a minimal amount of concern for employees' needs outside of work. The combination of electronic communication technologies such as e-mail and the

Internet and portable devices such as smart phones to access these technologies have made it possible for such organizations to pressure employees who wish to advance in their careers to be available at all times electronically no matter where they are physically. Many employees feel compelled to log in to their e-mail accounts late at night to scroll through and respond to messages received just to maintain the impression that they are on call at all times. As a result, even when at home, they are spending less time with their families.

Of course, not everyone wants to spend more time with their families. Some people relish what may be called **extreme jobs**—jobs that involve 60 hours or more per week, fast-paced work under tight deadlines, 24/7 availability, work-related events held outside normal work hours, frequent travel, and the like. Work is the primary source of satisfaction in life for many people, from young professionals to senior executives. A book titled *Better Than Sex: How a Whole Generation Got Hooked on Work* described the appeal of work as follows: "Where once sexual attraction and relationships drove humans, many now define themselves through work. From work comes [not only] money and the capacity to live and enjoy consumer items but also status, affirmation, and self-definition, especially if you are winning inside the system. . . . Survival of the species may have been about sex, but survival for corporate man or women is about work, to the exclusion, if necessary, of everything else."[2]

However, most people do not want to exclude everything other than work from their lives. Instead, they seek a sense of **work–family balance**, which comes from having their effectiveness and satisfaction in work and family roles be consistent with the value they attach to each role. If their work role is highly important to them, they want both to achieve a high level of work performance and to derive a high amount of satisfaction from work; if their work role is less important to them, being effective in it or satisfied with it is less critical to their work–family balance. In the same vein, if family is highly important in their life, people want both to be effective (however they define "effective") as a family member and to derive a high amount of satisfaction from their family role.[3]

Balancing work and family does not mean devoting equal time to one's work and family roles. Two people might distribute their time between work and family roles identically but differ in the sense of balance they experience. It also does not mean being equally involved in the two roles; one person may achieve a strong sense of balance from being primarily involved in family, whereas another person may achieve the same sense of balance from being primarily involved in work. Instead, the notion of work–family balance represents satisfaction with how things are going in one's work role in relation to how things are going in one's family role.

Most people would like to have some degree of control over how they allocate time and energy to the various roles in their lives, which may include worker, spouse, parent, child, part-time student, community service volunteer, and so on. To do so, they need to work for an employer that at least acknowledges that they have a life outside of work. If this is not the case, people may quit jobs working for others to start their own business just for the purpose of gaining control. Whether people work for themselves or others, they need to manage the **work–family interface**— how their work role influences their family role and vice versa.

This chapter is about how to manage the work–family interface to achieve a sense of balance, and what employers can do to help. First, we consider exactly what is meant by the term "family." As we shall see, even single employees have a family life that is likely to be important to them. Second, we consider the challenges involved in juggling work and family roles and how individuals' experiences in one role may influence their experiences in the other role, both positively and negatively. Third, we consider what constitutes "success" for individuals in their work and family lives. Fourth, we review how family factors influence important decisions individuals make in their work role that determine the nature of their work–family interface. We consider the role played by employers in shaping their employees' work–family interface, including different kinds of work–family programs and the impact of the organizational culture. Finally, we offer suggestions for how women and men may enhance their own sense of balance and manage the work–family interface successfully.

Throughout the chapter, we consider sex differences in various aspects of how people manage the work–family interface. According to gender roles and stereotypes, the linkage between sex and the work–family interface is straightforward. As discussed in Chapter 3, **gender roles,** consisting of beliefs about what role behaviors are appropriate for members of each sex, set norms for the roles that men and women should emphasize: Women's proper place is in the home and men's in the workplace. **Gender stereotypes,** consisting of beliefs about what psychological traits are characteristic of members of each sex, set expectations for the behaviors that men and women will exhibit: Women are more likely to exhibit "feminine" traits (e.g., compassion, nurturance, sensitivity to the needs of others) that are viewed as particularly important in the family domain, whereas men are more likely to exhibit "masculine" traits" (e.g., aggressiveness, decisiveness, independence) that are viewed as particularly important in the work domain. Both gender roles and stereotypes dictate that (1) men will regard their work roles as more important and their family roles as less important than women do and that (2) both men and women will make decisions about how to allocate their time and energy between work and family roles accordingly.[4]

However, given societal changes, the linkage between sex and the work–family interface no longer seems so simple. As the proportion of women in the labor force has increased, the traditional family structure of male breadwinner and female homemaker has given way to dual-career partnerships, single parenthood, and other family structures. Both men and women are less likely to endorse traditional gender roles, with the drop-off especially pronounced among men; now there is no statistical difference between men's and women's views. In addition, the most recent entrants to the labor force are the least likely to endorse gender roles. In times like these, sex differences in how individuals manage the interface between their work and family roles are no longer straightforward.[5]

We Are Family

To understand the work–family interface, we need to consider the nature of individuals' family lives. For example, if family life was fully determined by three variables—marital status (married or single), parental status (children or no children), and employment status of the spouse (employed or not employed)—there would be six possible combinations:[6]

1. Single, no children

2. Married, no children, spouse employed

3. Married, no children, spouse not employed

4. Single, children

5. Married, children, spouse employed

6. Married, children, spouse not employed

However, this categorization scheme for family life is much too simple. There are additional variations of marital status such as divorced, separated, widowed, or remarried. Due to court or legislative action, marriage has become an option in some states and countries for same-sex as well as opposite-sex couples. Single individuals may have a significant other who is as important as a spouse to them; unmarried couples also have family lives. Couples, married or unmarried, may or may not live together. The numbers and ages of children vary, of course, as well as their places of residence; blended families with stepchildren are prevalent. Younger children require different care than older children, and the rearing of multiple children is more demanding than that of a sole child. The employment status of the spouse or significant other also varies. Spouses and significant others differ in income contributed to the household and time and energy devoted to their work and family roles. Other family members such as parents, siblings, and extended family may also play important roles in people's lives.

Table 8.1 reports parental employment in U.S. families with children. The most prevalent combination of family and employment status is the dual-career couple, a married couple in which both parents are employed; 43% of families with children under age 18 and 40% with children under age 6 fall into this category. The second-most prevalent combination is the married couple in which only the father is employed; 21% of families with children under age 18 and 27% with children under age 6 fall into this category. This is the traditional family structure in which the father serves as breadwinner and the mother as homemaker. The third most prevalent combination is the female-headed family in which the mother is employed; 17% of families with children under age 18 and 14% with children under age 6 fall into this category.

The family structures of women and men differ. Women are more likely to be single parents than are men. In married couples, women are less likely to be the sole breadwinner than are men. Even at top management levels, there is a sex difference in family structure. As women assume managerial positions at increasingly higher levels, they are less likely to be married or to have children than are men with equivalent responsibilities. In general, the more successful the man's career in objective terms, the more likely he is to have a spouse and children. The opposite holds true for women.[7]

Family structures are becoming increasingly differentiated as the traditional pattern of male breadwinner and female homemaker gives way to dual-career couples, single-parent households, and other alternatives. Even the institution of marriage, traditionally the cornerstone of family life, is in flux as an increasing proportion of children are raised outside of marriage

Table 8.1   Employment Status of Parents in U.S. Families With Children

Type of Family	Own Children Under Age 18 Percentage of Total	Own Children Under Age 6 Percentage of Total
Married-couple families:		
Both parents employed	43	40
Mother employed, not father	4	3
Father employed, not mother	21	27
Neither parent employed	2	2
Families maintained by women:		
Mother employed	17	14
Mother not employed	7	8
Families maintained by men:		
Father employed	5	5
Father not employed	1	1
TOTALS:	**100%**	**100%**

SOURCE: U.S. Department of Labor, Bureau of Labor Statistics. (2009a). *Employment characteristics of families* in 2008 (computed from data in Table 4). Retrieved May 27, 2009, from http://www.bls.gov.

NOTE: No spouse was present in families maintained by women and families maintained by men. Own children include sons, daughters, stepchildren, and adopted children.

and the opportunity to marry is increasingly extended to same-sex as well as opposite-sex couples. This is an era of increasing family diversity.[8]

However, the workplace does not equally accommodate all types of family diversity. Individuals may be subject to biases in the workplace based on their marital status, parental status, and other dimensions of family diversity. For example, the stereotype of the workaholic single person with no family life is an example of **singlism,** or the pervasive stereotyping that single people experience in everyday life. Most single childless (or "child-free") employees are part of a family that may include parents, grandparents, siblings, aunts and uncles, cousins, and other extended family members. However, most corporate work–family programs focus on the family-related needs of married employees with children.[9]

Further, when companies offer paid maternity and paternity leaves for new parents, new fathers are much more hesitant to take advantage of the opportunity than new mothers because they fear that they will be stigmatized for doing so. Married men fear that their careers will suffer if they request a parental leave because they will not appear to be putting work first in their lives, thereby violating the male gender role. In contrast, married women know that they will be more likely to receive the approval of others if they request a parental leave because such a request is consistent with the female gender role.[10]

On the other hand, married women are offered fewer job opportunities requiring relocation, including international assignments, than married men. Job opportunities that require relocation enhance employees' development by providing them the chance to polish their skills, work on high-visibility projects, and gain exposure in a different geographic location. Organizational decision makers tend to assume that women will conform to the female gender role by being less likely to accept relocation offers than men because such a stance is less disruptive to their families. In reality, women do not express less of a willingness to relocate domestically or to accept international assignments than men. However, because they are perceived to be less willing to move their families, women experience lower geographic mobility than men, which restricts their career success.[11]

Thus, individuals' family status, often in combination with their sex, may be perceived to influence or may actually influence work-related decisions about them to their disadvantage. Although we live in an age of increasing family diversity, we do not live in an age of full acceptance of family diversity by all parties concerned. This lack of acceptance of the new range of family diversity presents a challenge for women and men who do not conform to their respective gender roles in managing the work–family interface.

A Juggling Act

There are different schools of thought about the linkage between work and family roles. According to an optimistic view, people benefit from juggling their work and family roles. When people participate heavily in multiple life roles (e.g., engaged in employment outside the home while caring for those within), they are able to avoid the worst aspects of any one role. Their involvement in one role enhances their functioning in the other. As a result, they have a heightened sense of well-being and subjective career success. According to a pessimistic view, people suffer from trying to juggle their work and family roles. When people attempt to participate in both work and family roles to any significant extent, they face an inevitable time bind. Either they flee home in response to the pressures or appeals of work, or they sacrifice career success to devote themselves primarily to their families.[12]

The reality for many families lies somewhere between these optimistic and pessimistic views. A "trade-offs" view suggests that there are benefits to juggling work and family roles as well as costs. The challenge for individuals of juggling the two roles then becomes to minimize the costs while maximizing the benefits.

Work and Family as Enemies

According to a **conflict perspective of the work–family interface**, individuals' work and family roles are inevitable "enemies" and continually interfere with each other. Individuals who attempt to juggle work and family roles are likely to experience some degree of **work–family conflict** as a result of simultaneous pressures from work and family roles that are mutually incompatible. Such conflict may come about because work interferes with family (work-to-family conflict), such as when long hours at work are required, or because family interferes with work (family-to-work conflict), such as when a child is sick and needs to stay home from school. Work–family conflict has considerable negative consequences for employees, their families, and their employers. High levels of work–family conflict produce feelings of dissatisfaction and distress within both roles that detract from well-being and life satisfaction. Three types of work–family conflict may occur for individuals: time-based, strain-based, and behavior-based.[13]

Time-based conflict results from the finite amount of time that is available to handle both work and family roles. Time spent working generally cannot be devoted to family activities and vice versa. Parents experience more time-based conflict than nonparents, parents of younger children more than parents of older children, and parents of large families more than parents of small families. In dual-career families, mothers are likely to experience more time-based conflict than fathers. This is because married mothers spend more time with their children and more time on household chores than married fathers do. This gap has narrowed as the proportion of women in the labor force, especially in managerial and professional jobs, has increased. Fathers have significantly increased the amount of time they spend with their children, and they have taken over more of the household chores as well. However, fathers who want to become more involved in family life tend to turn more to the nursery than to the kitchen or laundry room. One observer concluded, "Housework remains the last frontier that men want to settle."[14]

Strain-based conflict results when strain in one role spills over into the other role. Family strains may decrease performance at work and negatively affect objective career success. On the other hand, strain at work may affect one's behavior as a parent or spouse.

Behavior-based conflict occurs when incompatible behaviors are required for work and family roles, such as aggressiveness and objectivity at work and warmth and nurturance at home. Managers who adhere to the think manager—think masculine stereotype, whether female or male, may feel caught between the emotional detachment exhibited at work and the emotional expressiveness expected at home. "Shifting gears" between work and home is required to avoid this conflict.

Work-family conflict increases for individuals when the demands placed on them in either the work or family role increase. The greatest potential for conflict occurs when individuals face simultaneous demands to participate in both a work and a family activity and neither activity can be rescheduled. In the opening passage, Jennifer faced this kind of situation when she was forced to choose between an important work activity (emergency overtime work) and an important family activity (mother's birthday party). She made the difficult choice of going to work and missing the party. As a result, she experienced high work-to-family conflict that day and felt terrible about it. In general, when faced with conflicting demands, individuals are likely to choose the activity about which others (e.g., boss, spouse) are pressuring them most. They are also likely to choose the activity in the role that is most central to their identity.[15]

Work–family conflict may be alleviated by **social support** that people receive in both their work and family role for their involvement in the other role. Social support may be both tangible (e.g., information, advice, assistance) and intangible (e.g., affirmation, affection, trust). In addition, social support may be expressed as a willingness to reschedule activities so one can avoid potential work–family conflict. For example, if Jennifer's boss had been willing to reschedule or reassign weekend work so she could have attended her mother's 50th birthday party, this would have indicated that the organization supported her participation in an important family activity and would have resolved the conflict.[16]

Employees' experiences with work–family conflict and social support that may alleviate it differ across national cultures. For example, Chinese employees are more likely to have their parents as live-ins or dependents than U.S. employees. In addition, most adult children who do not reside with their parents live close to them. This high proximity facilitates the exchange of care between elderly parents and their married children. Elderly parents in China not only are more dependent economically and emotionally on their adult children than are their U.S. counterparts, but also are more important providers of child care and household assistance. Although the net amounts of work–family conflict felt by Chinese compared to U.S. employees may be similar, dual-career couples in China experience both greater stress from having to provide for their parents and greater support from their parents than dual-career couples in the United States.[17]

National culture influences the extent to which men's and women's experiences of work–family conflict differ. Cultures differ in **gender egalitarianism,** or the extent to which they minimize gender roles and stereotypes and promote equality of the sexes. Gender roles and stereotypes are more likely to be emphasized in less egalitarian cultures. As a result, members of cultures that are less egalitarian exhibit more pronounced sex differences in how they manage the work–family interface than members of cultures that are more egalitarian. In low-egalitarian cultures, women are likely to be more involved in their family roles and less involved in their work roles than men, leading to their experiencing higher levels of family-to-work conflict and lower levels of work-to-family conflict.[18]

Work and Family as Allies

According to an **enrichment perspective of the work–family interface,** individuals' work and family roles may be "allies" that continually enrich or enhance each other. **Work–family enrichment** is defined as the extent to which individuals' experiences in one role, work or family, improve their quality of life in the other role, either by improving their performance in the other role or by improving their positive affect or feelings about it. Work–family enrichment has considerable positive consequences for employees, their families, and their employers, including high job satisfaction and organizational commitment as well as high family satisfaction and good mental and physical health. As for conflict, enrichment may be present in either direction, work to family or family to work.[19]

Work–family enrichment takes place when resources generated in one role are applied in a way that promotes high performance or positive affect in the other role. Several types of resources may serve this purpose. **Skills** acquired in one's family or work role such as interpersonal skills and the ability to multitask may enhance one's effectiveness in the other role. **Perspectives** obtained in one role such as the importance of self-direction for personal development or respect for individual differences may also be applied in the other role. **Psychological and physical resources** developed or nurtured in one role can increase performance in the other role. For example, self-esteem, confidence, and good mental and physical health that are generated from positive experiences and attention to physical fitness in one's personal life may promote work performance and positive work-related attitudes.[20]

Individuals may also generate **social-capital resources,** or tangible support in the form of information, advice, or assistance in one role that benefit the other role. For example, information provided by an employee's spouse may be useful to the employee's career, and a colleague may use his or her clout to help one's child gain admission to the colleague's alma mater. **Flexibility** in the work or family role may also enrich performance in the other role. For example, flexibility in the work role as a result of flextime work arrangements may help an individual to meet family responsibilities better, and flexibility in the family role as a result of a spouse's handling child care may help him or her to perform more effectively on the job. Finally, **material resources** gathered in one role, such as bonus income from employment and inheritance or gifts from family members, may be used to enrich the other role.

Women experience greater work-to-family enrichment resulting from the application of nonmaterial resources than men. As discussed in Chapter 3, consistent with gender stereotypes, women tend to be higher than men in femininity, a psychological trait that places a high emphasis on interpersonal relationships. As a result, women may be especially committed to and knowledgeable about meeting their families' needs. Because they feel greater responsibility than men for the emotional well-being of their families, women may be particularly motivated to transfer nonmaterial resources acquired at work to enhance their families' well-being. However, because men earn higher pay than women to bring to their families, they are higher in work-to-family enrichment resulting from the application of material resources. Also, as for work–family conflict, sex differences in work–family enrichment tend to be greatest in national cultures that exhibit low gender egalitarianism in their endorsement of gender roles and stereotypes.[21]

Work and Family as Segmented or Integrated

Individuals vary in their preferences for segmenting or integrating their work and family roles. **Segmenters** prefer to keep these roles disconnected from each other by maintaining rigid boundaries between work and family. In contrast, **integrators** prefer to have these roles interwoven in their lives by merging or blending various aspects of work and family. The extent to which individuals prefer to segment work from family (e.g., by not taking unfinished work home) may differ from the extent to which they prefer to segment family from work (e.g., by not accepting routine family calls in the office). We will use the term **segmentation preferences** to refer to the extent to which individuals prefer to segment each role from the other.[22]

Segmenting work and family roles may have both advantages and disadvantages. Individuals who are successful in segmenting work from family are able to keep work demands from interrupting the time they devote to family, turn off work stressors when in their family roles, and leave behaviors at the office that would be dysfunctional at home. As a result, they experience less work-to-family conflict than individuals who are less successful at segmenting work from family or less inclined to do so. However, they are also less likely to transfer positive affect from work to family or see the relevance of applying skills or perspectives developed at work to their family roles, resulting in their experiencing less work-to-family enrichment. In the same vein, individuals who successfully segment from family from work restrict the amount of both family-to-work conflict and family-to-work enrichment they experience. Thus, there are trade-offs involved in the segmentation or integration of work and family roles.[23]

Sex differences are likely to emerge in individuals' segmentation preferences. According to gender roles, men should emphasize the primacy of work in their lives by segmenting their family roles from their work roles (e.g., by not accepting calls from family members at work) but not their work roles from their family roles (e.g., by bringing work home and being on call 24/7). In contrast, women should emphasize the primacy of family in their lives by segmenting their work roles from their family roles (e.g., by not bringing work home and restricting their availability outside of normal work hours) but not their family roles from their work roles (e.g., by accepting and initiating family calls at work).[24]

In conclusion, individuals may have negative experiences from juggling their work and family roles that result in work–family conflict (*work and family as enemies*), or they may have positive experiences that result in work–family enrichment (*work and family as allies*). They may experience both conflict and enrichment in different situations and at different points in time, and they may experience each in the direction of work to family or family to work. If they *disconnect* their work and family roles from each other (*work and family as segmented*), they will experience neither conflict nor enrichment.

The Meaning of Success

Individuals may experience success in both their work lives and family lives. In addition, they may be successful in achieving a satisfactory sense of balance between their work and family lives. However, as we shall see, the term "success" needs to be used with caution.

Career or work success is the more familiar concept. Both objective and subjective measures may be used to assess career success. In most research studies, **objective career success** is measured by variables such as earnings, level of position in the organizational hierarchy, and rate of advancement or promotion. When objective variables are used to measure career success, people's careers are deemed more successful when they receive more pay, hold positions at higher levels, and advance at a faster rate.[25]

In contrast, **subjective career success** is measured by variables that reflect individuals' satisfaction with various aspects of their work roles, including their current jobs, potential for advancement, job security, pay, relationships with coworkers, and so on. When subjective variables are used to measure career success, people's careers may be considered successful at any level in the organizational hierarchy, no matter how much they are paid and how rapid their advancement. What counts is that they are satisfied with where they are and with their future prospects.

Objective and subjective career success are positively related; people who achieve greater objective career success tend to be more satisfied with their careers. However, career success in objective terms does not necessarily lead to career satisfiaction. The factors that lead to objective career success may be very different from those that lead to subjective career success.[26]

Women and men tend to focus on different types of measures in assessing their career success, with men focusing more on objective measures and women focusing more on subjective measures. Men tend to regard **status-based satisfiers** such as earning a high salary, getting promoted faster than their peers, and rapidly advancing to higher organizational levels as more important than women. In contrast, women tend to regard socioemotional satisfiers such as having supportive coworkers, working as part of a team, and helping others at work as more important than men. Men's greater reliance on objective measures of success that emphasize "getting ahead" in organizations is consistent with the male gender role. When men achieve greater objective success, they are better able to fulfill their traditional responsibilities as breadwinners for their families. In contrast, women's reliance on subjective measures of success is consistent with the female gender role. Women's focus on their feelings about their careers corresponds with the stereotype of women as expressive. In addition, the high value that women place on positive interpersonal relationships necessitates the use of subjective measures. The quality of relationships is best captured by subjective, not objective, measures.[27]

The notion of "family success" is analogous to career success. We can envision objective measures that could serve as indicators of this type of success, such as marital (married or not married) or relationship (significant other or no significant other) status, number of children, number of sports in which children played (and their success in goals or points scored), prestige of children's colleges, number of family members who are friends on social networking Web sites such as Facebook, number of photos posted by family members on social networking Web sites in which one is tagged, and so on. However, measuring family success using only such variables would be absurd. Family success *has* to be measured subjectively. Satisfaction with family, which focuses on the perceived quality of family life, is more telling than objective measures of family status. In the same vein, satisfaction with career, defined in terms of its perceived quality, may be more important than objective career success as measured by promotions, salary, and the like.

The term *success* has been used in considering family life to make a point about what constitutes success for individuals. The traditional "male model" of career success emphasizes objective measures and focuses on work life. In contrast, what may be called a "female model" of career success emphasizes subjective measures and includes consideration of family life as well as work life. This is not to say that all men define success solely by objective measures or that all women define success solely by subjective measures. Instead, traditional notions of career success need to be expanded to include concepts that have been associated with how women as well as men view success.[28]

When we examine the actual levels of career success achieved by men and women, we find evidence of both sex similarities and sex differences. Several studies have tracked the career success of male compared to female MBA graduates who earned their degrees from the same institutions during the same period of time. These studies have found no sex difference in the level of subjective career success achieved. Over time, as their common educational experience recedes, female MBA graduates are no more or less satisfied with their careers than their male counterparts. However, the same studies have found a sex difference in the level of objective career success achieved as time passes. Eventually, female MBA graduates lag behind their male counterparts in indicators of objective career success such as income and managerial level.[29]

The phenomenon that women express no more dissatisfaction with their careers than men despite the fact that they hold jobs with less pay and authority has been called the **paradox of the contented female worker.** What would account for this paradox? Working men and women may experience similar levels of subjective career success because they perceive little discrepancy between what they obtain from their jobs in objective terms and what they feel entitled to obtain. If women *expect* less objective career success than men, perhaps they will be just as satisfied as men are when their expectations are met. In addition, if women *value* objective career success less than men, they will place less emphasis on it when subjectively evaluating their own success. The paradox of the contented female worker has been observed in occupations such as lawyers, human service workers, hospitality managers, and Protestant clergy and in part-time MBA students employed in full-time jobs across occupations.[30]

Issues of objective and subjective success also apply to business owners. Women-owned firms tend to rank lower than men-owned firms on measures of objective success such as sales, income, rate of growth, and business performance compared with competitors. However, there is no sex difference in business owners' subjective success. Despite differences in objective success, male and female business owners are similarly satisfied with the success of their business, supporting the **paradox of the contented female business owner.** Overall, female business owners place less value on achieving business success in traditional terms than male business owners. Instead, they are more concerned with the quality of their relationships with employees and contributions to society.[31]

It is not for us to say what being successful should mean for individuals in their work or family lives. However, it is important to recognize that men's and women's personal definitions of what constitutes success tend to differ. Sex differences in the meaning of success are likely to be reflected in the decisions individuals make in managing the work-family interface.

Work–Family Decisions

Throughout their lives, individuals make a stream of decisions in their work and family roles. **Work–family decisions** consist of decisions in one role, work or family, that are influenced by factors in the other role. Although they do not have full control over their lives and are subject to work and family pressures, people play an active role in shaping their lives. Earlier in the chapter, we examined work–family phenomena such as conflict and enrichment that individuals may experience as they manage the work–family interface. In this section of the chapter, we selectively examine work–family decisions that may influence the extent and direction of conflict and enrichment that individuals experience. In particular, we focus on how family factors influence the decisions individuals make at work.[32]

In general, individuals make three broad types of decisions regarding their work domain—role entry, participation, and exit decisions—that may be influenced by factors in their family domain. **Role entry decisions** involve choices about whether to enter a particular work role. **Role participation decisions** involve choices regarding how one engages in a particular work role. **Role exit decisions** involve choices regarding leaving a particular work role. We next consider examples of each type of work–family decision.[33]

Decision About Whether to Work Part-Time or Full-Time

The decision about whether to seek full-time or part-time employment represents a role entry decision. Part-time jobs are in the minority in the workplace, but their proportion is significant; the proportion of all jobs that are part-time is 17% in the United States and about 20% to 25% in most countries. Part-time work offers many workers the opportunity for a better balance between work and family. It can help to lower work-family conflict and increase life satisfaction. It may also provide a transition to or from full-time employment. However, part-time work also has drawbacks. Part-time employees have lower status in organizations than full-time employees doing the same kind of work. Their hourly wages are lower, they are less likely to receive health insurance benefits, their jobs are less secure, and their career prospects are more limited.[34]

Women and men differ in the propensity to hold part-time rather than full-time jobs. Women hold two thirds or more of all part-time jobs in most countries, which may be driven by their placing greater importance than men on work-family balance when seeking employment. In the United States, women hold 66% of all part-time jobs; 25% of the U.S. female labor force and 11% of the U.S. male labor force are employed part-time. Overall, although women's greater tendency than men to hold part-time jobs offers them a greater sense of work–family balance and subjective career success, it restricts their objective career success.[35]

Decision About Whether to Start a Business

The decision about whether to start a business represents a different type of role entry decision. Entrepreneurship is often depicted as a masculine preserve, with entrepreneurs described in terms that are associated more with men than women ("the conqueror of unexplored territories, the lonely hero, the patriarch"). Despite the masculine norm for entrepreneurship, women-owned business firms represent the fastest growth segment of privately held business firms, and female business owners are increasingly important contributors to their country's economic growth. However, although the sex difference in business start-ups is diminishing, women are still less likely than men to start a business.[36]

Several types of family factors influence individuals' decision to start a business. For example, having a self-employed parent, being married to another business owner, having one's career as a business owner receive high priority in the household, and being motivated to gain flexibility in meeting family demands and responsibilities and integrate work and family are positively related to the decision to start a business. Many of these factors differ according to owner sex. For example, women's careers as business owners receive lower household priority than those of men, which reinforces the sex difference in business start-ups favoring men. However, women's greater motivation to achieve work–family integration and flexibility through business ownership constrains the magnitude of this sex difference. Overall, women's decisions about whether to start a business are more driven by family considerations than those of men.[37]

Decision About Number of Hours to Devote to Job or Business

The decision about how many hours to devote to one's job or business represents a role participation decision regarding the distribution of time between the work domain and other life domains. This decision may have both positive (e.g., enhanced enjoyment from work, greater job and career satisfaction, higher compensation) and negative (e.g., workaholism, greater work-to-family conflict) consequences for individuals and their families. Over the past few decades, women have consistently devoted fewer hours to paid work than men. Although this sex difference is due in part to women's greater likelihood of working part-time, men work more hours than women even among full-time workers, and male business owners devote more hours to their business firms than female business owners.[38]

Several family factors are related to individuals' decisions about the number of hours to devote to their job or business. For example, playing the breadwinner role and having a spouse handle child care, which are more likely for men, contribute to individuals' working more hours. In contrast, spending more time on housework and child care oneself, which are more likely for women, contribute to individuals' working less hours. Also, some family factors influence women's decisions about work hours but not men's decisions. For women, having a greater number of children and a spouse who is more highly educated are negatively related to work hours, whereas having a spouse who devotes more hours to housework and having domestic help or a babysitter to handle child care are positively related to work hours. In contrast, these family factors are unrelated to work hours for men.[39]

Overall, men's decisions about work hours are less constrained by family-domain factors than women's decisions. For men, these results could be driven by the desire to get out of the house for the joys of work or by the need to fulfill their breadwinner role. For women, these results could be driven by the importance of family in their lives or by the need to restrict their work involvement to meet their family's needs. Both of these possible explanations are consistent with gender roles.

Decision About Whether to Have a Voluntary Employment Gap

Employment gaps, or periods during which individuals leave and then rejoin the labor force, represent a combination of role exit and role entry decisions. They may be either voluntary or involuntary on the part of the employee. Women are more likely than men to have employment gaps early in their careers. In addition, their employment gaps are more likely to be voluntary for purposes of child rearing.[40]

The voluntary employment gap violates the stereotype of a successful career, which is largely based on the experiences of men. An uninterrupted career pattern is assumed to demonstrate stability and commitment to work. Time away from work, unless for the purpose of enhancing educational credentials, is often assumed to lead to deterioration of skills and knowledge and to reflect less commitment to work. As a result, when people choose to take time out from their work careers for any reason, their subsequent advancement and earnings are likely to suffer. Thus, women's greater tendency to have voluntary employment gaps contributes to their achieving lower long-term objective career success.

Decision About Whether to Quit a Job

The decision to quit a particular job represents a role exit decision that has considerable ramifications for individuals, their families, and their employers. For some people, this decision is accompanied by a role entry decision to find alternative employment working for others, which may require relocation or other family adjustments, or to start a business. For others, this decision entails leaving the labor force altogether, which has financial and other implications for their families. Although women are more likely to have voluntary employment gaps than men, there is no sex difference in quit decisions overall.[41]

Family factors have both positive and negative influences on the decision about whether to quit a job. For example, being married and having more children, taking advantage of family-friendly corporate initiatives, and having supervisory support for meeting one's family needs are negatively related to the decision to quit. In contrast, having a spouse's job relocated is positively related to the decision to quit. High levels of work–family conflict make people more inclined to quit a job. However, family-to-work enrichment improves the work situation and makes people less inclined to quit a job. Some family factors, including having greater household responsibilities and being motivated to work closer to home and take time off for child rearing, not only have more positive effects on quit decisions for women than men but are also experienced more frequently by women than men. Overall, women are more likely to quit jobs for family-related reasons than are men.[42]

In summary, the evidence about how people make a wide range of role entry, participation, and exit decisions is clear: Women's decisions at work are more likely to be work–family decisions (i.e., decisions that are influenced by family factors) than those of men. However, the overall decline in endorsement of gender roles, especially among men and among recent entrants to the labor force, suggests that this sex difference is diminishing. Younger men in the present are increasingly expressing the desire to balance work and family compared with younger men in the past, who expected to devote their lives primarily to fulfillment of their breadwinner responsibilities. As a result, to attract and take advantage of the best new talent available from both sexes, employers need to be family-friendly.[43]

Being Family-Friendly

Individuals' success in managing the work–family interface is influenced by the work environments that their employers provide and the strategies they adopt. To understand the intersection of work and family more fully, we need to examine the roles of both employers and employees. In this section, we consider popular work–family initiatives and the influence of the organizational culture. Table 8.2 summarizes recommended actions for organizations to be family-friendly.

Family-Friendly Initiatives

Employers may be family-friendly through the programs they offer to help employees meet their family needs. Work–family initiatives that have been adopted by organizations include child and elder care assistance, alternative work arrangements, training on how to deal with common family issues, counseling for employees and their families when organizational decisions affect the family, employment assistance for spouses of relocated employees, partnerships with schools, gifts to community organizations, support groups for employees with similar family needs, and advisory task forces that address particular work–family issues. Firms with a higher proportion of professional employees and a higher proportion of female employees tend to develop more extensive work–family initiatives and experience greater gains in performance and shareholder returns as a result of such initiatives.[44]

Table 8.2   Recommended Actions for Organizations

1. Offer counseling when organizational decisions affect the family (e.g., relocation).

2. Offer employment assistance to spouses of relocated employees.

3. Offer assistance to employees in meeting child care and elder care needs.

4. Offer flexible work arrangements to employees when possible.

5. Make telecommuting available to qualified employees.

6. Offer training on how to deal with family issues (e.g., getting a child into college).

7. Provide incentives for managers to permit subordinates to take advantage of flexible work arrangements.

8. Adopt a flexible model of the successful career that does not penalize employment gaps, leaves of absence, and lateral moves.

9. Set reasonable standards for the number of hours employees are required to work.

Organizations may offer employees valuable assistance with care of children and elderly parents, including referrals, financial assistance, and corporate child or elder care centers. Employees' needs for dependent care vary greatly, and organizations need to consider their financial resources and the diversity of their employees' family lives when deciding how best to address these needs. Even when resources are scarce, there are many kinds of actions that can be taken to assist employees with meeting these needs. These actions have a positive impact on recruitment, absenteeism, job satisfaction, and organizational commitment.[45]

Organizations may also offer employees a wide array of alternative work arrangements, including flextime, telecommuting, part-time work, paid leaves and sabbaticals, unpaid leaves beyond what is legally mandated, job sharing, phased-in work schedules following leaves, and phased-in retirement. Alternative work arrangements are highly popular with many employees because flexibility in their work schedules enables them to gain greater control over their work and family lives. For example, parents may find it easier to accommodate their children's regular schedules and predictable events such as teacher conferences. In addition, they may respond better to emergencies and unanticipated events such as sudden illnesses, weather-related school closings, and breakdowns in child care arrangements. Flexibility in work arrangements appeals to all employees, not just parents, because it symbolizes a focus on getting the work done rather than how, when, or where it is done. Alternative work arrangements yield benefits for employers such as decreased absenteeism and turnover and increased productivity.[46]

The most popular type of alternative work arrangement is flextime, which allows planned variations from normal work hours. Managerial and professional employees make the greatest use of flextime programs. Flextime may consist of changes to the starting and ending times of the workday or of compression of the workweek into fewer days (e.g., four 10-hour days instead of five 8-hour days). It may also allow variation in the work schedule from one workday to the next. Flextime has a positive impact on employees' productivity, absenteeism, job satisfaction, and satisfaction with their schedules, which benefits their employers as well.[47]

Telecommuting, being paid to do some or all of one's work away from the work site, is an increasingly popular type of work arrangement as more work becomes virtual. As for flextime, telecommuting is most common for managerial and professional employees. It gives employees flexibility in the location and timing of work by allowing them to work out of a virtual office. Telecommuters report that working at home increases their productivity by reducing interruptions and distractions and enhancing their concentration. It also helps employees to balance work and family; their increased presence at home enables them to better fulfill their child care and household responsibilities and strengthens family relationships. However, telecommuting can blur the boundary between work and family roles in unproductive ways. Because work-related messages arrive electronically around the clock, telecommuters can feel pressures to be working (or appear to be working) around the clock. Telecommuters also face interruptions and distractions from being at home. Thus, telecommuting may both decrease work-to-family conflict and increase family-to-work conflict. The challenge for telecommuters then becomes how to segment work from family and how to segment family from work when desirable. When this challenge is met, telecommuting benefits both employees and employers.[48]

Organizations may take a proactive role in helping their employees minimize work–family conflict and maximize work–family enrichment through the training programs they offer. They may offer training in how to enlist a spouse's support to alleviate work–family conflict. Further, they may alleviate employees' stress by providing useful information about matters that concern employees outside work. For example, several firms offer educational programs about how to get one's child into and through college, including advice about the admissions process, testing, financial aid, and financial planning; this form of work-to-family enrichment is particularly appreciated by middle-aged parents. When employees' needs for low work–family conflict and high work–family enrichment are met, they are more likely to exhibit work-related attitudes and behaviors that benefit their employers.[49]

Family-Friendly Culture

Being family-friendly involves more than offering a variety of work-family programs. It also means providing an organizational culture in which employees feel comfortable in taking advantage of programs that are intended to benefit them. Supportive managers are a crucial link in creating a family-friendly culture. Employees are more likely to utilize work–family programs when they have a supportive manager who empathizes with their desire for work–family balance. Having a family-supportive manager reduces employees' work–family conflict, increases their work–family enrichment, and gives them more incentive to stay with the organization.[50]

Despite the benefits of work–family programs for both employees and employers, managers may resist implementing them. According to a study of the factors that affect managerial decisions about whether to approve requests for alternative work arrangements, the most important factor was the criticality of the subordinate's job assignment. Subordinates whose work was more critical to the work unit were less likely to have their requests approved than noncritical subordinates; subordinate sex had no effect on managers' decisions. These are curious results. Employees who are trusted with more critical job tasks would seem to deserve special treatment. However, in this study, their managers viewed such employees as the *least* desirable candidates for alternative work arrangements. Critical employees should not have to transfer to less critical jobs to qualify for these arrangements. To reap the benefits of work–family programs, organizations need to educate their managers on the corporate benefits of these programs and provide incentives to managers to implement them.[51]

Organizations also need to establish a culture that combats singlism. Most family-friendly initiatives are designed to meet the needs of married employees with children. Although single childless employees may not need work-family programs targeted toward them, they have other needs that may be addressed. They need to feel included in social events at work such as the annual company picnic for employees and their families, which should include both child-friendly activities (e.g., pony rides for small children) and singles-friendly activities (e.g., softball). They also seek equal access to employee benefits and respect for their family lives. Single childless employees need to know that there are similar work expectations for themselves and married employees with children. They should not be expected to travel more for business, to work more hours when coworkers miss work for family reasons, or to work at times when coworkers are not expected to work.[52]

Organizational cultures that define a successful career as an uninterrupted sequence of promotions to higher levels, or assume that requests to take time out from career for family reasons reflect a lack of career commitment, discourage employees from following any other career path. Organizations that want to create family-friendly cultures need to expand their notions of what constitutes career success to include interruptions and lateral moves. They should encourage, rather than discourage, employees to take advantage of work–family programs, recognizing that employees who do so are likely to be more committed, not less committed, to the organization.

In conclusion, when organizations recognize that they are employing whole individuals and not just jobholders, they are more likely to be family-friendly. They are also more likely to attract and retain productive employees.

Balancing Work and Family

The challenge for all individuals, whatever their family status may be, is to manage the interface between their work and family lives to achieve a sense of work–family balance. Meeting this challenge is no simple matter. The complexity of many employees' family situations can make the task of negotiating a balance between work and family interests seem like a full-time job in itself. Social support from family members and employers makes the task more manageable, but employees can do much to help themselves. Table 8.3 summarizes recommended actions for individuals to balance their work and family roles.

Table 8.3 Recommended Actions for Individuals

1. Be aware of your life values regarding the importance of work and family.

2. Cultivate social support from all possible sources.

3. Get a mentor if possible.

4. Deal with stresses in your work and family roles and in juggling the two roles by adopting appropriate coping strategies.

5. Reach accommodations with partners about the role that work and family concerns will play in each other's lives.

6. If you are a trailing partner, join a support group or form one with others in similar positions.

First, people need to be aware of their life values. What is the relative importance to them of the various roles in their life, which may include work and family as well as a host of other roles (volunteer, student, and so on)? With which role or roles do they identify the most? If individuals identify primarily with their work roles, decisions they make at work should seek to maximize their sense of success, whether measured objectively or subjectively, at work. Such individuals will experience balance primarily from being effective in and satisfied with their work roles. If they identify primarily with their family roles, their work decisions should take into account family considerations with the goal of maximizing their effectiveness in and satisfaction with their family roles. However, if individuals identify highly with both work and family, their work decisions need to be carefully calibrated to take into account the potential impact on their satisfaction and effectiveness in both roles.[53]

Next, people need to cultivate social support in both work and family roles for their involvement in the other role—from their managers and coworkers at work and from their spouses or partners and other family members at home. If they face pressures to participate in conflicting activities in both their work and family roles, they will benefit by mobilizing support in the form of release from time demands that will alleviate the need to make a choice. Through the support mobilization process, they may avoid work–family conflict.[54]

Mentors, or senior individuals with advanced experience and knowledge who provide guidance to their protégés, may be a valuable source of social support. Although some organizations have formal programs that assign mentors to protégés, informal mentoring relationships are most common. Mentors typically help protégés in their career development by acting as coaches and sponsors. Mentors also enhance protégés' satisfaction with their careers by offering friendship, counseling, and acceptance. Thus, mentors contribute to their protégés' objective and subjective career success. In addition, mentors may contribute to their protégés' management of the work–family interface by being sensitive to and supportive of their values and goals regarding attainment of work–family balance. Although women face greater barriers to forming formal mentoring relationships than men, they are equally likely to develop informal mentoring relationships.[55]

People also need to develop coping strategies to deal with stress from the demands of their work and family roles. Strategies that help individuals cope with stress in one role may not alleviate stress in the other role. For example, cognitive disengagement or detachment may be an effective strategy for coping with work-related stress, but not with family-based stress. Reassurances of emotional attachment and commitment may be effective when directed toward family members, but not when directed toward bosses, subordinates, and peers at work. Individuals need coping strategies for dealing effectively with stress in both spheres of their lives. In addition to unilateral coping strategies, couples may reduce their overall amount of stress by agreeing on what their work and family roles will be and by providing mutual support.[56]

Couples who relocate as a result of international assignments need to devote particular attention to developing coping strategies. Although relocated employees often receive employer assistance in coping with their new environments, trailing spouses of relocated employees need to act on their own behalf. For example, a group of men who trailed their executive spouses to Belgium formed their own support group, Spouses Trailing Under Duress Successfully (STUDS). The group provides the men a social network, which helps them settle in and adjust to their new location. STUDS brings these men together online and in person regularly for a weekly brunch, monthly lunch, winter black-tie ball with wives invited, and other events. These men are not only providing social support to each other. They also are acting to enhance their executive wives' career success and family satisfaction. The failure of the trailing spouse to adjust is a frequent cause of early returns home or resignations of executives from international assignments, which can derail or stall their career.[57]

Whether they work for themselves or others, individuals face a dilemma in deciding how much they want to segment or integrate their work and family roles. Segmenters take the risk of preventing work–family enrichment, the positive side of the work-family interface, in the interests of preventing work–family conflict, the negative side. Integrators, on the other hand, take the risk of increasing work–family conflict to an undesirable level while maximizing their opportunities for work–family enrichment. There is no simple solution to this dilemma.[58]

In conclusion, as their careers unfold, women and men may set goals for work–family balance in accordance with their life values and adopt plans for action to achieve these goals. With a little help from their friends, employer, and family, they may achieve their balance goals, thereby shaping their own lives.

The Rest of Jennifer's Story

After beginning the chapter with the story of Jennifer's fateful day, we conclude by presenting the aftermath. In the weeks that followed her decision to work overtime on the project that fateful Saturday and to miss the 50th birthday party for her mother, Jennifer felt considerable internal conflict and turmoil. She was very upset about what had happened. Shortly thereafter, she found a new job in her field with an employer who treated her with much more respect. She was still in that job and enjoying it 2 years later.

Notes

1. Powell, G. N. (1998). The abusive organization. *Academy of Management Executive, 12*(2), p. 95. ACADEMY OF MANAGEMENT EXECUTIVE by G. N. POWELL. Copyright 1998 by ACADEMY OF MANAGEMENT (NY). Reproduced with permission of ACADEMY OF MANAGEMENT (NY) in the format Textbook via Copyright Clearance Center.

2. Hewlett, S. A., & Luce, C. B. (2006). Extreme jobs: The dangerous allure of the 70-hour workweek. *Harvard Business Review, 84*(12), 49–59; Brett, J. M., & Stroh, L. K. (2003). Working 61 plus hours a week: Why do managers do it? *Journal of Applied Psychology, 88*, 67–78; Trinca, H., & Fox, C. (2004). *Better than sex: How a whole generation got hooked on work.* Sydney: Random House Australia, p. 67.

3. Greenhaus, J. H., & Allen, T. D. (in press). Work-family balance: A review and extension of the literature. In J. C. Quick & L. E. Tetrick (Eds.), *Handbook of occupational health psychology* (2nd ed.). Washington, DC: American Psychological Association.

4. Eagly, A. H., Wood, W., & Diekman, A. B. (2000). Social role theory of sex differences and similarities: A current appraisal. In T. Eckes & H. M. Trautner (Eds.), *The developmental social psychology of gender* (pp. 123–174). Mahwah, NJ: Erlbaum; Kite, M. E., Deaux, K., & Haines, E. L. (2008). Gender stereotypes. In F. L. Denmark & M. A. Paludi (Eds.), *Psychology of women: A handbook of issues and theories* (2nd ed., pp. 205–236). Westport, CT: Praeger.

5. Galinsky, E., Aumann, K., & Bond, J. T. (2009). *Times are changing: Gender and generation at work and at home.* New York: Families and Work Institute. Retrieved March 26, 2009, from http://familiesandwork.org.

6. Schneer, J. A., & Reitman, F. (1993). Effects of alternative family structures on managerial career paths. *Academy of Management Journal, 36,* 830–843.

7. Hewlett, S. A. (2002). Executive women and the myth of having it all. *Harvard Business Review, 80*(4), 66–73.

8. Marks, S. R. (2006). Understanding diversity of families in the 21st century and its impact on the work-family area of study. In M. Pitt-Catsouphes, E. E. Kossek, & S. Sweet (Eds.), *The work and family handbook: Multi-disciplinary perspectives, methods, and approaches* (pp. 41–65). Mahwah, NJ: Erlbaum.

9. DePaulo, B. M. (2006). *Singled out: How singles are stereotyped, singled, and ignored and still live happily ever after.* New York: St. Martin's Press.

10. Powell, G. N. (1997). The sex difference in employee inclinations regarding work-family programs: Why does it exist, should we care, and what should be done about it (if anything)? In S. Parasuraman & J. H. Greenhaus (Eds.), *Integrating work and family: Challenges and choices for a changing world* (pp. 167–174). Westport, CT: Quorum.

11. Brett, J. M., Stroh, L. K., & Reilly, A. H. (1993). Pulling up roots in the 1990s: Who's willing to relocate? *Journal of Organizational Behavior, 14,* 49–60; Stroh, L. K., Brett, J. M., & Reilly, A. H. (1992). All the right stuff: A comparison of female and male managers' career progression. *Journal of Applied Psychology, 77,* 251–260; Lyness, K. S., & Thompson, D. E. (2000). Climbing the corporate ladder: Do female and male executives follow the same route? *Journal of Applied Psychology, 85,* 86–101; Adler, N. J. (1984). Women do not want international careers: And other myths about international management. *Organizational Dynamics, 13*(2), 66–79.

12. Friedman, S. D., & Greenhaus, J. H. (2000). *Work and family—allies or enemies? What happens when business professionals confront life choices.* New York: Oxford University Press; Graves, L. M., Ohlott, P. J., & Ruderman, M. N. (2007). Commitment to family roles: Effects on managers' attitudes and performance. *Journal of Applied Psychology, 92,* 44–56; Ruderman, M. N., Ohlott, P. J., Panzer, K., & King, S. N. (2002). Benefits of multiple roles for professional women. *Academy of Management Journal, 45,* 369–386; Hochschild, A. R. (1997). *The time bind: When work becomes home and home becomes work.* New York: Metropolitan.

13. Greenhaus, J. H., & Beutell, N. J. (1985). Sources of conflict between work and family roles. *Academy of Management Review, 10,* 76-88; Eby, L. T., Casper, W. J., Lockwood, A., Bordeaux, C., & Brinley, A. (2005). Work and family research in IO/OB: Content analysis and review of the literature (1980–2002). *Journal of Vocational Behavior, 66,* 124–197.

14. Ng, T. W. H., & Feldman, D. C. (2008). Long work hours: A social identity perspective on meta-analysis data. *Journal of Organizational Behavior, 29,* 853–880; Shelton, B. A., & John, D. (1996). The division of household labor. *Annual Review of Sociology, 22,* 299–322; Gerson, K. (1993). *No man's land: Men's changing commitments to family and work.* New York: Basic Books, p. 141.

15. Greenhaus, J. H., & Powell, G. N. (2003). When work and family collide: Deciding between competing role demands. *Organizational Behavior and Human Decision Processes, 90,* 291–303; Powell (1998).

16. Powell, G. N., & Greenhaus, J. H. (2006). Managing incidents of work-family conflict: A decision-making perspective. *Human Relations, 59,* 1179–1212; Greenhaus, J. H., & Parasuraman, S. (1994). Work-family conflict, social support and well-being. In M. J. Davidson & R. J. Burke (Eds.), *Women in management: Current research issues* (pp. 213–229). London: Chapman.

17. Ling, Y., & Powell, G. N. (2001). Work-family conflict in contemporary China: Beyond an American-based model. *International Journal of Cross Cultural Management, 1,* 357–373.

18. Powell, G. N., Francesco, A. M., & Ling, Y. (2009). Toward culture-sensitive theories of the work-family interface. *Journal of Organizational Behavior, 30,* 597–616; Emrich, C. G., Denmark, F. L., & Den Hartog, D. N. (2004). Cross-cultural differences in gender egalitarianism: Implications for societies, organizations, and leaders. In R. J. House, P. J. Hanges, M. Javidan, P. W. Dorfman, & V. Gupta (Eds.), *Culture, leadership, and organizations: The GLOBE study of 62 societies* (pp. 343–394). Thousand Oaks, CA: Sage.

19. Greenhaus, J. H., & Powell, G. N. (2006). When work and family are allies: A theory of work-family enrichment. *Academy of Management Review, 31,* 72–92; McNall, L. A., Nicklin, J. M., & Masuda, A. D. (in press). A meta-analytic review of the consequences associated with work-family enrichment. *Journal of Business and Psychology.*

20. Greenhaus & Powell (2006); Friedman & Greenhaus.

21. Powell, G. N., & Greenhaus, J. H. (2010b). Sex, gender, and the work→family interface: Exploring negative and positive interdependencies. *Academy of Management Journal, 53;* Greenhaus & Allen.

22. Kreiner, G. E. (2006). Consequences of work-home segmentation or integration: A person-environment fit perspective. *Journal of Organizational Behavior, 27,* 485–507; Ashforth, B. E., Kreiner, G. E., & Fugate, M. (2000). All in a day's work: Boundaries and micro role transitions. *Academy of Management Review, 25,* 472–491.

23. Powell & Greenhaus (2010b).

24. Rothbard, N. P., Phillips, K. W., & Dumas, T. L. (2005). Managing multiple roles: Work-family policies and individuals' desires for segmentation. *Organization Science, 16*, 243–258; Pleck, J. H. (1977). The work-family role system. *Social Problems, 24*, 417–427.

25. Powell, G. N., & Mainiero, L. A. (1992). Cross-currents in the river of time: Conceptualizing the complexities of women's careers. *Journal of Management, 18*, 215–237.

26. Ng, T. W. H., Eby, L. T., Sorenson, K. L., & Feldman, D. C. (2005). Predictors of objective and subjective career success: A meta-analysis. *Personnel Psychology, 58*, 367–408; Judge, T. A., Cable, D. M., Boudreau, J. W., & Bretz, R. D., Jr. (1995). An empirical investigation of the predictors of executive career success. *Personnel Psychology, 48*, 485–519.

27. Eddleston, K. A., Veiga, J. F., & Powell, G. N. (2006). Explaining sex differences in managerial career satisfier preferences: The role of gender self-schema. *Journal of Applied Psychology, 91*, 437–445.

28. Powell & Mainiero (1992).

29. Kirchmeyer, C. (1998). Determinants of managerial career success: Evidence and explanation of male/female differences. *Journal of Management, 24*, 673–692; Schneer, J. A., & Reitman, F. (1995). The impact of gender as managerial careers unfold. *Journal of Vocational Behavior, 47*, 290–315; Cox, T. H., & Harquail, C. V. (1991). Career paths and career success in the early career stages of male and female MBAs. *Journal of Vocational Behavior, 39*, 54–75.

30. Crosby, F. J. (1982). *Relative deprivation and working women.* New York: Oxford University Press; Powell, G. N., & Eddleston, K. A. (2008). The paradox of the contented female business owner. *Journal of Vocational Behavior, 73*, 24–36.

31. Powell & Eddleston; Eddleston, K. A., & Powell, G. N. (2008). The role of gender identity in explaining sex differences in business owners' career satisfier preferences. *Journal of Business Venturing, 23*, 244–256; Brush, C. G., Carter, N. M., Gatewood, E. J., Greene, P. G., & Hart, M. M. (Eds.) (2006). *Growth-oriented women entrepreneurs and their businesses: A global research perspective.* Cheltenham, UK: Edward Elgar.

32. Poelmans, S. A. Y. (2005). The decision process theory of work and family. In E. E. Kossek & S. J. Lambert (Eds.), *Work and life integration: Organizational, cultural, and individual perspectives* (pp. 263–285). Mahwah, NJ: Erlbaum.

33. Powell, G. N., & Greenhaus, J. H. (2010a). Sex, gender, and decisions at the family→work interface. *Journal of Management, 36.*

34. U.S. Department of Labor, Bureau of Labor Statistics. (2009b). *Women in the labor force: A databook* (2009 ed., table 20). Retrieved December 14, 2009, from http://www.bls.gov/cps; Higgins, C., Duxbury, L., & Johnson, K. L. (2000). Part-time work for women: Does it really help balance work and family? *Human Resource Management, 39*, 17–32; Bollé, P. (2001). Part-time work: Solution or

trap? In M. F. Loutfi (Ed.), *Women, gender and work: What is equality and how do we get there?* (pp. 215–238). Geneva: International Labour Office.

35. U.S. Bureau of Labor Statistics (2009b); Bollé.

36. Bruni, A., Gherardi, S., & Poggio, B. (2004). Doing gender, doing entrepreneurship: An ethnographic account of intertwined practices. *Gender, Work and Organization, 11,* 406–429; Brush, Carter, Gatewood, Greene, & Hart; Langowitz, N., & Minniti, M. (2007). The entrepreneurial propensity of women. *Entrepreneurship Theory and Practice, 31,* 341–364.

37. Powell & Greenhaus (2010a).

38. Ng & Feldman; Jacobs, J. A., & Gerson, K. (2004). *The time divide: Work, family, and gender inequality.* Cambridge, MA: Harvard University Press; Humbert, A. L., & Lewis, S. (2008). "I have no life other than work"—Long working hours, blurred boundaries and family life: The case of Irish entrepreneurs. In R. J. Burke & C. L. Cooper (Eds.), *The long work hours culture: Causes, consequences and choices* (pp. 159–181). Bigley, UK: Emerald.

39. Powell & Greenhaus (2010a).

40. Reitman, F., & Schneer, J. A. (2005). The long-term negative impacts of managerial career interruptions. *Group & Organization Management, 30,* 243–262; Schneer, J. A., & Reitman, F. (1997). The interrupted managerial career path: A longitudinal study of MBAs. *Journal of Vocational Behavior, 51,* 411–434.

41. Mattis, M. C. (2005). "I'm out of here:" Women leaving companies in the USA to start their own businesses. In S. L. Fielden & M. J. Davidson (Eds.), *International handbook of women and small business entrepreneurship* (pp. 221–235). Cheltenham, UK: Edward Elgar; Griffeth, R. W., Hom, P. W., & Gaertner, S. 2000. A meta-analysis of antecedents and correlates of employee turnover: Update, moderator tests, and research implications for the next millennium. *Journal of Management, 26,* 463–488.

42. Powell & Greenhaus (2010a).

43. Galinsky, Aumann, & Bond.

44. Lobel, S. A. (1999). Impacts of diversity and work-life initiatives in organizations. In G. N. Powell (Ed.), *Handbook of gender and work* (pp. 453–474). Thousand Oaks, CA: Sage; Arthur, M. M. (2003). Share price reactions to work-family initiatives: An institutional perspective. *Academy of Management Journal, 46,* 497–505; Konrad, A. M., & Mangel, R. (2000). The impact of work-life programs on firm productivity. *Strategic Management Journal, 21,* 1225–1237; Perry-Smith, J. E., & Blum, T. C. (2000). Work-family human resource bundles and perceived organizational performance. *Academy of Management Journal, 43,* 1107–1117.

45. Rodgers, F. S., & Rodgers, C. (1989). Business and the facts of family life. *Harvard Business review, 67*(6), 121–129; Merrill, D. M. (1997). *Caring for elderly parents: Juggling work, family, and caregiving in middle and working class families.* Westport, CT: Auburn House; Lobel.

46. Lobel; Rodgers & Rodgers; Thomas, L. T., & Ganster, D. C. (1995). Impact of family-supportive work variables on work-family conflict and strain: A control

perspective. *Journal of Applied Psychology, 80,* 6–15; Grover, S. L., & Crooker, K. J. (1995). Who appreciates family-responsive human resource policies: The impact of family-friendly policies on the organizational attachment of parent and non-parents. *Personnel Psychology, 48,* 271–288.

47. Baltes, B. B., Briggs, T. E., Huff, J. W., Wright, J. A., & Neuman, G. A. (1999). Flexible and compressed workweek schedules: A meta-analysis of their effects on work-related criteria. *Journal of Applied Psychology, 84,* 496–513.

48. Golden, T. D., Veiga, J. F., & Simsek, Z. (2006). Telecommuting's differential impact on work-family conflict: Is there no place like home? *Journal of Applied Psychology, 91,* 1340–1350; Hill, E. J., Ferris, M., & Märtinson, V. (2003). Does it matter where you work? A comparison of how three work venues (traditional office, virtual office, and home office) influence aspects of work and personal/family life. *Journal of Vocational Behavior, 63,* 220–241; Hill, E. J., Miller, B. C., Weiner, S. P., & Colihan, J. (1998). Influences of the virtual office on aspects of work and work/life balance. *Personnel Psychology, 51,* 667–683.

49. Mesmer-Magnus, J. R., & Viswesvaran, C. (2006). How family-friendly work environments affect work/family conflict: A meta-analytic examination. *Journal of Labor Research, 27,* 555–574 ; Chaker, A. M. (2007, October 4). Employers offer help on college admissions. *Wall Street Journal.* Retrieved October 4, 2007, from http://online.wsj.com.

50. Hammer, L. B., Kossek, E. E., Yragui, N. L., Bodner, T. E., & Hanson, G. C. (2009). Development and validation of a multidomensional measure of family supportive supervisor behaviors (FSSB). *Journal of Management, 35,* 837–856; Mesmer-Magnus & Viswesvaran; Breaugh, J. A., & Frye, N. K. (2008). Work-family conflict: The importance of family-friendly employment practices and family-supportive supervisors. *Journal of Business and Psychology, 22,* 345–353; Thompson, C. A., Beauvais, L. L., & Lyness, K. S. (1999). When work-family benefits are not enough: The influence of work-family culture on benefit utilization, organizational attachment, and work-family conflict. *Journal of Vocational Behavior, 54,* 392–415; Thomas & Ganster.

51. Powell, G. N., & Mainiero, L. A. (1999). Managerial decision making regarding alternative work arrangements. *Journal of Occupational and Organizational Psychology, 72,* 41–56.

52. Casper, W. J., Weltman, D., & Kwesiga, E. (2007). Beyond family-friendly: The construct and measurement of singles-friendly work culture. *Journal of Vocational Behavior, 70,* 478–501; DePaulo.

53. Carlson, D. S., & Kacmar, K. M. (2000). Work-family conflict in the organization: Do life role values make a difference? *Journal of Management, 26,* 1031–1054.

54. Powell & Greenhaus (2006); Greenhaus & Parasuraman.

55. Allen, T. D., Eby, L. T., Poteet, M. L., Lentz, E., & Lima, L. (2004). Career benefits associated with mentoring for protégés: A meta-analysis. *Journal of Applied Psychology, 89,* 127–136; Greenhaus, J. H., & Singh, R. (2007). Mentoring

and the work-family interface. In B. R. Ragins & K. E. Kram (Eds.), *The handbook of mentoring at work: Theory, research, and practice* (pp. 519–544). Los Angeles: Sage; McKeen, C., & Bujaki, M. (2007). Gender and mentoring: Issues, effects, and opportunities. In B. R. Ragins & K. E. Kram (Eds.), *The handbook of mentoring at work : Theory, research, and practice* (pp. 197–222). Thousand Oaks, CA: Sage; Ragins, B. R. (1999). Gender and mentoring relationships: A review and research agenda for the next decade. In G. N. Powell (Ed.), *Handbook of gender and work* (pp. 347–370). Thousand Oaks, CA: Sage.

56. Eckenrode, J., & Gore, S. (Eds.). (1990). *Stress between work and family.* New York: Plenum; Davidson, M. J., & Fielden, S. (1999). Stress and the working woman. In G. N. Powell (Ed.), *Handbook of gender and work* (pp. 413–426). Thousand Oaks, CA: Sage.

57. *Belgium STUDS: Spouses Trailing Under Duress Successfully.* (2009). Retrieved December 16, 2009, from http://www.belgiumstuds.com; Lazarova, M., Westman, M., & Shaffer, M. A. (2010). Elucidating the positive side of the work-family interface on international assignments: A model of expatriate work and family performance. *Academy of Management Review, 35,* 93–117.

58. Powell & Greenhaus (2010b).

CHAPTER 9

Promoting Nondiscrimination, Diversity, and Inclusion

We Love Diversity

Company XYZ is committed to attracting, developing, and retaining the best people from the broadest possible employee pool to meet our business needs worldwide. Having a workforce that reflects the composition of the marketplaces we serve and the communities where we operate is an important competitive advantage. Our mission is to create a culture and a business environment based upon inclusion, mutual respect, responsibility, and understanding. We believe that business wins when everyone matters, and that the true strength of diversity is unleashed when each associate is encouraged to reach their full potential. We strive to be a great place to work, to be respectful and supportive of our diverse workforce and inclusive culture, and to recognize the benefits of our diverse suppliers, customers and business partners. The more we embrace our differences—diversity of thought, experience, perspective, race, gender, faith and more—the better we can deliver what the customers want and the more successful we will be.[1]

Does Company XYZ sound like a great place to work or what? Actually, it doesn't exist, at least as a single company. The six statements in the opening passage represent excerpts from the corporate diversity policies posted on the Web sites of six of the top 10 corporations in the *Fortune* 500, a list of America's largest corporations.[2] (See Note 1 for the sources of the six statements in order.) Can you tell the companies apart based on these excerpts from their diversity policies? Neither can I.

If such statements represented what the workplace is really like, it would be reasonable to conclude that the merits of having a diverse workforce have been fully recognized and embraced. However, the reality is more complex. Organizations are quite diverse in how they deal with the notion of diversity. Although some firms live up to such statements, many firms create diversity policies solely to reduce their liability, and many employees view such policies as lip service.[3]

In general, organizations may take three types of actions:

1. **Promote nondiscrimination** in treatment of people and decisions about people. This means promoting compliance by all employees with federal, state, and local equal employment opportunity (EEO) laws. Such laws ban discrimination on the basis of sex, race, ethnicity, national origin, age, religion, and other personal characteristics that are not relevant to the job at hand. It also means refraining from discrimination on the basis of job-irrelevant personal characteristics even if it not illegal. For example, there is no U.S. federal law banning discrimination on the basis of sexual orientation, but such discrimination is just as unacceptable as sex or race discrimination.

2. **Promote diversity** among employees in all jobs and at all levels. The focus of promoting diversity is on the number or quantity of employees from various groups in different jobs and at different organizational levels. Affirmative action programs, which are legally mandated for most employers, represent attempts to ensure that organizational practices enhance the employment, development, and retention of members of protected groups such as women and people of color. Organizations also may attempt to increase the diversity of their labor force for business reasons.

3. **Promote inclusion** of employees from all groups in the organizational culture. The focus of promoting inclusion is on the nature or quality of work relationships between employees who belong to different groups. There are no laws that say that organizations ought to provide a work environment in which members of all groups feel comfortable and accepted. Organizations may engage in this kind of action if they see some advantage to doing so.

Organizations benefit from pursuing all three types of actions: promoting nondiscrimination, promoting diversity, and promoting inclusion. An organization successful in these actions is less likely to be the target of costly litigation. Its employees bring a wider range of perspectives to work issues, which result in more creative solutions to problems facing the organization. Such an organization is most likely to attract and retain highly qualified employees from all groups and to take full advantage of their talents.

In this chapter, we consider what organizations need to do to achieve these benefits. First, we review the kinds of EEO laws with which organizations must comply. Second, we present the business case for going beyond minimal compliance with EEO laws. Third, we consider specific actions that organizations may take to promote a nondiscriminatory, diverse, and inclusive culture. We wrap up with the conclusions for the book.

Legal Requirements

Federal, state, and local laws govern the actions of employers, with federal laws having the broadest impact. Examples of federal EEO laws include Australia's Affirmative Action Act, Canada's Employment Equity Act, Japan's Equal Employment Opportunity Law, the United Kingdom's Sex Discrimination and Equal Pay Acts, the Netherlands' Equal Pay and Equal Treatment Acts, and Denmark's Equal Opportunities and Anti-Discrimination Acts. Although the details of these laws vary, they share the general objective of banning sex discrimination in employment practices and promoting diversity on the basis of sex in organizations.[4]

We focus our attention in this section on federal EEO laws in the United States. First, the legal requirements placed on employers to refrain from sex discrimination are described. Second, we consider the further requirements placed on many employers to take affirmative action to promote diversity on the basis of sex.[5]

Refraining From Discrimination

Title VII of the Civil Rights Act, enacted in 1964, and the Equal Pay Act, enacted in 1963, are the most significant pieces of U.S. federal legislation that address sex discrimination. Title VII prohibits discrimination on the basis of sex, race, color, religion, or national origin in any employment condition, including hiring, firing, promotion, transfer, compensation, and admission to training programs. It has been extended to ban discrimination because of pregnancy, childbirth, or related conditions and to ban sexual harassment (see Chapter 7). The Equal Pay Act makes it illegal to pay members of one sex at a lower rate than the other if they hold jobs that require equal skill, effort, and responsibility under similar working conditions in the same firm.

Several agencies are involved in the administration and enforcement of federal EEO laws. The Equal Employment Opportunity Commission (EEOC) is charged with administering Title VII and the Equal Pay Act. It investigates and reconciles charges of discrimination against employers, unions, and employment agencies. The Department of Justice enforces Title VII in cases involving a state or local government agency or political subdivision. Individuals may also go to court on their own behalf or in behalf of a class of employees or potential employees to seek compliance with the laws.

According to **Title VII of the Civil Rights Act,** two basic types of organizational practices are considered discriminatory under Title VII: those that involve disparate treatment and those that result in disparate impact. **Disparate treatment discrimination** occurs when sex is intentionally used as a basis for treating people unequally. For example, one employer violated Title VII by asking a female applicant whether she planned to get pregnant and quit, and if her husband would mind when she had to "run around the country with men." Male applicants, obviously, were not asked such questions. Another employer violated Title VII by asking questions about child bearing and child rearing of only female applicants.[6]

Disparate impact discrimination occurs when an employment practice affects women and men unequally, unless it is job-related and justified by the needs of the business. For example, a company's minimum height requirement for a certain job was rejected as discriminatory when it was shown to rule out more women than men and was not essential to job performance. Under the disparate impact standard, whether the employer discriminates intentionally is irrelevant. All that matters is whether a practice has unequal results, and, if so, whether it serves a legitimate need (such as apprenticeship training for skilled craft positions and licensing requirements for nurses and teachers) that cannot be met by an alternative practice with less disparate impact.

Employers are not required to meet hiring or promotion quotas for specific groups of workers (e.g., 45% of the area's labor force or population is female; thus, 45% of new hires should be female). Hiring quotas may be allowed, however, to remedy an imbalance caused by past discrimination.

If employers' past hiring practices promoted sex discrimination, they may be expected to take action to rectify these inequalities. In such cases, employers may give temporary preference to qualified applicants from underrepresented groups to achieve a long-term balance in the representation of those groups among their employees.

Although the vast majority of cases involving Title VII have dealt with discrimination against women, discrimination against men also is covered. For example, a court ruled against Pan American World Airways in the 1970s for limiting its flight attendants to women. Pan American cited survey results that passengers preferred female flight attendants, and a psychologist testified that women are better at comforting and reassuring passengers simply because they are women. Nonetheless, Pan American lost the case.[7]

The Title VII ban on sex discrimination makes an exception for discrimination based on a seniority system. For example, the U.S. Supreme Court ruled that an employer cannot be ordered to ignore a seniority system when making layoffs, even if the effect is to reduce the number of women hired under an affirmative action plan.

Another permissible exception to Title VII is when an individual's sex represents a legitimate condition of employment or **bona fide occupational qualification** (BFOQ). Employee sex may be specified as a BFOQ in situations involving hygiene (such as cleaning of washrooms during periods when they are in use), health care (such as counseling of rape victims), and safety. For example, women may be denied the opportunity to serve as guards in male prisons because of the possibility of assault by prisoners, but women cannot be denied the opportunity to be prison guards altogether. The sex of an employee also may be specified as a BFOQ for reasons of authenticity or genuineness. For example, it is legal for theaters and movie producers to hire only women to act female parts and only men to act male parts; however, this is not a requirement. The refusal to hire an individual because of customer preferences or stereotypical characterizations of the sexes (as in the Pan American case) is illegal.

In a well-publicized case, the EEOC filed charges against Hooters, a restaurant chain that features voluptuous waitresses in short shorts and formfitting tank tops or T-shirts, for requiring its waitstaff ("Hooters Girls") to be female. The issue was whether Hooters is in the restaurant business, as the EEOC saw it, or the sex business, as Hooters saw it. The EEOC claimed that no physical trait unique to women is required to serve food and drink to customers in a restaurant. In response, Hooters argued that the primary job function of

Hooters Girls is "providing vicarious sexual recreation" by wearing skimpy outfits that meet tight (pun intended) specifications. Hooters Girls also are expected to "enhance the titillation by their interaction with customers. They are to flirt, cajole, and tease the patrons." Ultimately, Hooters settled with the EEOC by paying compensation to men who were denied the opportunity to serve as Hooters Girls and by creating support jobs such as bartender and host that would be filled without regard to applicant sex. However, Hooters was allowed to continue luring customers with an exclusively female waitstaff of Hooters Girls. According to the triumphant company, "the settlement agreement acknowledged that 'being female is reasonably necessary' to the performance of the Hooters Girl's job duties, forever preserving the integrity of the Hooters Girl concept."[8]

The Equal Pay Act is based on the principle of equal pay for equal work. The equal work standard requires that jobs be only substantially equal, not identical. Equal work is defined by four factors: skill, effort, responsibility, and working conditions. Skill refers to the experience, training, education, and ability needed to perform the job. The skill level of the job, not the jobholders, determines whether two jobs are equal. For example, female nursing aides and male orderlies in hospitals perform equal work because similar skills are required. Effort refers to the amount or degree of effort, mental or physical, required for a job. Responsibility refers to the degree of accountability required in the performance of a job. For example, a wage differential may be justified for employees who are required to become acting supervisor in the absence of a regular supervisor. Working conditions refers to the physical surroundings and safety concerns of a job, such as inside versus outside work and adequate heat and ventilation. The fact that jobs are in different departments is not sufficient to demonstrate a difference in working conditions.

Pay differences are permitted between men and women engaged in equal work if they result from a seniority system, a merit system, a system that measures earnings by quality or quantity of production (e.g., a piecework incentive system), or some job-related factor such as a shift differential or a difference in experience. For example, a court upheld higher pay for salespeople in the men's department of a clothing store over those in the women's department because the company demonstrated that the men's department was the more profitable. In another case, however, women received 10% less pay than their male counterparts who did the same basic job. The men occasionally did heavier work, but this was infrequent and not done by all men. The court, ruling that the employer's lower wage rate for women was based on an artificially created job classification and that the extra duties of some men did not justify paying all of them more, awarded back wages to the women.

Pay disparities are often linked to **job evaluation,** a measurement procedure that rates jobs on factors such as skill, effort, responsibility, and working conditions. Job evaluations typically focus on a sample of *key jobs,* characterized as having a standard and stable content across organizations and within *job clusters,* which consist of groups of similar jobs. Job clusters may be determined on the basis of geographical location, stage of the production process, organizational level, or any other factor that makes the jobs comparable to one another and suggests that their wages be compared. Examples of job clusters include maintenance jobs, administrative assistant jobs, and an insurance claim processing team.[9]

The starting point for the setting of wages is what the marketplace currently pays for key jobs. Wages are assigned to key jobs according to the wages employers typically pay for that job. Wages for nonkey jobs are set according to how their job evaluation ratings compare with those for key jobs in the same job cluster. Ideally, the result is a pay structure that has both external equity—the pay for key jobs reflects the external marketplace—and internal equity—the relative pay for all jobs corresponds to their job evaluation ratings. Thus, wages for a software design job (typically a key job) should correspond to the wages for that job in the labor market. In addition, senior software design jobs that require familiarity with advanced design techniques or have more responsibilities should be rated higher, and thereby assigned higher wages, than lower-level jobs that require only familiarity with simple design techniques or have fewer responsibilities.

Employers need to make sure that sex discrimination does not enter into job evaluation or any other element of the compensation system. Sex discrimination does not legally exist if pay differences are due to differences in the value that the marketplace attaches to particular jobs or to differences in skill, effort, responsibility, or working conditions. However, if an organization has identified pay inequities that cannot be accounted for by job-related or market-related factors, then corrective action may be required. This does not necessarily mean immediately rectifying all differences or lowering anyone's pay, but it does mean fostering a commitment over the long run to eliminate unjustifiable disparities.[10]

Being charged with and convicted of illegal discrimination or failure to comply with affirmative action guidelines can be costly for a business firm. Convicted firms may incur direct costs from fines, punitive damages, and legal fees, and indirect costs from damage to their image and reputation. Current and prospective employees may have less regard for the firm and act accordingly. Firms also suffer long-term financial consequences when convicted of discrimination. A study of *Fortune* 300 companies found that those convicted of discrimination involving either disparate treatment or disparate impact had lower returns on assets and sales in the 5 years following the conviction compared to companies that were not convicted. Some of these costs are incurred even if an accused firm is not convicted or admits no guilt. Defending a firm against charges of illegal discrimination consumes top management attention that is better directed elsewhere. The costs of violating EEO laws and regulations provide a persuasive business argument for refraining from discrimination.[11]

In summary, EEO laws ban sex discrimination in several ways. Organizations may not discriminate in treatment of women and men in hiring, firing, promotion, layoff, compensation, and other types of employment decisions. They also may be held responsible for the unequal impact of their policies on men and women unless a legitimate business need is served by the policies in question. Organizations incur high costs, both intangible and tangible, if they are caught breaking EEO laws.

Taking Affirmative Action

Affirmative action represents an extension of the notion of nondiscrimination. Its purpose is to overcome the effects of past discrimination by allowing members of a victimized group to compete on equal terms with members of the favored group. Legally mandated practices for this purpose have been called affirmative action, employment equity, positive action, and other terms in various countries. They were first introduced in the United States in the 1930s to compensate for past unfair labor practices against union organizers and members. They were later used to assist veterans' reentry to the workplace after World War II.[12]

Executive Order 11246, instituted in 1965, requires U.S. organizations with 50 or more employees and federal contracts exceeding $50,000 per year to prepare and implement written affirmative action plans. An acceptable affirmative action plan must contain an analysis of the sex composition of all major job classes and an explanation for the underrepresentation of women in any job class. It must also contain goals and commitments to relieve any deficiencies revealed by the analysis. Finally, the plan must describe detailed steps that the organization will take to make a good-faith effort to meet its goals and to remedy all other EEO deficiencies. These steps should include a program for outreach to and recruitment of women for the job classes in which they are underrepresented.

Thus, the goal of an affirmative action plan is to promote diversity on the basis of sex in job classes in which women are underrepresented. If the plan has its intended result, the outcome is that male-intensive job classes become more balanced in their sex composition. Organizations are not under a legal requirement to take affirmative action for the purpose of making female-intensive job classes more balanced.

The Office of Federal Contract Compliance Programs (OFCCP) is responsible for administering Executive Order 11246. Its guidelines specify that unless sex is a BFOQ for a job, employers must actively recruit members of both sexes for the job. Advertisements for jobs in newspapers and other media cannot express a sex preference for jobholders. Employers must take affirmative action to encourage women to apply for jobs from which they previously have been excluded. This can be accomplished by various means. For example, recruitment at women's colleges may be regarded as evidence of a good-faith effort to meet affirmative action goals. In addition, if women are underrepresented in managerial jobs and specific training programs have been demonstrated to enhance employees' chances of attaining management positions, a commitment to include women in such programs is an important element of an affirmative action plan. The OFCCP requires organizations to file periodic reports on their affirmative action initiatives and to make their records available to federal administrators.

In summary, U.S. organizations must comply with EEO laws banning sex discrimination in the workplace. In addition, most federal contractors are expected to take affirmative action to remedy the effects of past sex discrimination. Although we have focused on U.S. laws and regulations, the governments of other countries make similar demands on organizations.

Business Imperatives

Business imperatives encourage organizations to go beyond minimal compliance with governmental requirements and aggressively promote diversity and inclusion. In this section, we summarize these imperatives.

Why Promote Diversity?

Several economic trends suggest that it is advantageous for organizations to promote diversity. First, the U.S. labor force has become more diverse in recent years. As in many other countries, it has become more heterogeneous on the basis of sex, race, ethnicity, national origin, religion, and many other dimensions of diversity. Organizations with management practices appropriate for a homogeneous group of employees need to rethink their human resource management strategies.

Second, the relative skills that members of different groups bring to the workplace have changed. In particular, the educational attainment of female entrants relative to that of male entrants has risen dramatically. Within all racial/ethnic groups in the United States, women now constitute the majority of individuals who earn bachelor's and master's degrees across all disciplines (Table 2.2); the proportion of women earning these degrees has increased in many other countries as well. As a result, more women worldwide are prepared to enter the high-paying occupations that require advanced degrees. Organizations that promote diversity by attracting highly educated women to historically male-intensive jobs and occupations are at an advantage in competing with organizations that do not.

Third, there has been a worldwide shift from a primarily manufacturing-based economy to an economy based more on the delivery of services. Service industries place greater importance on educational attainment and less on physical strength than do manufacturing industries. Because women and men compete for service jobs on more equal terms, service industries are more diverse on the basis of sex than are manufacturing industries. Companies in service industries have a greater proportion of women in jobs at all levels, including top management, than those in manufacturing industries. It is imperative that service firms implement human resource management programs and practices (e.g., work–family initiatives) that are appropriate for their diverse workforces.[13]

Service firms that aggressively promote diversity may be especially effective in the marketplace. Because services are both produced and consumed on the spot, employees have heightened contact with customers. Employees must be able to understand the customer's perspective, anticipate the customer's needs, and respond sensitively and appropriately. Employees whose demographic characteristics mirror the characteristics of their customers may be better able to do so. Also, customers may be more likely to purchase services from providers whose attributes match their own because they view such providers as more capable of understanding their needs. As the pool of potential customers becomes more diverse, the pool of employees with customer contact also needs to become more diverse for the organization to be successful.

Fourth, the increasing globalization of business, including multinational business operations and worldwide marketing of products and services, calls for organizations to be responsive to customers who are increasingly diverse in national origin. Organizations that want to take advantage of global business opportunities face greater challenges than do those that confine their business activities to the home market. They must learn to attract, interact with, and satisfy customers from a variety of national cultures. Overall, a diverse workforce may be better able to design, market, and sell products and services that meet consumer needs in an increasingly diverse marketplace.[14]

All of these trends suggest that organizations benefit from promoting diversity. Several studies have confirmed the relationship between sex diversity and organizational performance. Companies with higher proportions of female executives and female membership on the board of directors (i.e., greater diversity in their top management and governance ranks on the basis of sex) perform better on financial measures of return than other companies in their industries. In addition, firms with workforces that are about 50% female perform better in their industries than firms with lower or higher percentages of female employees. Because firms with a 50–50 split between male and female employees are the most diverse on the basis of sex, greater sex diversity throughout the ranks as well as in top management and governance ranks is associated with stronger firm performance.[15]

Correlation, of course, does not prove causality. Although a company's long-term record of hiring and promoting women to all levels of managerial positions could lead to higher profitability, more profitable firms may do a better job of attracting the best female talent or may feel freer to experiment with selecting women for previously male-intensive jobs. Profitable firms, however, typically attain their success by making smarter decisions than their competitors. One of these smart decisions may be promoting sex diversity.

Thus, the business case for promoting sex diversity is that it enhances firm performance and the bottom line. However, the appropriate culture needs to be in place for organizations to fully realize the benefits of sex diversity. Organizations need to promote inclusion as well as diversity to meet business imperatives.[16]

Why Promote Inclusion?

Taking steps to promote diversity, but ignoring the need for inclusion, may limit an organization's ability to reap the full benefits of a diverse workforce. Although increased employee diversity may enhance organizational performance, it also poses potential problems. It is easier to maintain a sense of cohesiveness in homogeneous organizations than in diverse organizations. People tend to be more attracted to and feel more comfortable in social settings in which they interact primarily with people like themselves. Thus, diversity may be a double-edged sword, increasing decision-making creativity and the congruence of the organization with the marketplace but decreasing employees' satisfaction with being a member of the organization. Unless the potential problems associated with diversity are addressed, its potential benefits may not be fully realized. The organization's diversity culture, as demonstrated by how it deals with group differences, influences the extent to which these problems appear.[17]

Taylor Cox distinguished among three types of diversity cultures.[18] **Monolithic organizations** are characterized by a large majority of employees from one group (e.g., White men), especially in the managerial ranks. Differences between majority and minority group members are resolved by the process of assimilation, whereby minority group employees are expected to adopt the norms and values of the majority group to survive in the organization. Such organizations are characterized by low levels of intergroup conflict because there are few members of minority groups and these members have outwardly adopted, if not inwardly embraced, the majority's norms and values. Changes in workforce demographics have led to a reduction in the number of monolithic organizations with White male majorities. The diversity culture of monolithic organizations conveys a straightforward message to employees and potential job applicants: We do not particularly welcome diversity.

Plural organizations have a more heterogeneous workforce than do monolithic organizations, primarily because they have taken steps to promote diversity. These steps may include hiring and promotion policies that stress recruitment and advancement of members of minority groups and managerial training on equal opportunity issues. Plural organizations focus on the numbers of majority versus minority group members in different jobs and levels, not on the quality of work relationships between members of different groups. The primary approach to resolving cultural differences in plural organizations is assimilation, just as for monolithic organizations. Intergroup conflict is high in plural organizations if members of the majority group resent practices used to boost minority group membership. Even though overt discrimination may have been banished, prejudice is still likely in plural organizations. The diversity culture of plural organizations conveys a mixed message: We promote diversity, but we expect employees from minority groups to fit in with the majority group.

Multicultural organizations do more than promote diversity; they also promote a culture of inclusion. They respond to cultural differences by encouraging members of different groups to respect the norms and values of other groups, in contrast to the assimilation required by monolithic and plural organizations. Multicultural organizations attempt to bring about qualitative changes in their work environments through increased appreciation of the range of skills and values that dissimilar employees offer and increased use of teams that include members culturally distinct from the dominant group. The goal is to create a culture in which employees from all groups feel comfortable and appreciated and are given a chance to make meaningful contributions. In an inclusive culture, the knowledge, skills, insights, and experiences of employees from different groups are regarded as valuable resources that the organization may use to advance its mission. Intergroup conflict in multicultural organizations is low due to the absence of prejudice and discrimination accompanied by the appreciation of individuals from different groups. The diversity culture of multicultural organizations conveys a consistent message: We welcome members of all groups as full participants in our organizational culture, and we strive to take full advantage of what they have to offer.[19]

It is more difficult to assess the effects of promoting inclusion on organizational performance than the effects of promoting diversity. Researchers may obtain data on the sex composition and performance of corporations from publicly filed reports. Researchers, however, do not have the opportunity to assess the diversity cultures of organizations unless they are granted permission to do so. Organizations that do not want their business practices to be scrutinized, particularly those that are doing little to promote inclusion, are reluctant to grant researchers such permission. Organizations that are doing a better job of promoting inclusion may be more eager to showcase their progress.[20]

As noted in Chapter 4, inclusive cultures make it easier for organizations to attract employees. A study of college students' reactions to a fictitious recruitment brochure demonstrates the importance of an inclusive culture for applicant attraction. Students received either of two forms of the brochure. Both forms stated that the company is an affirmative action/equal opportunity employer, as many companies do in their recruitment literature. One of the forms also stated that the company values the contributions of a diverse workforce and has adopted programs to help teach all employees to recognize the strengths that individuals from diverse backgrounds can bring to the company. Students of both sexes and different races were more attracted to the company when they received a brochure with the additional statement about the inclusive culture.[21]

In conclusion, promoting inclusion is likely to contribute to full utilization and retention of valued employees from all groups and enhance the bottom line. Employees from different groups, especially minority groups, can tell whether their organization is monolithic, plural, or multicultural. They are well aware of the message that the organization's diversity culture sends to people like themselves. They are most likely to be attracted to and commit themselves to an organization that promotes a culture in which members of all groups are valued and respected. Such organizations are likely to have a business advantage over competitors that are weaker in promoting inclusion or that fail to make the attempt.

Organizational Actions

We have presented the legal and business cases for promoting nondiscrimination, diversity, and inclusion. In this section, we consider these issues from a practical perspective—what organizations need to do. First, appropriate goals should be adopted and communicated. Second, the representation of women and men in different jobs and at different levels should be analyzed and a cultural audit performed to determine how well the company is achieving its diversity goals. Third, a management system should be adopted that sets concrete objectives for critical employees and provides incentives for them to meet these objectives. Fourth, employee network groups and advisory councils should be sponsored to stimulate employee involvement as well as to identify obstacles to the achievement of diversity goals. Fifth, employees should receive education and training that enhances their abilities and readiness to meet assigned objectives. Finally, changes in the organizational culture should be implemented as needed to ensure that goal achievement is sustained. Table 9.1 summarizes recommended actions for organizations and their employees.[22]

Table 9.1   Recommended Actions

1. Set and communicate the organizational goals of promoting nondiscrimination, diversity, and inclusion.

2. Comply with all EEO laws.

3. Encourage employees to be champions of diversity, to take strong stands on diversity issues in the workplace and behave as a role model for others.

4. Assign responsibility for achieving organizational goals to a highly placed executive.

5. Make sure that employees understand how affirmative action works in the organization.

6. Work with employee network groups formed out of employees' common interests in planning and implementing cultural change.

7. Provide diversity training that educates employees about organizational goals and gives them the knowledge and skills they need to work toward these goals.

8. Analyze the organization's composition and culture to determine what specific improvements are needed, and then set objectives for attaining them.

9. Ensure that the achievement of organizational goals and objectives is rewarded by the management system and supported by the organizational culture.

10. Continually monitor the organization's progress relative to its goals and take appropriate actions to ensure that improvements are permanent.

Setting and Communicating Goals

The first step to be taken is to set goals for the organization's diversity culture. The appropriate goals for *all* organizations—large or small, public or private, profit or nonprofit—are to be nondiscriminatory, diverse, and inclusive in their employment practices.

Assuming that an organization sets these goals, it then needs to communicate them to key employees. How organizational goals are sold to employees plays a large role in determining whether they are achieved. They may be presented to employees as moral, legal, or business issues. Appeals to morality seldom work because few people do the "right thing" unless it is personally advantageous. The legal argument does not fully work either; it suggests that compliance with the law is most important, and thereby promotes only a minimal effort to achieve diversity goals. A sales pitch is most effective in promoting nondiscrimination, diversity, and inclusion throughout the organization when it points to bottom-line profits, which most employees see as ultimately affecting their own livelihoods.[23]

Corporate communications should convey the message that promoting nondiscrimination, diversity, and inclusion are important organizational goals. These communications may include speeches by top executives, with transcripts or videos available to internal and external groups, newsletters, status reports, recognition events, special awards, and publicity for employees who have done good work toward these goals. The mission statement of the organization should state that the organization regards achievement of these goals as critical to its success.[24]

Top management commitment is critical to achieving organizational goals. The chief executive of an organization plays an important role in setting its primary values. In organizations with strong track records in managing diversity, the CEOs galvanize employees to take diversity seriously by making them aware of diversity issues facing the firm and by personally stimulating change. In addition, **champions of diversity** are needed—people who take strong public and personal stands on the need for cultural change in the organization and behave as role models in creating change. What better champion of diversity than the top executive?[25]

Assignment of responsibility and allocation of resources also demonstrate top management commitment. The person with primary responsibility for achievement of organizational goals should either report to or be a top-line executive. This person should have immediate access to and control over the managers who determine program success or failure. If this responsibility is buried in the professional ranks of the human resource management department, employees infer that promoting nondiscrimination, diversity, and inclusion are not top priorities, and there is less impact on the organization as a whole.[26]

Identifying and Rewarding the Right Behavior

Making a good sales pitch for promoting nondiscrimination, diversity, and inclusion does not ensure that employees will act accordingly. An organization also needs a sound management system that encourages employees to engage in the right kinds of behavior on a regular basis. As one executive said in a Conference Board survey:

How do you go about achieving [diversity] results in a company? The same way you achieve any other results. You analyze the problem carefully, determine what you need to do, and then set up an overall management planning and control system to make very sure that it happens—and on schedule.[27]

First comes an analysis of what the organization needs to do to achieve its goals. This analysis begins with an assessment of whether women are equitably represented throughout the organization. Required by Executive Order 11246 for U.S. government contractors, it should compare the number of women in each job category with the number of women in the relevant labor force who are qualified to fill jobs in that category. The relevant labor force may be defined as that located in the immediate city or town, the metropolitan area, or the nation, depending on the job category. Areas in which women are underemployed then become the appropriate targets of affirmative action programs. Although not required by law, this analysis could also identify areas in which men are underemployed.

The organizational analysis also includes a **cultural audit,** a snapshot of the current organizational culture. It assesses the nature of the organizational culture as experienced by employees, which is not necessarily what top management thinks the culture is or should be. It also assesses how the organizational culture influences the treatment of members of different groups. Surveys, interviews, focus groups, and meetings may be used to gather information for the audit. A successful audit uncovers obstacles to the full attainment of organizational goals. Obstacles may include stereotypes and prejudices that affect employees' interactions with one another and managers' decisions regarding recruitment, performance appraisals, promotions, compensation, and other employment practices.[28]

Next comes the specification of objectives. Managers will put more effort into promoting nondiscrimination, diversity, and inclusion if they are expected to meet concrete objectives in pursuit of each of these goals. For example, the PQ Corporation, a manufacturer of specialty chemicals and glass materials, implemented a unique procedure to meet the objective of promoting nondiscrimination in employment decisions. The key to the procedure was the "selection checklist," a two-part document that a manager completed for each candidate interviewed for a position. The first part contained questions about each step in the selection process and the degree of possible discrimination (e.g., "Did you perform or do you have a current job analysis for this position?" "Was the position posted internally?" "Were reasons for rejection based on job-related deficiencies and not related to non-job-related factors such as a handicap or religious beliefs?") Each question had to be answered yes, no, or not applicable. The questions answered with a *no* reflected possible incidents of discrimination by the manager. The second part documented the correlation between the job criteria (i.e., skills and knowledge required to perform major job functions) and the attributes of the candidate.[29]

PQ's selection checklist was intended to make managers aware of the process they used to make their decisions. Objectives for managers were stated in terms of percentages of discriminatory incidents. Managers' checklists were passed on to their superiors, who could then assess how well the corporate goal of nondiscrimination was being achieved. If a manager fudged the checklist to cover up discrimination, he or she did so with the knowledge that this behavior could expose the company to an EEO lawsuit.

Managers should be expected to meet the objective of promoting diversity in their work units. In pursuing this objective, they could adopt either of two opposing affirmative action policies. According to one policy, competence is the first screening criterion for hiring or promoting individuals. Members of underrepresented groups such as women are then given preference if they pass the screen. According to the opposite policy, membership in an underrepresented group is the first screen, and competence is then used to choose among the candidates who remain. The first policy yields qualified and competent employees. The second policy yields the best of the available "affirmative action" candidates, whether qualified or not.

Instructing managers to follow the first policy in meeting their diversity objectives is advantageous to both organizations and individuals. The second policy tends to be detrimental to its intended beneficiaries and the organization in the long run. When employees believe that a woman has been hired under the second policy, they conclude that she must be incompetent. Such beliefs place women managers at a disadvantage. When women managers believe that they were hired primarily because of their sex, they tend to be less committed to the organization and less satisfied with their jobs than those who believe that sex was not an important factor in their selection. In contrast, when the organization makes it clear that merit considerations are central to the selection process, employees' reactions to the selection of a woman to be their boss are less pronounced. A woman who is selected for a leadership position under such conditions is more likely to see herself as competent and want to remain in the position. Other employees, even those who have been bypassed for the position, are less likely to stigmatize her as incompetent and grumble about her selection. Thus, organizations need to set objectives for promoting diversity that emphasize the role of merit in selection decisions.[30]

Managers also should be expected to meet the objective of providing their employees an inclusive work environment. Achievement of this objective may be measured by employee surveys. Monitoring of employee complaints will provide additional information about whether a manager has problems in this area that need to be addressed.

Once an organization develops and assigns specific objectives, they should become part of the manager's overall performance appraisal. Managers should be made aware that their success at promoting nondiscrimination, diversity, and inclusion will be evaluated by their supervisors. Good performance in these areas should be reinforced with tangible rewards such as promotions, salary increases, and favorable task assignments; failure to meet objectives should result in the withholding of such rewards. Actions speak much louder than words of approval or disapproval. By giving managers explicit knowledge of the organization's diversity goals and incentives to meet personal objectives consistent with these goals, an effective management system overcomes resistance from managers.

Stimulating Employee Involvement

Organizations benefit when employees from all groups feel personally involved in attaining the goals of nondiscrimination, diversity, and inclusion. For example, Xerox stimulates employee involvement through its sponsorship of employee network groups, including Hispanic Association for Professional Advancement, Black Women's Leadership Council, National Black Employee's Association (for all Black employees),

Galaxe Pride at Work (for gay, lesbian, transgender, and bisexual employees), The Women's Alliance, and Asians Coming Together. Each group has a Corporate Champion assigned to it. Groups elect their own officers and run their own functions, including meetings, conferences, professional development activities, and outreach activities in the community. For instance, Black Women's Leadership Council takes an active role in encouraging and developing young Black women through a high school scholarship program. It also promotes mentoring and sponsorship of Black women at Xerox, celebrates their accomplishments, and surveys its members about corporate issues.[31]

Microsoft supports a wide variety of employee network groups initiated by its employees. Separate groups, some with overlapping interests, target women, fathers, parents, adoptive parents, single parents, military reservists, the hearing-impaired, the visually impaired, employees affected by attention deficit disorder, and gay, lesbian, bisexual, and transgender employees. In addition, there are employee network groups for African, Arab, Black, Brazilian, Chinese, Filipino, Hispanic, Indian, Japanese, Israeli, Korean, Malaysian, Native American, Nepali, Pakistani, Portuguese, Romanian, Russian, Singaporian, Taiwanese, Turkish, Thai, Ukranian, and Vietnamese employees. These groups provide career development and networking opportunities and assist the company with college recruiting and cultural awareness activities.[32]

Organizations may form groups to involve employees in dealing with diversity issues. For example, one organization established an advisory council of a cross section of employees. The council met monthly to discuss issues related to a diverse workforce. Corporate activities that resulted from the council included a diversity booth at the annual family picnic, articles on diversity in the company newsletter, training on refraining from discrimination, guidelines for first-line supervisors on appraising employees, and a suggestion box called "Dr. Equality." The council also assisted in the design of employee opinion surveys.[33]

Employee network groups and advisory councils serve several purposes that benefit both the organization and its members. Such groups help the organization to be aware of and address the concerns of employees. As a result, employees are more likely to feel that the organization cares about their concerns, which fosters their commitment to the attainment of corporate goals. The outreach activities of such groups also help the organization to be a good citizen in the community. Finally, they act as a vehicle for employee self-help by providing opportunities for networking, personal support, and career development.

In addition, given the preponderance of men in leadership positions, engaging men in the attainment of organizational goals is in a company's best interest. It helps to prevent a win–lose mentality that gains for women mean losses for men. In general, when men become more aware of sex bias in organizational practices, they are more likely to believe that it is important for the organization to set and achieve the goals of nondiscrimination, diversity, and inclusion. Men with a strong sense of fair play are more likely to be aware of sex bias and become champions of diversity, which makes them powerful change agents in stimulating the involvement of other men who are disengaged.[34]

Educating Employees

Educational initiatives serve to promote the organizational goals of nondiscrimination, diversity, and inclusion. Specific education and training programs may be offered to employees at all levels to meet a range of objectives:[35]

1. Increase participants' knowledge about diversity issues, including EEO laws, changing societal demographics, and the business case for attention to these issues.

2. Increase participants' familiarity with organizational policies regarding inappropriate workplace behavior (e.g., sexual harassment) and what they should do if they experience or witness such behavior.

3. Increase participants' awareness of their own stereotypes and prejudices based on sex, race, ethnicity, age, national origin, sexual orientation, abilities/disabilities, and other primary and secondary dimensions of diversity.

4. Increase participants' skills in moving beyond their stereotypes and prejudices as they work with dissimilar customers and coworkers.

5. In multinational organizations, increase participants' fluency in other languages and knowledge of other national cultures.

6. Increase managers' skills in making bias-free decisions, such as decisions about selection, compensation, performance appraisal, promotion, and development.

7. Increase managers' skills in dealing with diversity-related incidents.

8. By addressing the above objectives, change the organization's diversity culture itself.

Diversity training programs should have an expected outcome: As a result of the program, something should change. To determine whether the desired change has occurred, program outcomes should be measured on a long-term basis, not just at the end of the last session. For example, participants' assessment of what was most useful about a program and how it helped them may be solicited 3, 6, or 12 months afterward. If the program's objective is to modify the organization's diversity culture, periodic employee surveys of employees' attitudes toward diversity may provide information on whether this objective is being met.[36]

One issue that arises is whether participation in a diversity training program should be mandatory for employees. For example, Marriott has mandatory diversity training every month to make sure that all of the company's employees are culturally competent when dealing with customers from different backgrounds. Voluntary training may be more effective than mandatory training because participants who volunteer are more aware of the need for change. However, allowing employees to opt out of diversity training may signal that top management does not regard it as particularly important to achievement of corporate objectives. Making participation mandatory sends the message that top management regards the training as critical to achievement of corporate goals.[37]

If participation in diversity training is mandatory, the program facilitator faces the challenge of dealing with reluctant participants. Under these circumstances, the facilitator must get *all* participants to believe that they have something to gain from the training or its objectives may be thwarted. Programs that are designed to get everyone working toward the same corporate goals, not to embarrass or blame anyone, are most likely to encourage involvement.

According to a survey of human resource professionals, a diversity training program is more likely to be effective when (1) top management support for achievement of organizational goals is strong and visible; (2) participation is mandatory for managers; (3) program success is evaluated over the long term; (4) managers are rewarded for promoting diversity in their work units; and (5) a broad definition of "diversity" is used that acknowledges the needs and concerns of all employees, including White males. Achievement of organizational goals is enhanced if employees know why they are being asked to work toward these goals and are taught the necessary skills.[38]

Implementing Cultural Change

An organization's diversity culture influences how group differences are taken into account. It consists of a general perception of the value the organization places on being nondiscriminatory, diverse, and inclusive. Organizational culture is an elusive concept. It lies beneath the surface of organizational life, yet it influences every aspect of how employees are treated and work is conducted. Because organizational culture is deep-seated, often going back to the values of the founder, it cannot be changed overnight. If an organization sets goals of promoting nondiscrimination, diversity, and inclusion and its culture does not fully support achievement of these goals, some form of cultural change is needed.[39]

The first step in implementing cultural change is to decide, based on a cultural audit and corporate goals, how the culture needs to be improved. Cultural change will be especially critical for monolithic organizations. Plural organizations, which promote nondiscrimination and diversity but not inclusion, will also need to make some cultural changes. Even organizations that are already multicultural may benefit from some modifications to their diversity cultures.

The second step is to develop a plan that charts the course for cultural change. The plan may include revisions to existing policies and practices, including the management system, and new programs such as education and training initiatives. Top management support of the plan for cultural change is crucial, but not sufficient, to bringing about cultural change. The participation of first-line supervisors in development of the plan also is critical to its success. First-line supervisors are those most responsible for getting work done in organizations. If they are told by top management to implement a plan for cultural change but do not participate in its development, they will not be committed to the plan. Long-lasting cultural change can be brought about only when the change is accepted and owned by all of the employees who will be involved in making the change effective.

The third step is to launch the change effort itself. For the launch to be effective, leaders of the change effort need to specify objectives, achieve early results to demonstrate the value of the effort, and assess progress along the way. The management system should reward behavior that contributes to achievement of needed cultural change.

The final step, once the initial change effort is complete, is to ensure that cultural changes take hold and are not temporary. Long-term maintenance of the organizational culture is necessary. Maintenance involves monitoring the results of the change effort to guard against backsliding and motivating employees to confront and overcome obstacles to sustained cultural change. Cultural audits should be repeated on a regular basis to determine whether intended changes are in place and to identify further needs for change.

Multinational corporations face additional challenges in changing their diversity cultures. Change efforts are especially likely to fail if managers in the home office impose their notions of diversity on operations in other areas of the world. Such efforts may be viewed as cultural imperialism and resented by managers outside the home office. The challenge for a multinational organization is to engage in efforts to influence the *organizational* culture while taking internal differences in *national* culture into account.[40]

All organizations benefit from promoting nondiscrimination, diversity, and inclusion. Even organizations with a history of such actions need to continue to make special efforts to attract qualified applicants from all groups, offering satisfying jobs and a welcoming culture. When organizations take such actions and achieve the goal of being multicultural in their management practices, they are likely to attract the best talent available, stimulate employee involvement and commitment, and enhance the bottom line.

Conclusions for the Book

In Chapter 1, the following question was posed: "Is it only a matter of time until the proportions of women and men in all managerial levels and all occupations become essentially equal, until women and men are paid equal wages for equal work, and until individuals' work experiences are unaffected by their biological sex?" As we have seen, the answer to this question is that it depends on actions that organizations and individuals take.

Throughout this book, we describe the effects of sex and gender in the workplace. We identify issues that arise as women and men seek employment, work together in teams, serve as leaders, exhibit sexual behavior at work, and manage the interface between their work and family roles. In previous chapters as well as this one, we offer numerous recommendations for improving interactions between, and promoting the full utilization of, women and men in the workplace. Overall, more actions are recommended for organizations than for individuals. However, organizations consist of people who work together to provide products or services. Thus, *all* of the recommended actions are ones that people may take. Although this book's title stresses the managerial role, *all* of us—current and future members of the labor force, managers and nonmanagers—may contribute toward making a better workplace.

In all likelihood, some sex differences in workplace preferences, experiences, and behaviors will remain. We need to be clear on what the facts about sex differences are, but not suggest what they should be. Instead, our overriding concern should be with gender differences, beliefs about how males and females differ and should behave. When gender differences are guided more by stereotypes than by facts about sex differences, they have a corrosive impact on interactions between the sexes at work.

The goal is to create a nondiscriminatory, diverse, and inclusive workplace—a world in which members of both sexes are valued for what they bring to the workplace and are granted the opportunity to make full use of their talents. By taking actions such as the ones recommended, all of us can contribute to establishment of such a world. What a wonderful world this would be.

Notes

1. ExxonMobil Corporation. (2009). *Our diverse workforce.* Retrieved December 19, 2009, from http://www.exxonmobil.com; Chevron Corporation. (2009). *Diversity.* Retrieved December 19, 2009, from http://www.chevron.com; General Motors Company. (2009). *I am GM.* Retrieved December 19, 2009, from http://www.gm.com; Walmart Corporation. (2009). *Diversity.* Retrieved December 19, 2009, from http://walmartstores.com; AT&T Corporation. (2009). *Investing in people.* Retrieved December 19, 2009, from http://www.att.com; Ford Motor Company. (2009). *A word about diversity and inclusion from our CEO, Alan Mulally.* Retrieved December 19, 2009, from http://www.ford.com.

2. Fortune. (2009, April 19). Fortune *500: Our annual ranking of American's largest corporations.* Retrieved December 19, 2009, from http://money.cnn.com/magazines/fortune.

3. Roth, L. M. (2007). Women on Wall Street: Despite diversity measures, Wall Street remains vulnerable to sex discrimination charges. *Academy of Management Perspectives, 21*(1), 24–35.

4. Myors, B., Lievens, F., Schollaert, E., Van Hoye, G., Cronshaw, S. F., Mladinic, A., et al. (2008). International perspectives on the legal environment for selection. *Industrial and Organizational Psychology, 1,* 206–246.

5. The description of legal requirements placed on U.S. employers is based primarily on the following two sources: Sedmak, N. J., & Vidas, C. (1994*). Primer of equal employment opportunity* (6th ed.). Washington, DC: Bureau of National Affairs; Gamble, B. S. (Ed.). (1992). *Sex discrimination handbook.* Washington, DC: Bureau of National Affairs.

6. Sedmak & Vidas, pp. 39, 138.

7. Ledvinka, J., & Scarpello, V. G. (1991). *Federal regulation of personnel and human resource management* (2nd ed.). Boston: PWS-Kent, p. 60; Sedmak & Vidas, p. 44.

8. Bovard, J. (1995, November 17). The EEOC's war on Hooters. *Wall Street Journal,* p. A18; Hooters. (2009). *About Hooters.* Retrieved December 18, 2009, from http://www.hooters.com.

9. Schwab, D. P. (1984). Job evaluation and pay setting: Concepts and practices. In E. R. Livernash (Ed.), *Comparable worth: Issues and alternatives* (2nd ed., pp. 49–77). Washington, DC: Equal Employment Advisory Council; Mahoney, T. A. (1990). Compensation functions. In G. R. Ferris, K. M. Rowland, & M. R. Buckley (Eds.), *Human resource management: Perspectives and issues* (2nd ed., pp. 226–236). Boston: Allyn & Bacon.

10. Sape, G. P. (1985). Coping with comparable worth. *Harvard Business Review, 63*(3), 145-152.

11. Baucus, M. S., & Baucus, D. A. (1997). Paying the piper: An empirical examination of longer-term financial consequences of illegal corporate behavior. *Academy of Management Journal, 40,* 129–151.

12. Konrad, A. M., & Linnehan, F. (1999). Affirmative action: History, effects, and attitudes. In G. N. Powell (Ed.), *Handbook of gender and work* (pp. 429–452). Thousand Oaks, CA: Sage; Crosby, F. J., Iyer, A., & Sincharoen, S. (2006). Understanding affirmative action. *Annual Review of Psychology, 57,* 585–611.

13. Gutek, B. A., Cherry, B., & Groth, M. (1999). Gender and service delivery. In G. N. Powell (Ed.), *Handbook of gender and work* (pp. 47–68). Thousand Oaks, CA: Sage.

14. Cox, T., Jr. (1993). *Cultural diversity in organizations: Theory, research and practice.* San Francisco: Berrett-Koehler.

15. Catalyst. (2004). *The bottom line: Connecting corporate performance and gender diversity.* New York: Author; Welbourne, T. M., Cycyota, C. S., & Ferrante, C. J. (2007). Wall Street reaction to women in IPOs: An examination of gender diversity in top management teams. *Group & Organization Management, 32,* 524–547; Campbell, K., & Mínguez-Vera, A. (2007). Gender diversity in the boardroom

and firm financial performance. *Journal of Business Ethics, 83,* 435–451; Frink, D. D., Robinson, R. K., Reithel, B., Arthur, M. M., Ammeter, A. P., Ferris, G. R., et al. (2003). Gender demography and organization performance: A two-study investigation with convergence. *Group & Organization Management, 28,* 127–147.

16. Dwyer, S., Richard, O. C., & Chadwick, K. (2003). Gender diversity in management and firm performance: The influence of growth orientation and organizational culture. *Journal of Business Research, 56,* 1009–1019.

17. Milliken, F. J., & Martins, L. L. (1996). Searching for common threads: Understanding the multiple effects of diversity in organizational groups. *Academy of Management Review, 21,* 402–433.

18. Cox (1993); Cox, T., Jr. (1991). The multicultural organization. *Academy of Management Executive, 5*(2), 34–47.

19. Ely, R. J., & Thomas, D. A. (2001). Cultural diversity at work: The effects of diversity perspectives on work group processes and outcomes. *Administrative Science Quarterly, 46,* 229–273.

20. Gilbert, J. A., & Ivancevich, J. M. (2000). Valuing diversity: A tale of two organizations. *Academy of Management Executive, 14*(1), 93–105.

21. Williams, M. L., & Bauer, T. N. (1994). The effect of a managing diversity policy on organizational attractiveness. *Group & Organization Management, 19,* 295–308.

22. Lobel, S. A. (1999). Impacts of diversity and work-life initiatives in organizations. In G. N. Powell (Ed.), *Handbook of gender and work* (pp. 453–474). Thousand Oaks, CA: Sage.

23. Cox (1993).

24. Lobel.

25. Cox, T. H., & Blake, S. (1991). Managing cultural diversity: Implications for organizational competitiveness. *Academy of Management Executive, 5*(3), 45–56; Gilbert & Ivancevich.

26. Cox & Blake.

27. Schaeffer, R. G., & Lynton, E. F. (1979). *Corporate experiences in improving women's job opportunities.* New York: Conference Board, p. 21.

28. Cox & Blake.

29. PQ Corporation. (2009). *Diversity at PQ.* Retrieved December 18, 2009, from http://www.pqcorp.com; Poole, J. C., & Kautz, E. T. (1987). An EEO/AA program that exceeds quotas—It targets biases. *Personnel Journal, 66*(1), 103-105.

30. Heilman, M. E., & Welle, B. (2006). Disadvantaged by diversity? The effects of diversity goals on competence perceptions. *Journal of Applied Social Psychology, 36,* 1291–1319; Heilman, M. E., & Alcott, V. B. (2001). What I think you think of me: Women's reactions to being viewed as beneficiaries of preferential selection. *Journal of Applied Psychology, 86,* 574–582; Heilman, M. E., Battle, W. S., Keller, C. E., & Lee, R. A. (1998). Type of affirmative action policy: A determinant of reactions to sex-based preferential selection? *Journal of Applied Psychology, 83,* 190–205; Heilman, M. E. (1994). Affirmative action: Some unintended consequences

for working women. In B. M. Staw & L. L. Cummings (Eds.), *Research in organizational behavior* (Vol. 16, pp. 125–169). Greenwich, CT: JAI.

31. Xerox Corporation. (2009). *Xerox diversity: Different ideas, diverse people, dramatic results.* Retrieved December 18, 2009, from http://www.xerox.com; Xerox Corporation, Black Women's Leadership Council. (2002). *Mission.* Retrieved March 22, 2002, from http://www.bwlc.com; Sessa, V. I. (1992). Managing diversity at the Xerox Corporation: Balanced workforce goals and caucus groups. In S. E. Jackson & Associates (Ed.), *Diversity in the workplace: Human resources initiatives* (pp. 37–64). New York: Guilford.

32. Microsoft Corporation. (2009). *Diversity advisory councils at Microsoft.* Retrieved December 18, 2009, from http://www.microsoft.com.

33. Gilbert & Ivancevich.

34. Catalyst. (2009). *Engaging men in gender initiatives: What change agents need to know.* New York: Author.

35. Arredondo, P. (1996). Chapter 8, The role of education and training. In *Successful diversity management initiatives: A blueprint for planning and implementation* (pp. 125–145). Thousand Oaks, CA: Sage; Ferdman, B. M., & Brody, S. E. (1996). Models of diversity training. In D. Landis & R. S. Bhagat (Eds.), *Handbook of intercultural training* (2nd ed., pp. 282–303). Thousand Oaks, CA: Sage.

36. Arredondo.

37. Kulik, C. T., & Roberson, L. (2008). Common goals and golden opportunities: Evaluations of diversity education in academic and organizational settings. *Academy of Management Learning and Education, 7,* 309–331; DiversityInc. (2009). Top 50 companies for diversity: No. 4, Marriott International. *DiversityInc, 8* (3), 46.

38. Rynes, S., & Rosen, B. (1995). A field survey of factors affecting the adoption and perceived success of diversity training. *Personnel Psychology, 48,* 247–270.

39. Kossek, E. E., & Zonia, S. C. (1993). Assessing diversity climate: A field study of reactions to employer efforts to promote diversity. *Journal of Organizational Behavior, 14,* 61–81; Reardon, K. K., & Reardon, K. J. (1999). "All that we can be": Leading the U.S. Army's gender integration effort. *Management Communication Quarterly, 12,* 600–617.

40. Fulkerson, J. R., & Schuler, R. S. (1992). Managing worldwide diversity at Pepsi-Cola International. In S. E. Jackson & Associates (Ed.), *Diversity in the workplace: Human resources initiatives* (pp. 248–276). New York: Guilford.

Index

About the Author

Gary N. Powell, PhD, is Professor of Management and Director of the PhD Program in the School of Business at the University of Connecticut. He is author of the first two editions and coauthor (with Laura M. Graves) of the third edition of *Women and Men in Management,* editor of *Handbook of Gender and Work,* and author of *Managing a Diverse Workforce: Learning Activities* (3rd ed.). He is an internationally recognized scholar and educator on gender and diversity issues in the workplace. His graduate course on women and men in management won an award on innovation in education from the Committee on Equal Opportunity for Women of the American Assembly of Collegiate Schools of Business (AACSB) and first led to the writing of this book. He has won the University of Connecticut School of Business Outstanding Graduate Teaching Award (three times) and Outstanding Undergraduate Teaching Award. He also has received the University of Connecticut President's Award for Promoting Multiculturalism.

He has served as Chair, Program Chair, and Executive Committee member of the Women in Management (now Gender and Diversity in Organizations) Division of the Academy of Management, and received both the Janet Chusmir Service Award for his contributions to the division and the Sage Scholarship Award for his contributions to research on gender in organizations. He has published over 100 articles in journals such as *Academy of Management Journal, Academy of Management Review, Journal of Applied Psychology, Organizational Behavior and Human Decision Processes, Journal of Management, Personnel Psychology, Human Relations, Journal of Organizational Behavior, Organizational Dynamics,* and *Academy of Management Executive;* contributed over 20 chapters to edited volumes; and presented over 120 papers at professional conferences. He is a Fellow of the British Academy of Management and Eastern Academy of Management. He has served on the Board of Governors of the Academy of Management and as President and

Program Chair of the Eastern Academy of Management. He also served as Co-Chair of the Status of Minorities Task Force of the Academy of Management and has served on the Editorial Board of *Academy of Management Review, Academy of Management Executive, Journal of Management, Human Relations,* and *Journal of Management Studies.*

Prior to joining the faculty at the University of Connecticut, he worked at General Electric, graduating from its Manufacturing Management Program. At GE, he designed and implemented automated project scheduling systems as well as systems for inventory control, materials procurement, and so on. He has provided management training and development for many companies, including Webster Financial Corp., The Hartford Financial Services Group, The Implementation Partners (TIP), GE-Capital, General Signal, Apple Computer, Monroe Auto Equipment, AllState, and CIGNA, and has conducted numerous other workshops.

He holds a doctorate in organizational behavior and a master's degree in management science from the University of Massachusetts and a bachelor's degree in management from MIT.

About the Contributor

Laura M. Graves, PhD (co-author of Chapters 4 and 5), is Associate Professor of Management at the Graduate School of Management at Clark University. She is a recognized scholar on diversity in the workplace. Her work has examined gender and race effects in organizations, particularly gender bias in employment interviewers' decision processes and the effects of demographic diversity on work teams. She has also explored issues related to work-life integration and well-being. She received the Sage Scholarship Award from the Gender and Diversity in Organizations Division of the Academy of Management for her contributions to the management literature. Her research has appeared in leading academic journals including *Academy of Management Review, Journal of Applied Psychology,* and *Personnel Psychology.* In addition, she has contributed chapters to several books and presented numerous papers at academic meetings. She has served on the Editorial Board of *Academy of Management Journal* and as a Guest Editor for an *Academy of Management Journal* special research forum.

She is a former Chair, Chair-Elect, Program Chair, and Executive Committee member of the Gender and Diversity in Organizations Division of the Academy of Management. She also has held several positions in the Eastern Academy of Management, serving on its Board and chairing both the Organizational Behavior and Human Resources Management programs for its annual meeting.

Prior to joining the faculty at Clark, she worked in Corporate Human Resources at Aetna, where she was engaged in internal management consulting. She was also a member of the management faculty at the University of Connecticut. She holds a doctorate and a master's degree in social psychology from the University of Connecticut and a bachelor's degree in psychology from the College of William and Mary.